M000207760

Health Equity in Brazil

Health Equity
in Brazil

Intersections of Gender, Race, and Policy

KIA LILLY CALDWELL

UNIVERSITY OF ILLINOIS PRESS
Urbana, Chicago, and Springfield

© 2017 by the Board of Trustees
of the University of Illinois
All rights reserved
1 2 3 4 5 C P 5 4 3 2 1
♾ This book is printed on acid-free paper.

Library of Congress Cataloging-in-Publication Data
Names: Caldwell, Kia Lilly, 1971– author.
Title: Health equity in Brazil : intersections of gender, race, and
    policy / Kia Lilly Caldwell.
Description: Urbana : University of Illinois Press, [2017] |
    Includes bibliographical references and index.
Identifiers: LCCN 2016058967 (print) | LCCN 2016059477
    (ebook) | ISBN 9780252040986 (hardback : alk. paper)
    | ISBN 9780252082474 (paperback : alk. paper) | ISBN
    9780252099533 (e-book)
Subjects: | MESH: Health Equity—history | African
    Continental Ancestry Group | Health Policy—history
    | Racism | Sexism | Socioeconomic Factors—history |
    Women's Health | History, 20th Century | History, 21st
    Century | Brazil
Classification: LCC RA448.4 (print) | LCC RA448.4 (ebook) |
    NLM W 76 DB8 | DDC 362.108900981—dc23
LC record available at https://lccn.loc.gov/2016058967

*This book is dedicated to the memory and lasting legacy
of my grandparents.*

Contents

Acknowledgments

This book, like most, has been a journey of both the mind and the heart. It has also been a collective endeavor. I first want to thank my friends and colleagues in Brazil who helped me learn more about health issues and challenges there. Fátima Oliveira stands out as someone who has been extremely helpful since I first visited Brazil in the 1990s. Her deep commitment to women's health, reproductive rights, and the health of the black population has inspired me and provided an important model of feminist scholarship and advocacy over the years. Maria Noelci Homero has also been an important friend and interlocutor and I deeply cherish the insights she has shared with me. I also want to thank Edna Araujo for her important work on racial health disparities in Brazil and for being a wonderful collaborator. While numerous people have contributed to this book in large and small ways, Maria Ines Barbosa, Fernanda Lopes, Jurema Werneck, and Luis Eduardo Batista provided important models for the analysis this book offers through their writings, activism, and advocacy. Finally, my friends in Brazil have been a source of support and camaraderie as I completed this project.

I have also been fortunate to have a number of friends and colleagues in the United States who have provided support and encouragement as I wrote this book. Michele Berger, Tanya Shields, Renya Ramirez, and Eunice Sahle all formed part of a special group that provided intellectual and emotional sustenance for me during critical times. I also want to thank Keisha-Khan Perry,

Tiffany Willoughby-Herard, Millie Thayer, Tanya Hernandez, Michele Rivkin-Fish, Lydia Boyd, Jocelyn Chua, and Sonia Alvarez for providing feedback on various chapters of the book. Special thanks to Allison Mathews for assistance with the book's bibliography. I also deeply appreciate the guidance provided by my editor at the University of Illinois Press, Dawn Durante, and the press staff for their support of this project.

Finally, to my husband and children, thank you for the love, understanding, and numerous sacrifices that have made my research and this book possible. You are loved more than you know.

Abbreviations

ABPN	Associação Brasileira de Pesquisadores/as Negros/as (Association of Black Brazilian Researchers)
ACMUN	Associação Cultural de Mulheres Negras (Black Women's Cultural Association)
AMNB	Articulação de Organizações de Mulheres Negras Brasileiras (Articulation of Black Brazilian Women's Organizations)
ARV	Anti-retroviral therapy
ASPERS	Assessoria de Promoção da Equidade Racial em Saúde (Office for Promoting Racial Equity in Health)
BEMFAM	Sociedade Civil de Bem-Estar Familiar no Brasil (Civil Society for Family Well-being in Brazil)
CEDAW	Convention on the Elimination of All Forms of Discrimination against Women
CERD	Convention on the Elimination of All Forms of Racial Discrimination
CLADEM	Comitê Latino Americano e do Caribe para a Defesa dos Direitos da Mulher (Latin American and Caribbean Committee for the Defense of Women's Rights)
CNDM	Conselho Nacional de Direitos da Mulher (National Council on Women's Rights)

CPAIMC	Centro de Pesquisas de Assistência Integral à Mulher e à Criança (Research Center for Integral Assistance to Women and Children)
DFID	British Department for International Development
FUNASA	Fundação Nacional de Saúde (National Health Foundation)
GTI	Grupo de Trabalho Interministerial
HDI	Human Development Index
IBGE	Instituto Brasileiro de Geografia e Estatísica
ICPD	International Conference on Population and Development
MNU	Movimento Negro Unificado (Unified Black Movement)
MP	Medida Provisória (Provisional Measure)
NGO	Non-governmental organization
PAF	Programa de Anemia Falciforme
PAISM	Programa de Assistência Integral à Saúde da Mulher (Program for Integral Assistance to Women's Health)
PCRI	Programa de Combate ao Racismo Institucional (Program to Combat Institutional Racism)
PNAISM	Política Nacional de Atenção Integral à Saúde da Mulher (National Policy for Integral Attention to Women's Health)
PNSIPN	Política Nacional de Saúde Integral da População Negra (National Policy for the Integral Health of the Black Population)
PT	Partido dos Trabalhadores (Worker's Party)
SEPPIR	Secretaria para a Promoção de Políticas de Igualdade Racial (Secretariat for the Promotion of Racial Equality Policies)
SPM	Secretaria para a Promoção de Políticas para a Mulher (Secretariat for the Promotion of Women's Policies)
STD	Sexually transmitted disease
STI	Sexually transmitted infection
SUS	Sistema Único de Saúde (Unified Health System)
UN	United Nations
UNDP	United Nations Development Programme
UNESCO	United Nations Educational, Scientific, and Cultural Organization
UNFPA	United Nations Population Fund
UNICEF	United Nations Children's Emergency Fund

Health Equity in Brazil

Introduction

In 2002, Alyne da Silva Pimentel, a twenty-eight-year-old Afro-Brazilian woman, died several days after experiencing complications resulting from a stillbirth that was inadequately treated at a public health center. The circumstances leading to her death highlighted gross inadequacies and failures in the quality of maternity care and emergency obstetric care provided to poor, Afro-descendant women in Brazil. A number of missteps and instances of medical neglect led to Alyne's premature and preventable death, including inadequate provision of services to pregnant women and a lack of high-quality emergency obstetric care in the region where she lived.

Since her death in 2002, Alyne da Silva Pimentel has become a symbol of the disparate medical treatment Afro-Brazilian women receive. In 2011, the Committee for the Convention on the Elimination of All Forms of Discrimination against Women (CEDAW) issued a ruling in the case *Alyne da Silva Pimentel v. Brazil*. The Committee found that the Brazilian state violated the right to life, as enshrined in the International Covenant on Civil and Political Rights,[1] which is a foundational human rights treaty, as well as the right to effective protection of women's rights and the right to health under CEDAW (CEDAW 2011, 13). In addition, the Committee found that, as a maternal mortality case, Alyne Pimentel's death was gendered and was also compounded by the discrimination she experienced due to her race. As I discuss in chapter 5, this case highlighted the intersecting forms of discrimination that led to the death of Alyne Pimentel and set a precedent for both recognizing and calling for reparations to address intersectional health inequities as they impact racially marginalized women in Brazil as well as in other countries.

Health Equity in Brazil examines the ways in which structural and institutional factors contributed to Alyne's death and similarly poor health outcomes for scores of nameless Afro-Brazilian women and men. By exploring how health activists and policy makers have attempted to address gender and racial health inequities over a thirty-year period, from the early 1980s to the mid-2010s, this book highlights Brazil's successes and challenges in its quest to provide quality health care to all of its citizens, particularly women and Afro-Brazilians. In the opening years of the twenty-first century, state action to address and challenge racial discrimination and racial inequality began to take place at an unprecedented pace in Brazil. High-level discussions of affirmative action and other measures to promote racial equality signaled a move toward the development of race-conscious public policies. This shift contrasted sharply with how the Brazilian state and society at-large approached racial issues in previous time periods. During most of the twentieth century, Brazil was viewed, both domestically and internationally, as a racial democracy or a society that was free of racism and racialized forms of discrimination. As a result, public policies focused on redressing racial inequalities or targeting Afro-Brazilians were believed unnecessary. In addition, research on issues affecting the Afro-Brazilian population, particularly health-related research, was rarely conducted and race was rarely incorporated in data on health and other social indicators, including in the census (Nobles 2000; Paixão 2013; Telles 2004).

The development of affirmative action policies, health policies for the black population, and legislation such as the 2010 Statute of Racial Equality and the 2012 Law of Quotas for Higher Education were virtually unthinkable when I first began doing research in Brazil in the early 1990s. This largely owed to the continued dominance of the ideology of racial democracy in Brazil, which fostered official and popular beliefs that discussions of race and racism were not necessary in the country. As a result, prior to the early 2000s, policymakers and politicians rarely spoke about or took seriously the possibility of addressing racial discrimination or racial inequality in the policy arena.

I first visited Brazil in 1994 with the intention of doing research on black women's reproductive health. At that time, I met several prominent black women activists in the city of São Paulo, including Edna Roland, Sueli Carneiro, and Fátima Oliveira. While my research focus has changed over time, I have continued to follow black women's health activism and the black women's movement, as well as broader issues of health policy development from a distance as well as close up. This book reflects a twenty-year process of engagement with activists, issues, initiatives, and texts that have been central to the effort to create greater health equity in Brazil. In this study, I document the development of the feminist health movement and black women's movement and their significant policy interventions related to women's health, particularly at the federal level. This book also analyzes the role of black movement activism in pushing for government policies to address and challenge racial disparities in health. The analysis explores the ways in which social movements have shaped health policy and Brazil's continuing challenges in achieving health equity by posing the following questions: How have policies focusing on gender and racial equity in health been developed in Brazil from the early 1980s to the mid-2010s? What are the strengths and shortcomings of Brazil's public health system (SUS) with respect to gender and racial equity in health? What role have activists in the women's movement, black movement, and black women's movement played in developing policies focused on gender and racial equity in health? Finally, in what ways is an intersectional approach, which frames gender, race, and class as interlocking aspects of social identity and experience, useful in addressing the health needs of Afro-Brazilian women?

The methodological approach used in this book combines analysis of health activism within the women's movement, black movement, and black women's movement with examination of health policies and programs at the local, state, and federal level. In many ways, this study offers a history of health policy development in Brazil and the impact of feminist and antiracist activism on health policy formulations from the 1980s to the mid-2010s. Between 2007 and 2014, I conducted interviews with health activists and researchers in several Brazilian cities, as well as with municipal, state, and federal government employees who worked in the health sector. I also did participant observation at seminars and conferences focusing on women's health and the health of the black population, as well as at national congresses of the *Associação Brasileira de Pesquisadores/as Negros/as* (Association of Black Brazilian Researchers, ABPN) that were held in 2008, 2010, and 2014. During these national congresses, I observed and participated in multiple sessions focused on the health of the black population, including state-of-the-art research and policy discussions.

My analysis also examines the impact of transnational advocacy by feminist and antiracist activists in Brazil, particularly in relation to United Nations world conferences, on health policy development and implementation in the country. By engaging the development of health policies since the early 1980s, this book provides new insights into the Brazilian government's efforts to meet the needs of populations that are often marginalized on the basis of race and/or gender. In addition, the intersectional approach used in this project places health policies focusing on women's health in dialogue with policies focusing on the health of the black population. Through use of an intersectional approach that views race, gender, and class as co-occurring and inseparable aspects of identity and social experience, as well as policy formulation (Collins 1998; Crenshaw 1989, 1995), this book seeks to shed light on the effectiveness of Brazilian health policies in meeting the needs of African-descendant women in the country.

While Brazil has enjoyed notable successes with regard to health care and health policy in recent decades, many of these achievements have owed to the active engagement of civil society and social movements with the state, particularly as the country transitioned from a military dictatorship to civilian rule beginning in the late 1970s. Although activists in the women's health movement have organized around women's health needs for several decades, activists in the black women's movement have also made women's health a priority since the mid to late 1980s. In addition, activists in the black women's movement have led efforts to address the health needs of the black population and to develop health policies that focus on the impact of both race and gender on black women.

Brazil offers an instructive case for examining policies focused on gender and racial health equity. On one hand, it has been at the forefront of policies for HIV/AIDS prevention and treatment at the global level, and its public health system has offered free health care to all citizens since the early 1990s. On the other hand, Brazil has faced extremely high levels of infant and maternal mortality, female sterilizations, and cesarean sections, all of which highlight ineffectiveness in efforts to address the health needs of women and children (Victora et al. 2011). As a society widely believed to be a racial democracy, or essentially one in which race and racial divisions held little to no significance, for much of the twentieth century, Brazil's racial composition provides added complexity to issues of health equity. The 2010 census found that close to 51 percent of the Brazilian population self-identified as being of African descent (Instituto Brasileiro de Geografia e Estatística 2011), when the *preto* (black) and *pardo* (brown) census categories are combined. However, until the early 2000s, there was minimal discussion of comprehensive policies to address the health needs of the African-descendant population.

The ideology of racial democracy was central to conceptualizations of Brazilian national identity and views of race and racism in Brazil for most of the twentieth century. Racial democracy also severely limited options for mobilizing against racism, since individuals and organizations that focused on racism were accused of creating racial divisions where they did not previously exist (Hanchard 1994; Twine 1998). During the early twentieth century, Brazilian sociologist Gilberto Freyre was one of the primary ideologues responsible for popularizing the belief that Brazil was a society that had avoided the pitfalls of U.S.-style racism. Freyre also advanced the notion that Brazil was a "Luso-tropical" society, or "new world in the tropics," that had developed out of a uniquely Portuguese style of colonization that encouraged racial egalitarianism and social, as well as sexual, interaction across racial lines (Freyre 1959). His 1933 book, *The Masters and the Slaves*, solidified Brazil's image as a society in which more "cordial" and "harmonious" racial dynamics found their roots in the colonial slave era (Freyre 1986[1933]). However, in Freyre's representation of Brazilian colonial history, the sexual violence and exploitation experienced by enslaved African women and indigenous women was discursively erased and reimagined as the foundation of Brazil's egalitarian and raceless *mestiço* (mixed-race) society (Caldwell 2007).

Idealization of racial and cultural mixing, or *mestiçagem,* was central to the Brazilian version of racial democracy. Similar to other Latin American *mestizaje* ideologies, in Brazil elites argued that the country's largely mixed-race or *moreno* (brown) population was a reflection of a nonracist society in which distinctions between "black" (*negro*) and "white" (*branco*) populations did not matter (Freyre 1974). Although black activists critiqued and challenged the ideology of racial democracy beginning in the early decades of the twentieth century, it was difficult to completely break its hold on both official and popular views of race and racism in the country (Alberto 2011; Butler 1998; Andrews 1991). This was particularly true during periods of severe political repression and authoritarian rule, such as Getúlio Vargas's *Estado Novo* dictatorship (1937–1945) and the military dictatorship (1964–1985).

This book's focus on health activism within the black women's movement and women's movement is both fitting and important because these movements have made health and health policy a central part of their activism since the 1980s. Moreover, health, and women's reproductive health in particular, have been important citizenship demands of both movements. Focusing on health activists in the black women's movement and the larger women's movement underscores the specificities of women's citizenship rights and human rights, especially as they relate to reproductive and bodily autonomy. The book documents and analyzes the history of these movements' interventions related to gender health equity, as well as civil society-state interaction related to both gender and racial equity in health. The contributions and critiques of black women activists are also central to this analysis, because their activism and political work highlight the relationship between gender and racial health equity.

The Development of Brazil's
Unified Health System

During Brazil's transition to democracy, following a twenty-one-year period of military rule (1964–1985), health activists struggled to create a universal health-care system, which would meet the needs of the entire population. The idea of health as a citizenship right was consolidated in the 1988 Brazilian Constitution, which declared that health "is a right of every individual and a duty of the state, guaranteed by social and economic policies that seek to reduce the risk of disease and other injuries, and by universal and equal access to services designed to promote, protect, and restore health" (Presidencia da República 1988). The Brazilian Constitution thus established health as the right of every Brazilian citizen and a state responsibility; it also enshrined the principles of universal and equal access to health services and called for the development of the *Sistema Único de Saúde* (Unified Health System, SUS), which was an important step in efforts to broaden access to health care in the country.[2]

During the late 1970s and early 1980s, a broad-based movement for the right to health emerged in Brazil. It developed in response to precarious health conditions and inefficiencies in the health system. Brazil's health reform movement, known as the *movimento sanitário* (sanitary reform movement), brought together researchers, health professionals and administrators, students, union leaders, and community residents to work for health reform, the universal right to health, and the creation of a single health system under the auspices of the state (Costa and Aquino 2000). The 8th National Health Conference, which took place in 1986, was an important milestone in the success of the health reform movement. Two years after the conference, as part of Brazil's transition to democracy, health reform activists made an important intervention in the 1988 constitution, which declared health to be a right of every Brazilian citizen and a duty of the state to provide. It thus established the principle of universality in the provision of health care and established a basis for the creation of the SUS two years later. It has been estimated that a third of the Brazilian population became part of the public health system with the promulgation of the 1988 constitution (Paim 2006). Prior to this time, only formal workers and their families were covered by social insurance. This meant that approximately 85 percent of the population received care at charity health facilities, at the public services provided by some cities and states, or at federal hospitals (Negri Filho 2013).

Development of the SUS was closely linked to efforts to democratize health, as well as ensure human rights and citizenship in Brazil (Paim 2006). The three core principles of the SUS were universality, integrality or comprehensiveness, and equity. A new concept known as *controle social* (citizen control) called for broad and meaningful civil society participation in health policy development. In addition, public funding was also an important guiding principle for the SUS (Berkman et al. 2005, 1167). Members of Brazil's health reform movement viewed these principles as a means of ensuring that the system would serve all Brazilian citizens in a holistic manner and in democratic dialogue with civil society. However, the implementation of Brazil's universal health system faced serious challenges at the outset, since it began in an unfavorable political and economic climate in which a market-oriented approach to health was promoted (Paim et al. 2011). A neoliberal government led by Fernando Collor de Mello was elected in 1989, which "presented significant barriers for the implementation of legislation and regulation necessary for the financing of the new universal health system" (Negri Filho 2013, 174).[3] The implementation of SUS was delayed until the end of 1992, following the impeachment of President Collor de Mello. During subsequent years, neoliberal economic policies increased the complexities of establishing a decentralized public health system that would meet the needs of all sectors of the Brazilian population.

In 1990, Federal Law 8.080 specified the "attributions and organization of the SUS" (Paim et al. 2011, 1786) and Law No. 8.142 called for the public health system to be controlled through municipal, state, and federal health councils. In Brazil's reformed public health sector, the practice of citizen control called for citizen representation on health councils and in health conferences at every level of government. By creating mechanisms that would ensure civil society participation in policy development and budgeting for the public health sector, advocates of health reform sought to create a public health system that would be inclusive and democratic (Costa and Aquino 2000). Researchers such as Cornwall and Shankland have highlighted the importance of citizen participation in health conferences at the municipal, state, and national level. As they note:

> Stimulating waves of engagement that ripple throughout the country, drawing together hundreds of thousands of people in deliberating health policies, and creating spaces for mobilisation as well as sites for social movements to press their claims on the state, the Conferências (health conferences) are an instance in which some of the promise of radical democracy comes to be lived out. [2008, 2181]

Creating a rights-based, participatory public health system was in line with democratic values that social movements and civil society advocated as Brazil transitioned from a military dictatorship during the mid to late 1980s and early 1990s. Citizen control of health was also viewed as an important means of ensuring universal citizenship with respect to health, as well as the democratization of public services (Paim 2012). However, it is important to note that the socialist and universalist principles undergirding the creation of the SUS did not recognize race as a significant factor shaping access to health or health outcomes. Indeed, this is one of the major paradoxes examined in this book.

Race-Conscious Public Policies in Brazil

Since 2001, policy developments focusing on affirmative action in employment and university admissions, as well as in health, have marked a sharp break with longstanding approaches to public policy in Brazil, which tended to elide race and advocate universalist approaches to address social and economic inequalities. The increased discussion and implementation of affirmative action policies at the federal, state, and local level in the early 2000s was an important and unprecedented development in Brazil. In the legal sphere, passage of the 2010 Statute of Racial Equality was an important milestone in efforts to acknowledge and challenge racial discrimination. However, it should also be noted that the final version of the statute was significantly altered, and provisions for affirmative action quotas in higher education were removed from it (Jeronimo 2010).

The issue of affirmative action in university admissions was revisited again in August 2012 when President Dilma Rousseff signed Federal Law 12.711, the *Lei de Ingresso nas Universidades Federais e nas Instituições Federais de Ensino Médio Técnico*, also known as the Law of Quotas for Higher Education. This law mandated that 50 percent of students admitted to federal universities come from public schools. It also required federal universities to increase their racial/ethnic diversity by admitting *preto* (black), *pardo* (brown), and *indígena* (indigenous) students in proportion to their population numbers in each federal unit or state. Although legislation such as the Statute of Racial Equality and Law 12.711 were passed, conservative sectors of Brazilian society and many academics often opposed such measures, and there were heated debates in the media and public sphere about the appropriateness and efficacy of using race as a factor in public policy (Fry et al. 2007a, 2007b; Kamel 2006; Santos et al. 2011).

Conceptualizing Racial Health Equity in Brazil

While affirmative action policies in employment and university admissions have been a popular topic of academic research (Cicalo 2012; Racusen 2010;

Santos 2006, 2009, 2014; Santos and Rocha 2007; Santos et al. 2008), health policies focused on the black population have been an equally important development and one that has received less scholarly attention.[4] The increased discussion and implementation of health policies for the black population have been especially significant considering, in many cases, they reflect concerns that black activists, particularly activists in the black women's movement, had focused on since the 1980s.

The Brazilian census utilizes two color categories to refer to and collect data on the African-descendant population, *preto* and *pardo*. Researchers and black activists have long criticized the use of two color categories on the census, since it divides the "black" or African-descendant population and traditionally has portrayed this population as being smaller than it actually is (Nobles 2000; Telles 2004). This has been particularly true when only the *preto* population is counted as "black" in official records, which was a common practice during the twentieth century. According to the 2010 census, the *preto* and *pardo* populations comprised 50.7 percent of the total Brazilian population (Instituto Brasileiro de Geografia e Estatística 2011). In addition, *preta* and *parda* women comprised 50 percent of the total female population (Instituto Brasileiro de Geografia e Estatística 2011). Demographic data provided by the Pan-American Health Organization in the early 2000s has also shown the size of the African-descendant population to vary from 46 percent to 70 percent (Torres and del Rio 2001, 94). These numerical ranges reflect the difficulties of gathering accurate data on the size of the African-descent population in Brazil. The use of color categories and the tendency for individuals to lighten or whiten their identities in government surveys have increased the difficulty of assessing the "true" size of the African-descendant population (Telles 2004).

Given the fact that people of African descent constitute a sizable percentage of Brazil's overall population and also constitute the majority of the country's poor (Beato 2004), I advocate use of the term *minoritized group,* rather than *minority group,* to describe their status in Brazilian society. Referring to Afro-Brazilians as a minoritized group highlights the ways in which social, economic, and political processes have positioned Brazilians of African descent as a numerically significant group that has largely been excluded from power. While Brazilian of African descent are overrepresented in the ranks of the country's poor, they have been drastically underrepresented politically (Johnson 1998). However, it is important to note that my use of the term minoritized group contrasts sharply with terminology that has been used by researchers such as Torres and del Rio, who have classified Afro-Brazilians as "the most important minority due to their numbers" (2001, 96, 97). Torres and del Rio also describe

Latin American countries that have large African-descendant populations, such as Brazil, in the following terms:

> ... despite the importance of the absolute number of people of African descent in these countries ... these populations do not enjoy significant political power but are part of a national reality in which their participation is limited. From the standpoint of ethnic identity, the population is not distributed uniformly and includes groups that are very active and others comprised of individuals who do not participate in public, community, or political activities. Examples are: Brazil, Colombia, Venezuela, and Panama, among others. [2001, 97]

Drawing on critiques of official data collection methods that have been made by black activists and antiracist scholars (Oliveira 2002; Roland 1999; Telles 2004),[5] I seek to challenge use of the term *minority group* owing to its tendency to perpetuate the view that Afro-Brazilians are a numerical minority, and that white Brazilians constitute the majority of the national population. When I conducted research in Brazil following the publication of the 2010 census data, it was striking to hear people, including federal government employees, say that Brazil was now a majority black country. Hearing these statements was unprecedented in my previous experiences, and black activists often said this with a great deal of pride. It should also be noted that black activists had long claimed that Brazil was a predominantly black nation, despite the fact that census data portrayed the country as having a small black population, because official statistics tended to only count the *preta* segment of the population as being black. For example, in the 2000 national census, the *preta* population was 6.2 percent of the total population and 7.6 percent of the total population in 2010. Although researchers now routinely combine both the *preto* and *pardo* segments of the population to calculate the size of the black population, a marked difference can be noted when only data for the *preto* population is used. As noted earlier, when this is done, the black population appears to be a small fraction of the total.

Examining health disparities in Brazil highlights the Afro-Brazilian population's status as a minoritized group. Though Brazil has long been considered a racial democracy, or a society that accords equal opportunities to all of its citizens, regardless of race or ethnicity, a growing body of research has documented health disparities between white Brazilians and Afro-Brazilians. Beginning in the 1990s, an increasing, though still relatively small, number of researchers began to investigate the health status of Afro-Brazilians.[6] Much of this research was prompted by concerns about health disparities that had long been expressed by black movement activists. For more than two decades, members of Brazil's black movement, particularly black women activists, have called on the government to address the health status of African-descendant men, women, and children as part of the struggle to achieve racial equality (Damasco et al. 2012; Santos 2009; Werneck 2007).

The concept of health equity is particularly useful when thinking about differences in health outcomes and rates of illness among different social and racial groups in Brazil. Braveman (2010, 31) describes health equity as "the concept underlying a commitment to reducing health inequalities—that is, systemic, plausibly avoidable differences in health, varying according to levels of social advantage, with worse health occurring among the disadvantaged." The concept of health equity moves beyond the notion of health inequalities by highlighting how issues of justice are related to and produce health inequalities. As Braveman (2010) notes, health equity is also grounded in the principle of redistributive justice and focuses on ways to reduce health inequalities. In this book, the concepts of racial health equity and gender health equity are used as ways to think about and assess health outcomes among women, among the African-descendant population in general, and among African-descendant women in particular.

A number of illnesses and health concerns that have a disproportionate impact on Afro-Brazilians have been identified by scholars and health activists, including sickle cell anemia, type II diabetes, hypertension, and infant mortality (Fundação Nacional de Saúde 2005; Kalckmann et al. 2010; Leal et al. 2005; Lopes 2005). Researchers have also found striking disparities in life expectancy for different color/racial groups in Brazil. Based on data from Brazil's national census for 2000, the life expectancy for the *branca* (white) population was found to be 73.99 years, while the life expectancy for the *preta* population was found to be 67.64 years and 68.03 years for the *parda* population. This translates into a 6.35 year difference in life expectancy for the *preta* population and 5.96 years for the *parda* population, when compared to the *branca* population (Lopes 2005).

Racial/ethnic disparities in health are further compounded for Afro-Brazilian women by gender-specific conditions and illnesses. When compared to white women, Afro-Brazilian women have often been disproportionately affected by a number of reproductive health issues such as fibroid tumors, maternal mortality, and clandestine abortions (Koshimizu 2011; Martins 2006; Volochko 2010).[7] In addition, activists in the black women's movement have long suspected that Afro-Brazilian women have been subjected to sterilization, including forced sterilizations, at higher rates than white women (Damasco et al. 2012; Geledés 1991b; Roland 1999; Santos 2009). As Sonia Santos has noted:

The majority of the time the black population has experienced traumatic situations and ones of deep disrespect of their human rights in the health services; they have to confront institutional racism historically and on an everyday basis (as well as sexism, heterosexism). These circumstances, joined with adverse socio-economic situations—poverty, racial segregation, low educational levels, low salaries and unemployment—and the effects of racial/ ethnic illnesses (sickle cell anemia, hypertension, type II diabetes, among others), have placed the black population in a profound situation of vulnerability and inequality. [2009, 282]

Beyond "Pior Ainda": Developing an Intersectional Framework for Health Equity in Brazil

In my frequent conversations with a black woman health activist in the city of Porto Alegre during the late 2000s and early 2010s, she would often mention that health professionals and white feminists commonly referred to black women's health status as being *pior ainda,* which means "even worse" in English. The notion of *pior ainda* captures the sense that black women's health status is being compared to that of white women; however, while this phrase highlights worse health outcomes for black women, it fails to specify what is worse about these outcomes or how they came to be that way. As a result, describing black women's health as *pior ainda* may obfuscate more than it clarifies. The vagueness of this notion can also leave one feeling powerless to change a situation that appears to be worse than one would like. Instead, the reality of black women's worse health outcomes is normalized and rendered as something immune to change.

This study is centrally concerned with examining the effectiveness of Brazil's health system in meeting the needs of women, Afro-Brazilians, and Afro-Brazilian women. My focus requires simultaneous consideration of gender health equity, racial equity, and the intersection of the two. The analysis seeks to advance an intersectional view of health equity that addresses the ways in which gender, race, class, and other forms of social marginalization shape differential health outcomes for marginalized populations. By examining health activism by feminist health activists, particularly black women, and black movement activists, this study offers new perspectives on how gender and race have entered the health policy arena in Brazil, as well as efforts to achieve gender and racial equity in health. Employing an intersectional approach to health policy analysis is particularly important for black women, because their treatment in the health-care system and health outcomes lie at the crossroads of gendered and racialized forms of social experience and social inequality.

The framework of intersectionality, as developed by feminist activists and scholars in Brazil, the United States, and other national contexts is central to the analysis provided in this book. The social thought and writings of African American feminists in the United States have been instrumental in the development of the concept of intersectionality. While the concept of intersectionality, as formulated by African American feminist legal scholar Kimberlé Crenshaw (1989, 1995), was not originally developed to address issues of health policy, it provides an effective and important means to broaden health policy beyond a race- or gender-only focus.[8] In addition, despite the fact that the concept of intersectionality originally sought to address the experiences of U.S. women of color, it offers a basis for understanding the ways in which Afro-Brazilian women's experiences with regard to health and health care are shaped by multiple axes of identity and inequality, including gender, race, class, sexuality, and regional location. As I argue in chapter 2, the concept of intersectionality has also developed along distinctly Brazilian lines and has been central to much of the work of black women activists in the country. Given the fact that intersectionality has become a transnational and diasporic concept, it is important to consider resonances and dissonances in how it is conceptualized and utilized, particularly in and by African diaspora communities that are linked by similar histories of racial slavery and contemporary forms of gendered antiblack racism.

Kimberlé Crenshaw's (1995) work uses the concept of structural intersectionality to describe how African American women, and other U.S. women of color, are positioned within interlocking structures of domination. Crenshaw's discussion of domestic violence underscores the importance of examining the "intersectional location" of women of color when considering the development of policies and remedies to address the social, economic, and political disempowerment of racially dominated groups (1995, 360). Crenshaw also proposes the use of political intersectionality as a heuristic tool for examining how U.S. women of color are positioned in relation to various political concerns and struggles. For Crenshaw, the concept of political intersectionality provides a means of describing "the location of women of color within overlapping systems of subordination and at the margins of feminism and antiracism" (1995, 367).

African American feminist sociologist Patricia Hill Collins has further elaborated the concept of intersectionality by examining its significance as a tool for understanding "the ability of social phenomena such as race, class, and gender to mutually construct one another" (1998, 205). As Collins observes, African American women "can be seen both as a group that occupies a distinctive social location within power relations of intersectionality and as one wherein intersectional processes characterize Black women's collective self-definitions and actions" (1998, 205). In Collins's view, intersectionality is most usefully applied as a conceptual framework or heuristic device for examining structural power relations, rather than as a framework for describing "any actual patterns of social organization" (1998, 208). As she notes, "intersectionality provides an interpretive framework for thinking through how intersections of race and class, or race and gender, or sexuality and class, for example, shape any group's experience across specific social contexts" (1998, 208).

A growing number of U.S. and Canadian feminist scholars of health have also begun to openly advocate use of an intersectional approach in research on health disparities and health policy. Work by Lynn Weber and Deborah Parra-Medina argues for the value of intersectional approaches to health noting:

> On the one hand, intersectional approaches complicate the traditional models of health and illness by incorporating more dimensions, situationally specific interpretations, group dynamics and an explicit emphasis on social change. On the other hand, they provide a powerful alternative way of addressing questions about health disparities that traditional approaches have been unsuccessful in answering. [2003, 222]

Lynn Weber's subsequent work has highlighted the contributions of "social justice-driven health disparities research," arguing that "feminist intersectional scholarship, which is empirically based (that is, resting on direct observation of behavior), not positivist (assuming distance and disengagement between researcher and researched)" suggests new ways to bridge the gap between theory in the academy and social action (2006, 33).

Hankivsky and Cormier's (2009) work offers a rare discussion of the use of intersectionality in health policy. They highlight the benefits of developing intersectional perspectives for health policy design and implementation, in order to address how multiple, overlapping social identities and experiences shape policy needs and outcomes, as well as policy efficacy. Their discussion of the limitations of using single identity and single-issue frameworks in policy design is particularly important. In contrast to single identity or single-issue frameworks, Hankivsky and Cormier (2009) argue that intersectionality provides a way to see, acknowledge, and address the complexity and dynamism found in real life. As they note:

By bringing to the foreground the various background dimensions that inter-
act to create layers of inequality, a more complete and sophisticated analysis
can be developed, one that better captures the ways in which public policy
is experienced by various groups of women and men who may experience
multiple forms of discrimination. Policy-makers may be persuaded to in-
corporate this approach into their work if they understand that it has the
potential to lead to more effective, more responsive, and therefore, more
efficient policy decisions. [Hankivsky and Cormier 2009, 41–42]

Books, articles, reports, and pamphlets published by black women's NGOs
and individual black women scholar-activists have been instrumental in establishing a corpus of literature focusing on black women's health and intersectional
perspectives on health in Brazil (Cruz et al. 2008; Geledés 1991a, 1991b; Oliveira
2002; Werneck et al. 2000). Though many of these publications were not the
result of traditional academic research (Lebon 2007), they have been important
intellectual interventions in the nascent field of health disparities research in Brazil. Furthermore, given the paucity of research focusing on the black population,
particularly in the 1990s and early 2000s, these publications were an important
means of producing alternative forms of knowledge that challenged the longstanding tradition of color-blind health research, policy, and practice in Brazil.
They also offered early analyses of black women's health that have served to guide
more recent academic research in this area. I use work published by black women
activists and black women's organizations as valuable and important primary
sources for understanding the intersectional relationship among gender, race,
and class in shaping health, as well as for thinking about ways to enhance and
expand academic research and government policy in this area.

Outline of the Book

Chapter 1 examines the development of health policies for women in Brazil
since the early 1980s and the central role that feminist health activists have
played in calling for gender health equity. Women's health, particularly reproductive health and abortion, has been a central issue for Brazilian feminists
for several decades. This chapter explores the following questions: How have
state policies on women's health developed and changed since the early 1980s?
What role have feminist health activists played in developing health policies
for women? What challenges exist in efforts to achieve gender health equity
in Brazil? This chapter also considers some of the major challenges that arose
related to gender health equity during the first and second administrations of
Dilma Rousseff, Brazil's first female president.

Using the lens of intersectionality, chapter 2 explores black women's health activism in Brazil since the mid-1980s. I argue that black women's location at the nexus of gender, racial, and class-based forms of discrimination has provided them with a unique perspective on health and has enabled them to develop an intersectional approach to health policy. This approach has been particularly important given the tendency for policymakers to focus either on women or Afro-Brazilians, which often renders Afro-Brazilian women invisible in the policy arena. The analysis focuses on black women's activism at the local level, primarily through the actions of non-governmental organizations, as well as at the national and transnational level. Discussion of black Brazilian women's organizing for the III World Conference against Racism, which was held in 2001, figures prominently in this chapter.

Chapter 3 examines the development of state policies focusing on the health of the black population in Brazil and examines them in the context of political shifts since 1988, a year that marked the one-hundredth anniversary of Brazilian abolition and the promulgation of a new democratic constitution. Given Brazil's longstanding image as a society in which race and skin color hold little importance as a basis of social division and discrimination, this chapter explores how the relationship between race and health and the health status of Afro-Brazilians have been conceptualized in recent decades. The analysis is guided by the following questions: How have health policies for the black population developed at the federal level and within the context of Brazil's Unified Health System (SUS), particularly since the Zumbi march[9] was organized by black activists in 1995 and the World Conference against Racism was held in 2001? How have advocates and critics of race-conscious health policies conceptualized the relationship between race, racism, and health? How does the development of health policies for the black population and other race-conscious public policies, such as affirmative action, since the early 2000s provide insight into changing state discourses and practices related to race and racism?

Chapter 4 examines some of the key issues and challenges related to the effective implementation of health policies for the black population in Brazil. The analysis centers on the development of initiatives to combat institutional racism in the health sector, as well as on the complexities of fully and consistently implementing collection of the *quesito cor* (color/race data) in epidemiological records and health research. These two issues highlight the racial implications of health policies for the black population and the impact that beliefs that racism is either nonexistent in Brazil or confined to individual prejudice have had on possibilities for the effective implementation of policies to promote racial health equity.

Chapter 5 uses the circumstances surrounding Alyne da Silva Pimentel's 2002 death and the subsequent legal decision to examine maternal mortality in Brazil, particularly as it affects poor, Afro-descendant women. I analyze the ways in which Alyne's death and the legal case that her family pursued shed light on Afro-Brazilian women's experiences of maternal death. The analysis addresses the following questions: What role do gender, race, and class play in shaping Afro-Brazilian women's vulnerability to maternal mortality? How has the Brazilian state sought to address and reduce maternal mortality? What are the strengths and limitations of these approaches, particularly for Afro-Brazilian women? What are some potential benefits that can be gained from using a human rights approach to address maternal mortality among Afro-Brazilian women?

Chapter 6 examines efforts to address the HIV/AIDS prevention needs of the Afro-Brazilian population and places such efforts within the broader context of Brazil's universalist HIV/AIDS prevention and treatment programs. The analysis maps the development of Brazil's HIV/AIDS policies and initiatives at the federal level and explores the extent to which race and the specific needs of the Afro-Brazilian population have been addressed in recent decades. Given the fact that Brazil has been internationally recognized as a model of successful prevention and treatment of HIV/AIDS, it is important to consider the impact of these initiatives on the African-descendant population in order to more fully understand issues of health equity in the country. This chapter also examines HIV prevention and support initiatives that have been developed by black women's organizations and how their work in local communities highlights the racial, gender, and class dimensions of the HIV/AIDS epidemic.

The conclusion ties the various strands of the book's argument together and examines current and future challenges related to Brazilian health policy. It also assesses the limits of universalist policies in achieving racial and gender health equity in Brazil, as well as the promise of intersectionality for advancing change in this area. It also discusses political and policy challenges that Brazil faced in the mid-2010s, particularly the Zika virus outbreak and the political crisis that led to President Dilma Rousseff's impeachment and removal from office. As the conclusion points out, many of the advances made with regard to women's health and the health of the black population that are discussed in this book were extremely fragile and subject to being reversed by 2016 when President Rousseff was forced from office.

Feminist Dreams and Nightmares

The Struggle for Gender Health Equity in Brazil

On December 26, 2011, Brazilian President Dilma Rousseff issued Provisional Measure 557 (*Medida Provisória*), also known as MP 557, which called for the creation of a National System of Registration, Tracking and Follow-up of Pregnant and Puerperal Women for the Prevention of Maternal Mortality (*Sistema Nacional de Cadastro, Vigilância e Acompanhamento de Gestante e Puérpera para a Prevenção da Mortalidade Materna*). MP 557 sought to establish a nationwide system for registering pregnant women, which would place them under state surveillance and possibly subject them to penal action if they were suspected of having an induced abortion. It also called for the provision of financial assistance to low-income pregnant women to cover transportation costs for medical appointments.

On May 31, 2012, MP 557 expired before being voted on by the Brazilian Congress. However it raised important issues related to state intervention in the areas of reproductive health and women's health; it also created a firestorm of controversy and critique, particularly from public health professionals, including the Brazilian Center for Health Studies (CEBES) and the Brazilian Association of Collective Health (ABRASCO), as well as feminist activists. The National Health Council, a body comprised of health professionals, users of the public health system, and civil society representatives, also disapproved of the measure. The provisional measure was criticized for violating women's human rights, since it sought to create surveillance mechanisms for pregnant women (Leme 2009). Given that MP 557 was issued during the 2011 Christmas and New Year's Holiday, this timing further heightened activists' concerns that it was a stealthy and ill-conceived policy.

Provisional Measure 557 reflected an authoritarian posture by Rousseff, Brazil's first female president, that undermined the longstanding participation of feminist health activists in shaping health policies for women. This tradition of civil society involvement in policy development and implementation emerged during Brazil's transition from a military dictatorship to democratic rule in the early 1980s, in large part due to the demands of feminist health activists and health reform advocates, and has been a key feature of health policy in recent decades. This chapter traces the development of health policies for women in Brazil since the early 1980s and examines the central role feminist health activists have played in calling for gender health equity. Women's health, particularly reproductive health and abortion, has been a central organizing issue for Brazilian feminists for several decades. The analysis in this chapter explores the following questions: How have state policies on women's health developed and changed since the early 1980s? What role have feminist health activists played in developing health policies for women? What challenges continue to exist in efforts to achieve gender health equity in Brazil?

PAISM and Feminist (Re)Conceptualizations of Women's Health in Brazil

During the early 1980s, Brazilian feminists began to advance new conceptualizations of women's health that challenged biomedical and maternal-child health paradigms that viewed women's health as being limited to their biological function as reproducers (Diniz 2012). In addition, by 1980–1981, feminists began to insist that women had a "'right' to control their fertility and that the State had an 'obligation' to provide the means for women of all social classes to exercise that right'" (Alvarez 1990, 185). Feminist views of women's health challenged population-control policies that were promoted by the military regime and private institutions such as BEMFAM, *Sociedade Civil de Bem-Estar Familiar no Brasil* (Civil Society for Family Well-being in Brazil) and CPAIMC, *Centro de Pesquisas de Assistência Integrada à Mulher e à Criança* (Research Center for Integrated Assistance to Women and Children) during the late 1970s and early 1980s.

BEMFAM was created in 1965 as a private, nonprofit organization and was the first institution to provide family planning services in Brazil (Costa 2009). The organization became affiliated with the International Planned Parenthood

Federation (IPPF) and attained federal recognition in 1971. BEMFAM was heavily involved with creating contraceptive clinics in poor communities throughout the country. It was active in hundreds of municipalities, particularly in the Brazilian northeast. Writers such as Ana Maria Costa have noted that BEMFAM distributed contraceptive methods "without criteria and without clinical monitoring," which posed a danger to women who received services from the organization (2009, 1075). CPAIMC also held nonprofit status and was financed by the United States' Agency for International Development (USAID) by means of Family Planning International Assistance (FPIA), the Pathfinder Foundation, and other organizations. CPAIMC's activities promoted an interventionist ideology regarding contraception within the Brazilian medical community (Costa 2009). The organization financed professionals who provided medical training for doctors and nurses, and supported a network of doctors who performed surgical sterilizations by donating equipment and subsidizing their activities (Costa 2009). Organizations such as BEMFAM and CPAIMC were also instrumental in promoting population-control policies in Brazil, which sought to curb reproduction, particularly among poor and non-white populations. Such policies gave little regard to women's health needs beyond reproduction.

The Program for Integral Assistance to Women's Health (*Programa de Assistência Integral à Saúde da Mulher,* PAISM) was elaborated in 1983 and adopted by the Brazilian government in 1985, the final year of a military dictatorship that began in 1964. Close examination of the development of PAISM provides important insights into how women's health policies developed within the context of the military dictatorship and the subsequent lag in their full implementation. An integral or comprehensive approach to women's health was central to the conceptualization of PAISM. The program sought to meet women's health concerns on a lifelong basis and to move beyond the emphasis on reproductive health that had characterized earlier initiatives. PAISM was intended to address a range of health issues, including cancer prevention, gynecological care, contraception, and fertility treatment, as well as all phases of women's lives, from infancy to advanced age.

PAISM represented a sharp break with earlier population-control policies and marked the first time women's health came under focus within the Brazilian federal government. In addition, fertility regulation was viewed as a social right, women were viewed as subjects, not only as reproducers, and there was also an educational dimension of the program that focused on altering the sexist character of health values and practices (Costa and Aquino 2000). Surprisingly PAISM was developed during the military dictatorship and at a time when little dialogue between women's health advocates and the military regime was possible (Oliveira 2005a). During the military dictatorship of the early 1980s, President João Batista Figueiredo created a Parliamentary Inquiry Commission (*Comissão Parlamentar de Inquérito*, CPI) to study issues related to population growth. Then Minister of Health, Waldir Arcoverde, participated on the commission and decided to create a proposal for attention to women's health. Minister Arcoverde's proposal for the creation of PAISM was presented to the commission in June 1983. After receiving criticisms from the women's movement and health professionals about the ways in which PAISM promoted population control, the Ministry of Health incorporated the demands of civil society and reconceptualized its approach to maternal-infant health (Oliveira 2005a).

Although women's groups initially rejected the proposal for PAISM because they opposed collaboration with the military government, they eventually supported its development. Due to concern that the program not become subject to bureaucratic manipulation, women's health activists became involved in the development of technical guidelines and educational materials for PAISM, as well as in the implementation of policies at the national, state, and municipal levels (Alvarez 1990).[1] As Sonia Alvarez has observed, the Brazilian feminist movement "successfully mobilized against those State factions who promoted *controlista* solutions and 'beat' the outgoing authoritarian regime 'at its own game'" (1990, 194). In addition to having to contend with the anti-natalist policies of the military regime, feminist activists also had to navigate claims from the political Left that any form of family planning was inherently anti-natalist (Alvarez 1990). PAISM's emphasis on an integral or comprehensive approach to women's health sought to be more holistic than previous efforts. According to Simone Diniz:

> "Comprehensive" health (*integralidade*) is a complex concept, more used in Latin America than elsewhere. In the case of the PAISM, comprehensiveness included the notions of primary, secondary and tertiary care; the physical, emotional and social aspects of health, and of care for women from infancy until old age, not only for the reproductive years. [2011, 126]

The establishment of PAISM within the context of the military regime has been attributed to three main factors: the move toward decentralization of health care, the presence of women activists within the government, and the call for a wider choice in contraceptives from within the women's movement (Alvarez 1990; Dixon-Mueller 1993). As Ruth Dixon-Mueller has observed: "Designed by feminists and physicians, the program intended to correct inadequacies in the provision of contraception and other basic health services for women, to emphasize high quality care, and to raise the consciousness of health providers to respect women's rights and autonomy" (1993, 89). However, some feminist scholars and activists have noted that a shortcoming of PAISM was its failure to address abortion, even in cases where it was legally allowed (Pitanguy 1999). Brazil's 1940 Penal Code criminalizes abortions except in cases of pregnancies resulting from rape and when there is a risk to the mother's life. Moreover, the Penal Code has continued to be important, because it set the terms for defining when abortion is legally allowed during the twentieth and into the early twenty-first century in Brazil.

During the mid-1980s, developments regarding women's issues at the federal level facilitated greater discussion of reproductive rights and programs such as PAISM. In 1984, the women's movement proposed the creation of a national council focused on women's issues (Alvarez 1990). The *Conselho Nacional de Direitos da Mulher* (National Council on Women's Rights, CNDM) was created by Law 7.353 in August 1985 (Bohn 2010). Establishment of the CNDM provided an important opening for feminists to affect political change and influence state policy as Brazil returned to civilian rule. However, there was not universal agreement among feminists about the creation of the CNDM, since it would encourage a close relationship with the state. Though some feminists supported the creation of the CNDM and wanted to be directly involved with it, others supported it from a distance, and still others believed that the council would lead to the cooptation of the feminist movement by the state (Pitanguy 1993). The CNDM mirrored state and city councils for women that had been established in the city and state of São Paulo and the state of Minas Gerais in the early 1980s (Alvarez 1990; Dixon-Mueller 1993).[2] The CNDM played a critical role in supporting the women's movement in its efforts to promote reproductive rights. The *Comissão de Estudos dos Direitos da Reprodução Humana* (Commission on Reproductive Rights) of the *Secretaria Nacional de Programas Especiais da Saúde* (National Secretariat for Special Health Programs, SNPES) was established by the Brazilian Ministry of Health in 1985 to coordinate and implement PAISM. The commission included representatives from the women's movement, the CNDM, members of other government ministries, and the academic community (Dixon-Mueller 1993). The commission existed until 1988, with prominent demographer Elza Berquó serving as its first president from 1986 to 1987 (Oliveira 2005a).[3]

Feminists who participated in the health reform movement (*movimento sanitário*) of the 1980s were important advocates of women's health issues. Women made up a significant number of the participants in the 8th National Health Conference, which was held in March 1986 (Costa 2009). The conference had five thousand participants and was an important milestone in efforts to create a new public health system with input from civil society as Brazil returned to democratic rule, following federal elections in January 1985. This national conference is often seen as the origin of the development of Brazil's public system, the *Sistema Único de Saúde* (Unified Health System, SUS), and an important marker and victory in the health reform movement's efforts to achieve an equitable health system that would address the needs of all Brazilian citizens. The resolutions from the 8th National Health Conference also called for the immediate convocation of a national conference on women's health.

The National Conference on the Health and Rights of Women took place in October 1986 and was organized by the CNDM, with support from some sectors of the women's movement, the Ministry of Health, and the Ministry of Social Welfare. Nine hundred representatives from every state in Brazil attended the conference. Proposals related to women's health were also developed in regional pre-conferences held prior to the national conference. This event "reaffirmed and detailed the guiding directives of policies for women's health in line with PAISM, transforming them into programmatic resolutions" (Costa 2009, 1077). The final report from the conference contained resolutions addressing the importance of including a comprehensive approach to women's health in the development and consolidation of the new health system. The resolutions also called for the reinforcement of PAISM, the provision of family planning services to challenge the influence of private agencies with population-control objectives, and the legalization of abortion (Costa 2009). The resolutions addressing reproductive rights focused on women's free choice of contraceptive methods, access to all existing methods, with proper orientation regarding their use, and the involvement of the state and its health-related entities, as well as the women's movement, in actions related to conception and contraception. The resolutions on reproductive rights also stated that private interests, whether domestic or international, should not interfere with reproductive health policies and practices.

The resolutions from the 1986 National Conference on the Health and Rights of Women were transformed into a political document known as the *Carta das Mulheres Brasileiras aos Constituentes* (Letter from the Brazilian Women to the Constituents). While this letter addressed women's political rights and their expectations for Brazil's new democracy, it also reaffirmed health as the central theme in the agenda of the women's movement and was used as part of the process of drafting the 1988 constitution. It also emphasized that health was a right of all Brazilians and a duty of the state, and that women had the right to have their health attended to, regardless of whether or not they were mothers (Costa 2009).

The ideas and demands articulated in the resolutions from the 1986 National Conference on the Health and Rights of Women and "Letter from the Brazilian Women to the Constituents" have played a fundamental role in how health has been conceptualized in Brazil since the mid-1980s. Furthermore, the impact of feminist health activists on the 1988 Constitution is evident in article 226, paragraph 7, which states that "family planning is the free decision of the couple, it is the responsibility of the State to provide educational and scientific resources for the exercise of this right and to impede any coercion on the part of official and private institutions" (*Constituição da República Federativa do Brasil* 1988). This description of family planning was important symbolically, since it was included as part of the democratic "people's constitution" of 1988, which conferred new rights on previously marginalized sectors of society and also called for state recognition of health as a citizenship right. Moreover, despite pressure from the Catholic Church to include a statement in defense of life beginning at conception, the 1988 Constitution did not include provisions related to abortion, neither those in favor nor those in opposition (Costa 2009).

PAISM's Incomplete Implementation

Though PAISM represented a progressive approach to addressing women's health comprehensively, it was never fully implemented. PAISM included nearly all of the reproductive health-care elements that were called for ten years later in the Program of Action from the 1994 International Conference on Population and Development (ICPD), which was held in Cairo, Egypt (Corrêa et al. 1998). Ironically, in the *Carta de Brasília* (Letter from Brasília), which resulted from a 1994 preparatory national meeting for the Cairo conference, Brazilian women's health activists called for the immediate implementation of PAISM. This highlights the fact that Brazilian feminists recognized that PAISM was in peril and were attempting to use the U.N. conference process as a way to call attention to its precarious state. As later sections of this chapter discuss, feminist health activists in Brazil repeatedly have used the U.N. conference process to push for the implementation of PAISM and other forward-looking policies designed to meet women's health needs and promote gender health equity.

During the height of PAISM's implementation (1984–1994), women's health services improved in some municipalities and states; however the progress and results were uneven (Corrêa et al. 1998). As discussed above, the first women's health program was implemented in the city of São Paulo, and the departments of health of both the city of Recife and state of Pernambuco made investments in reproductive health. Initiatives focusing on prenatal and obstetric assistance had already been developed in the northeastern state of Ceará, and PAISM trainings led to a more comprehensive approach to women's health there. Correa et al. (1998) note that, in the early 1990s, only 20 percent of the state services and 46 percent of the municipal services offered prenatal assistance to more than 40 percent of the population. In addition, only three municipal health departments provided contraception services to more than 40 percent of the women of reproductive age in their areas.

Original plans for the implementation of PAISM called for the program to be launched in the Brazilian northeast in 1984 and to be extended throughout the country by 1988. However, by the late 1980s, the program had not been fully implemented. In 1989, only the state of São Paulo was offering contraception in its Social Security health facilities (INAMPS). The relative success of PAISM in the city of São Paulo largely owed to the efforts of the administration of Luiza Erundina, the city's first female mayor and a member of the *Partido dos Trabalhadores* (Worker's Party, PT), and the unprecedented presence of and collaboration with feminists in her municipal administration.

Between 1988 and 1992, implementation of PAISM resulted in an increase of 110 family-planning posts in the city of São Paulo (Costa 1992). Services devoted to legal forms of abortion were also established in two municipal hospitals. In addition, a reduction in maternal deaths was recorded during this period (Costa 1992). However, despite the relative success of family planning efforts in the city of São Paulo, a 1988 study of the state showed that of the 1,797 health units that had implemented some aspects of this program by 1988, only 7 percent offered access to contraceptive methods (Barroso 1989).

Corrêa et al. (1998) have argued that PAISM's failed implementation occurred because it remained a stand-alone program never funded as part of the SUS. Similarly, Oliveira (2005a) has noted that, in practice, PAISM was never a directive of the SUS, although the Ministry of Health was responsible for developing norms for the program. In addition, PAISM was never linked to other important programs, such as the Adolescent Health Program, the National HIV/AIDS Prevention Program, or the Family Health Program (*Programa de Saúde da Família*, PSF). In 1995, more than ten years after the creation of PAISM, Brazil's public health services continued to lack "basic interventions in prenatal and maternity care, and cervical and breast cancer screening and treatment" (Corrêa et al. 1998, 3).

Ruth Dixon-Mueller has noted that a "*partial institutionalization of a feminist perspective* on women's health and rights at the federal level" had been achieved in Brazil by the early 1990s (1993, 91; original emphasis). According to Dixon-Mueller, although the Brazilian women's movement served as an example for feminists seeking to influence state policy in other countries, implementation of PAISM and other women's health programs proved difficult, "because of the deepening economic crisis and spending cuts, the decentralization of health planning to the state level, and a lack of political support in all but a few states" (1993, 91). Changes within the state, including the weakening of the CNDM beginning in 1989, also posed a challenge to complete institutionalization of feminist health policies.[4] In addition, during the 1990s, more than one hundred private family planning agencies,[5] including BEMFAM, continued to operate in the country, and implementation sustained opposition by the Catholic Church to the use of contraceptive methods considered to be artificial (Dixon-Mueller 1993). By the late 1990s, PAISM was more a feminist dream than reality.

Feminist Health Activism at the National Level

Though a strong feminist health movement exists in Brazil, it is also important to recognize that women's health has been a central concern and area of mobilization for the women's movement more generally in the country since the 1970s (Pitanguy 1999). In addition to challenging population-control policies and advocating for the full implementation of PAISM, Brazilian feminists have brought attention to the extremely high rates of female sterilization in the nation. They have also called for the decriminalization of abortion, which would remove it as a crime from the Brazilian Penal Code, as well as the provision of abortion services in situations where it is legally allowed, including rape and risk to the mother's life. Moreover, despite challenges to the full implementation of PAISM, feminist health activists continued to view it as a model for women's health and call for its implementation well into the 1990s.

Activists in Brazil's black women's movement have been the leading advocates for the development of research and policies focusing on both racial/ethnic and gender health disparities. In most cases, black women's calls for health programs and initiatives that attend to the needs of the Afro-Brazilian population have been grounded in their personal experiences and observations, as well as their activism in black organizations and women's organizations. The emergence of the black women's movement in the late 1980s marked a new phase of political activism that began to bridge the struggles for racial and gender justice in Brazil. During the late 1970s and 1980s, a number of important black movement and women's movement organizations were formed throughout the country, including Geledés and Maria Mulher in São Paulo and Porto Alegre (Caldwell 2007; Lebon 2007; Santos 2012). These organizations played a crucial role in placing issues of race and gender on the political agenda as the country gradually returned to democratic rule and civil society mobilization increased during the early and mid-1980s.

While the black movement and women's movement both achieved a measure of success in promoting discussion of racism and sexism during the late 1970s and 1980s, the relationship between both forms of discrimination and their combined impact on black women was rarely emphasized. As a result, although black women were involved with both movements from their inception, they often found that their concerns were marginalized (Caldwell 2007). The marginalization of black women's concerns led to the development of a strong black women's movement during the 1980s and 1990s that made health, especially reproductive health, a major focus.

Feminist non-governmental organizations such as the *Rede Nacional Feminista de Saúde, Direitos Sexuais e Direitos Reprodutivos* (Feminist Network for Health, Sexual Rights and Reproductive Rights), CEPIA (*Cidadania, Estudo, Pesquisa, Informação e Ação*), CFEMEA (*Centro Feminista de Estudos e Assessoria*), *Coletivo Feminista Sexualidade e Saúde, SOS Corpo,* and *Geledés* (a black women's NGO based in São Paulo) actively organized around reproductive rights issues at the local and national level during the 1980s. In the mid-1990s, the feminist movement chose citizen control of health policies as the focus of its efforts at the municipal, state, and federal level (Oliveira 2005a). As noted earlier, the concept and practice of citizen control was central to the conceptualization of Brazil's public health system, the SUS. Through participation on municipal, state, and federal health councils, as well as in conferences at each of these levels, feminist health activists have pushed for the development and implementation of programs and policies that address women's health needs and promote gender health equity. Scholars such as Rosalind Petchesky (2003) have argued that feminist health activists' engagement with the Brazilian state led to an unprecedented degree of institutionalization of the women's health movement at federal, state, and municipal levels by the early 2000s.

Early feminist health organizations included SOS Corpo, which was founded in the city of Recife in 1981, and the *Coletivo Feminista Sexualidade e Saúde* (Feminist Sexuality and Health Collective), which was founded in the city of São Paulo in 1985. The *Comissão de Cidadania e Reprodução* (Commission for Citizenship and Reproduction, CCR) was founded in 1991 and functions at the national level (Oliveira 1998). Feminist organizations that have supported reproductive rights and women's health, while not exclusively focusing on these issues, included CFEMEA, *Centro Feminista de Estudos e Assessoria* (Feminist

Center of Study and Support), which was founded in Brasília in 1989, and CE-PIA, which was founded in the city of Rio de Janeiro in 1990. These organizations played a critical role in promoting a feminist health agenda and enforcing social accountability mechanisms that place pressure on the state to address women's health needs. Feminist organizations were also instrumental in helping sustain Brazil's independence against external political pressures that would weaken policies and initiatives focusing on women's health (Petchesky 2003).

Rosalind Petchesky has highlighted four features of the "partnership" model that developed between women's health groups such as *SOS-Corpo, Fala Preta* (a black women's non-governmental organization in the city of São Paulo),[6] the *Coletivo Feminista Sexualidade e Saúde,* CEPIA, and the Brazilian government. This partnership involves "(a) strong representation on government-civil society monitoring bodies by (b) nationally coordinated networks of independent women's NGOs that in turn represent (c) major participation and leadership in transnational women's coalitions and caucuses (including in U.N. and alternative forums, like the World Social Forum) as well as (d) organic links with local CBOs [community based organizations] and health professionals and managers" (2003, 230). As Petchesky notes, these organizations serve as a vital link between global policy and discourse, "while translating and implementing human rights principles into local and national policy" (2003, 230).

Millie Thayer's (2010) work analyzes the organizational evolution of SOS Corpo and its involvement with transnational feminist discourses and practices. Thayer notes that, while SOS Corpo was initially developed to focus on issues of sexuality and to provide popular sexual education to low-income and poor women in the city of Recife, over time it became more involved with the Brazilian state and transnational feminist practices. During the early 1980s, along with other feminists, members of SOS Corpo were involved in the development of PAISM in the State of Pernambuco (Thayer 2010). They trained groups of state health professionals as a way "to increase their sensitivity to women's needs" (Thayer 2010, 65). This was the organization's first interaction with the state during the *abertura* period of the dictatorship, which was a time of political opening led by the military regime. Interaction with the state was initially viewed with some suspicion by members of SOS Corpo. However, the benefits of being involved with women's health programs was seen as a way "to influence the medical care provided to their working-class constituency in the public health system" (Thayer 2010, 65). A member of SOS Corpo was later invited to serve on the CNDM and the organization participated in the process of lobbying for the inclusion of women's issues in the 1988 constitution (Thayer 2010).

The *Rede NacionalFeminista de Saúde, Direitos Sexuais e Direitos Reprodutivos* (Feminist Network for Health, Sexual Rights and Reproductive Rights), also known as the RedeSaúde, was formed in 1991, following feminist mobilization for the XI National Feminist Encounter, which took place earlier that year.[7] By the early 2000s, the RedeSaúde was comprised of 180 institutions, including women's groups, non-governmental organizations, research centers, professional and labor organizations, and women's rights councils, as well as health professionals and feminist activists. The RedeSaúde had ten regional areas, organized in the states of Pará, Paraíba, Pernambuco, Goiás, Minas Gerais, Rio de Janeiro, Santa Catarina, São Paulo, Rio Grande do Sul, and the Federal District (Brasília). It was also represented on various councils, committees and commissions at national, state, and municipal levels.

During the early 1990s, the RedeSaúde began to focus on three main areas: conceptualizing reproductive rights as human rights, the defense of PAISM, and advocacy related to women's right to have abortions (Oliveira 1998, 35). Maternal mortality was also a key area of activism for the Rede since its founding. The Rede Feminista de Saúde began to focus on neonatal mortality, following the elaboration of the *Pacto Nacional pela Redução da Morte Materna e Neonatal* (National Pact to Reduce Maternal and Neonatal Mortality) in 2003. In an interview published in 2006, Fátima Oliveira, then executive secretary of the Rede Feminista de Saúde, noted that the network considered neonatal mortality to be important, but also recognized the tendency to focus on neonatal, rather than maternal mortality because of the emotional issues neonatal mortality raised, even among health professionals. She noted that in cities and states that lacked a strong feminist presence on the committees to prevent maternal death or where there was not a tradition of debate and struggle on such committees, they tended to be called "Committees for Life." In addition, financial resources also tended to go toward prevention of neonatal death, rather than maternal death ("Mortalidade Materna Persiste" 2006).

The RedeSaúde was instrumental in initiating campaigns focusing on maternal mortality and abortion, as well as publishing books, dossiers, newsletters, and other publications that called attention to health issues affecting women. These publications played an important role in documenting and analyzing these issues. In many cases, they also served as key texts that have been used to call attention to and address gender health disparities. In addition, publications by the RedeSaúde have highlighted health issues that disproportionately affect African-descendant women, thus supporting initiatives undertaken by black women activists that are discussed in chapter 2.

United Nations Conferences and
Transnational Feminist Health Activism

In addition to mobilizing at the national level, Brazilian feminists also used the United Nations conferences of the 1990s as an opportunity to articulate an alternative vision of reproductive rights and gender health equity. SOS Corpo entered the transnational activist arena through its participation in the United Nations Conference on Women in Nairobi in 1985 (Thayer 2010). Subsequently, representatives from SOS Corpo participated in ICPD, the U.N. International Conference on Population in Cairo (1994), and the Fourth World Conference on Women in Beijing (1995). The organization also took part in a transnational research network (IRRAAAG), a network of documentation centers focusing on women's health and reproductive rights, and the *Red de Salud de las Mujeres Latinoamericanas e del Caribe* (Latin American and Caribbean Women's Health Network, RSMLAC), in addition to participating in other regional and transnational networks (Thayer 2010).

The ICPD was one of the first times feminists from around the world organized to challenge population-control policies on such a massive scale. Feminists had largely been excluded from the First World Conference on Population (1974), which was held in Bucharest, Hungary, as well as the Second World Conference on Population (1984), which took place in Mexico. As Fátima Oliveira has argued, both conferences focused on policies controlling the bodies of "poor women and of the ethnicities considered to be inferior" (1998, 37). The ICPD provided an important opportunity for feminists to challenge anti-natalist population policies that promoted development at the expense of women's bodies and reproductive rights.

In preparation for the ICPD, a national encounter, *Encontro Nacional Mulher e População, Nossos Direitos para Cairo,* was held in the Brazilian National Congress in September 1993. The encounter sought to give greater visibility to issues of gender, reproductive health, and population. Approximately 550 people from all over Brazil participated in the encounter. The *Carta de Brasília* (Letter from Brasília) was written during the conference and later distributed to political authorities and diverse organizations throughout the country. This letter articulated a feminist standpoint on issues of population and development that could be used to inform discussions at the ICPD. Mobilization by Brazilian feminists prior to ICPD, particularly in relation to policies and programs such as PAISM, led to important outcomes from the conference. Brazilian feminist Sonia Corrêa has argued that "the Brazilian experience in the 1980s, both in advocacy and in policy formulation, must be interpreted as one of the relevant contributions to the paradigm change that occurred at the ICPD" (cited in Petchesky 2003, 226).

Scholars such as Jacqueline Pitanguy have highlighted the role of the U.N. conferences of the 1990s in "widening the international mark of human rights and providing instruments that allowed for the legitimization and support of the work developed by women's movements and organizations at the national level" (1999, 37). Along similar lines, Ana Maria Costa (2009) has noted that the U.N. conferences of this time period provided an opportunity for Brazilian feminists to "articulate" with feminists from other countries and consolidate strategic alliances which subsequently conferred a great deal of respect on the movement at the international level.

Abortion and Female Sterilization in Brazil

Despite decades-long feminist mobilization and advances in some areas related to women's health, policies and laws regarding abortion have been slow to change in Brazil. Since the 1970s, feminist activists in Brazil worked to decriminalize abortion and make legal abortion procedures accessible within the public health system. Efforts to decriminalize abortion have been rooted in efforts to ensure reproductive justice in Brazil, as well as to address the role unsafe abortions play in causing maternal deaths.

Since the 1980s, there have been ongoing debates regarding abortion in Brazil. These debates have been heavily influenced by the antiabortion views of the Catholic Church and conservative evangelicals, who have strongly opposed the legalization of abortion and have tried to restrict the provision of abortion in situations in which it is legally allowed. In their efforts to achieve full reproductive rights for women in Brazil, feminist health activists have focused on abortion as a key issue. Abortion has typically been a taboo and hidden topic in Brazil; however, during the 1980s, feminist health activists developed strategies to make it more visible. In the early 1980s, there was a growing number of repressive actions by the police and the judicial system against women and doctors involved with abortion in the city of Rio de Janeiro (Pitanguy 1999). Feminist health activists responded by writing for newspapers, organizing roundtable discussions about abortion, and supporting women who were affected by penal processes related to induced abortions (Pitanguy 1999). As a result, the right to voluntary abortion became a key political issue in Brazil during the 1980s.

Although decriminalization of abortion was discussed during the process leading to the promulgation of the 1988 constitution and as part of the larger democratization process, there were not significant changes in abortion legislation during this time (Rocha 2006). The lack of legislative advances related to abortion has often been attributed to the influence of the Catholic Church and its historical emphasis on religion and the family. Though there were no major changes in abortion legislation, and the provisions of the 1940 Penal Code remained in force into the early 2000s, feminist activists were successful in establishing technical norms for abortions and made some progress in guaranteeing abortions in legally allowed situations, as well as increasing the likelihood that women who had an induced abortion received proper medical attention (Rocha 2006). In April 2012, the Brazilian Supreme Court issued a ruling allowing abortion for women carrying fetuses suffering from anencephaly, a severe fetal anomaly in which parts of the brain are missing and the fetus has no chance of survival after birth. This ruling resulted from pressure placed on the Brazilian judicial system by feminist health activists regarding the issue of anencephaly, beginning in 2004. Provision of abortion in legally permitted cases has been a longstanding challenge and something feminist health activists have fought to ensure.

Brazil's Penal Code criminalizes women who undergo induced abortions with one to three years of imprisonment. Physicians who perform abortions may be imprisoned for up to twenty years (Presidência da República 1940). During the late 2000s, there was a marked increase in rates of criminalization and arrests for induced abortions. Brazilian abortion and reproductive rights advocate Beatriz Galli has called attention to the high stakes involved in seeking abortion services, noting that women "fear stigmatization, criminal investigation, revelation of their private medical histories to their families, coworkers or the public at large" (2011, 975). Important cases in Campo Grande, Mato Grosso do Sul, and the city of Rio de Janeiro highlight the impact of criminalization of women seeking abortions. In April 2007, police raided a family planning clinic in Mato Grosso do Sul and confiscated the medical records of more than nine thousand female patients. Several members of the clinic staff were also prosecuted for carrying out abortions. Four health care providers were found guilty and sentenced. Three nursing auxiliaries also received prison sentences between one and seven years (Galli 2011). The clinic owner was also found dead, owing to an apparent suicide, two years after police raided the clinic. By late 2008, more than 1,200 women suspected of having abortions were being investigated by the police and 150 had been charged. In addition, at least thirty women had been sentenced to community work in daycares or schools for disabled children by that time (Duffy 2008).

During August 2009, police raided four clinics in the city of Rio de Janeiro (Galli 2011; Kane et al. 2014). Abortion-related arrests also took place and were part of a larger trend in the state of Rio de Janeiro. Between 2007 and 2011, the state registered 351 police reports related to abortion (Kane et al. 2014). These practices also fit into global trends in the criminalization of abortion. As Kane et al. (2014) have noted, from 2006 to 2011, women were arrested for illegal abortion in at least thirty countries. The majority of women arrested were poor, African-descendant or indigenous, young, and lacked a competent legal defense. These dynamics can be seen in the arrests made in the state of Rio de Janeiro, considering 55 percent of the women arrested were nonwhite, more than half had only a secondary education, and only 8 percent finished high school (Kane et al. 2014).

While abortion is often focused on in Brazil and elsewhere as the preeminent reproductive rights issue, female sterilization has long been an important issue focused on by activists, researchers, and policymakers. High rates of female sterilization among women of all racial/ethnic backgrounds and social classes historically have reflected the lack of contraceptive options available in Brazil. The country has long had some of the highest rates of female sterilization in the world. Although voluntary sterilization is not permitted by the Brazilian constitution, and health ministry guidelines only recommend sterilization for women older than thirty-five whose health would be affected by another pregnancy, female sterilization has been widely and clandestinely performed when women undergo cesarean sections (Vieira and Ford 1996).

The Brazilian Parliament passed a 1996 law meant to curb the practice of tubal ligation; however, this measure has not been systematically enforced. Federal Law 9.263, also known as the Law of Family Planning, limited male and female sterilizations to individuals above twenty-five years of age and cases where conception posed a risk to the life of the mother. A 2006 National Study of Demography and Health of Women and Children found that female sterilization was the most frequent contraceptive method (29 percent), with 25 percent of women using the pill and 12 percent using condoms. This study also found a substantial decline in the frequency of female sterilization between 1996 and 2006. The rate stood at 40 percent in 1996 and 29 percent in 2006. There was also an increase in the use of birth control pills, which went from 4 percent in 1996 to 12 percent in 2006 (Pesquisa Nacional de Demografia e Saúde de Criança e da Mulher 2006). As chapter 2 details, concerns about racially motivated female sterilization led to the creation of autonomous black women's organizations during the late 1980s and early 1990s.

Federal Policies for Women
during the Early 2000s

Although the CNDM was an important force pushing for gender-specific public policies in the 1980s, by the early 1990s its influence had significantly declined, largely owing to backlash against its successes. During the two terms of President Fernando Henrique Cardoso (1995–1998 and 1999–2002), the administration did little to improve the status of the CNDM. At the end of his second term, Cardoso created the *Secretaria dos Direitos das Mulheres* (Secretariat for the Rights of Women, SEDIM) in response to demands by feminists in the PT (Bohn 2010). Like the CNDM, the SEDIM was located under the auspices of the Ministry of Justice and, thus, did not have a direct connection to the administration (Bohn 2010). When President Luiz Inácio Lula da Silva took office, one of his first actions was the creation of the *Secretaria Especial para a Promoção de Políticas para a Mulher* (Special Secretariat for the Promotion of Policies for Women, SPM) by means of Provisional Measure 103 in January 2003. This measure later became Law 10.683, and the SPM gained a permanent status as a federal secretariat that was part of the presidential cabinet. The Lula administration described the SPM as the realization of the "commitment of the federal government to women of the country" (cited in Bohn 2010, 88).

That the SPM was located within the presidential cabinet distinguished it from earlier entities focusing on women's issues within the federal government, such as the CNDM or the SEDIM.[8] In addition, the SPM was granted the status of federal ministry, which "translated not only in closer access to the President of the Republic, but also in a better administrative structure and the capacity to formulate and implement public policies" (Bohn 2010, 88). Although the SPM had a miniscule budget, it grew between 2003 and 2009 and was not reduced as significantly as those of other federal ministries. In comparison, the *Secretaria para a Promoção de Políticas de Igualdade Racial* (Secretariat for the Promotion of Racial Equality Policies, SEPPIR) experienced a substantial decrease in federal funding during the same time period (Bohn 2010).

In 2004, the Brazilian Ministry of Health instituted the *Política Nacional de Atenção Integral à Saúde da Mulher* (National Policy for Integral Attention to Women's Health, PNAISM). This policy resulted from dialogue with various sectors of civil society, including the feminist movement, rural women workers, black women, lesbians, and individuals with special needs (Oliveira 2005a). The PNAISM built upon the emphasis on integral or comprehensive women's health that was central to the conceptualization of PAISM. Two key areas emerged from the PNAISM that had a high level of visibility: the 2004 *Pacto Nacional pela Redução da Mortalidade Materna* (National Pact for the Reduction of Maternal Mortality) and the *Política Nacional de Direitos Sexuais e Direitos Reprodutivos* (National Policy for Sexual Rights and Reproductive Rights), which was instituted in 2005. In addition, the following year brought creation of the *Política Nacional de Planejamento Familiar* (National Policy for Family Planning).

Following the launch of the National Pact for the Reduction of Maternal Mortality, a booklet was published focusing on issues of equity as they related to maternal mortality among black women (Ministério da Saúde 2005). The booklet included information on *quilombo* communities—predominantly black communities, many of which were formed by fugitive slaves—as well as the impact of illnesses such as high blood pressure, type II diabetes, and sickle cell anemia on pregnant black women. Raising health professionals' awareness of these issues was important given the high rates of maternal mortality among black women in Brazil, a topic that is examined in detail in chapter 5.

Dilma Rousseff's 2010 Election, and Abortion

President Luíz Inácio Lula da Silva ("Lula") was elected in 2002 as a candidate from the Worker's Party (*Partido dos Trabalhadores*, PT), making him the first president of non-elite origins in Brazil's history. Lula was a founder of the PT and a former labor organizer who had run for president several times prior to his election. Abortion became highly politicized in 2010 during Lula's second term. Early in 2010, the issue took center stage as part of discussions for the III National Plan for Human Rights. Feminist activists were a driving force behind two sections of the plan, which called for the decriminalization of abortion (Corrêa 2010a). Ultimately, however, abortion was not decriminalized. During her 2010 presidential campaign, Dilma Rousseff was forced to openly address the issue. In March 2009, Rousseff stated in an interview for *Marie Claire* magazine that abortion was difficult, but should be legalized because it posed a major public health problem (Corrêa 2010b). However, by May 2010, Rousseff shifted to stating that "abortion is a matter of public health services," a position in line with the III National Plan for Human Rights (Corrêa 2010b). Two days before the first round of elections in October 2010, Rousseff met with representatives of the National Pastors Conference and with Catholic leaders to discuss her positions on abortion and gay marriage. Rousseff declared her personal position as being opposed to abortion, but defended public health services for women who have undergone the procedure (Corrêa 2010b). It is important to note that these statements did not address whether abortion should be decriminalized or legalized.

Rousseff also addressed the issue of abortion during her 2010 campaign in two open letters focusing on religion and politics. Both letters came in response to the growing political influence of Brazilian evangelicals and charges by her opponent, Marina Silva, that Rousseff had made inconsistent declarations about her position on abortion. Silva was a former senator and evangelical Christian who ran as a Green Party candidate in the 2010 presidential election. Rousseff's August 2010 *"Carta Aberta ao Povo de Deus"* (Open Letter to the People of God) borrowed its title from Lula's 2002 *"Carta Aberta ao Povo Brasileiro"* (Open Letter to the Brazilian People); however, as the contrasting titles suggest, Rousseff's letter was intended for a narrower segment of the Brazilian electorate than was Lula's. While Lula's letter was intended to calm fears about the negative impact a leftist president might have on the Brazilian economy, Rousseff's letter was an appeal to Christian voters and sought to allay concerns about her intentions regarding policies that would affect families. Rousseff also appeared with Lula in some of her campaign materials targeting Christian voters. In her "Open Letter to the People of God," Rousseff referenced policies enacted during the Lula administration that supported families, such as *Bolsa Família* and *Minha Casa, Minha Vida*. These programs provided economic and housing assistance to poor and low-income Brazilian families. Rousseff's letter described the family as the "bulwark of a healthy society," stating "The more structured the family is, the less social chaos we will have." The letter also touched on issues such as child abandonment, street children, and domestic violence. Given the controversy surrounding Rousseff's position on abortion, her failure to address the issue of abortion in her letter is somewhat surprising.

Rousseff's second letter, *"Mensagem da Dilma"* (Message from Dilma) was published on October 15, 2010 (Bonin 2010). Unlike Rousseff's first letter, this letter directly addressed abortion, as well as policies focusing on families. The letter touched on six key issues: (1) Rousseff's defense of the coexistence of different religions and religious freedom, as assured in the federal constitution; (2) Rousseff's personal position against abortion and support of maintaining the existing legislation on abortion; (3) If elected president, Rousseff stated she would not take steps to propose changes in abortion legislation and other themes related to the family and the free expression of any religion in the country; (4) Rousseff referenced the III National Human Rights Plan and stated her intention to not promote any initiatives that affront the family;

(5) Rousseff referenced the bill, *Projeto de Lei Complementar 122* (PLC 222), which was under review in the Senate, and affirmed her commitment to articles of the bill that did not violate freedom of belief, religion, and expression as well as other individual constitutional guarantees that existed in Brazil; and (6) Rousseff affirmed her commitment to creating laws and programs that would have the family as the principal focus, such as Bolsa Familia and Minha Casa, Minha Vida, if elected.

When Dilma Rousseff was elected in October 2010 she became Brazil's first female president. During the 1970s, Rousseff had been imprisoned by the military dictatorship for her political views and was tortured while in prison. Like her predecessor, President Lula, Rousseff was a member of the Worker's Party (PT). However, while in office, she often received criticism for implementing less-progressive policies and also for approaching her role more as a technocrat than as visionary leader with a social justice agenda. International observers have highlighted the gender focus of Rousseff's first administration, particularly in areas such as the Maria de Penha Law, which addresses domestic violence, equal pay for women, and prenatal care (Sweig 2012). In addition, Rousseff chose an unprecedented number of women to lead federal ministries during her first term as president. Many viewed this decision as signaling her commitment to women's leadership and gender equality.

Despite making several seemingly gender-sensitive administrative decisions, a number of Rousseff's policy decisions undermined a comprehensive approach to women's health, replacing it with a maternalist approach that emphasized women's reproductive role. During Rousseff's first year in office, the Brazilian Ministry of Health issued *Portaria* 1459, which called for the creation of the *Rede Cegonha*, or Stork Network. This network was designed to increase women's access to prenatal care and lessen challenges associated with childbirth, particularly in public hospitals. One of the main goals of the program was to decrease the maternal mortality rate in Brazil, which was in line with the United Nations' Millennium Development Goals.[9]

A good number of feminist activists and scholars criticized the Rede Cegonha as being a regressive response by Rousseff's administration to conservative religious and political forces (Diniz 2012). The notion of creating a "stork network" can also be seen as an effort to erase women's role in childbearing by perpetuating mythical ideas about reproduction that failed to adequately address or expand reproductive rights. Rede Cegonha's emphasis on maternal health also fell in line with the maternalist politics of conservative political sectors, which drew attention away from the widespread practice of unsafe and clandestine abortions by Brazilian women who did not have access to legal abortion. This perspective emphasized women's roles as reproducers and did not engage with the public health consequences of abortion being illegal, most notably how this historically has led to high rates of maternal mortality and morbidity in the country (Diniz 2012; Galli 2011; Mariz et al. 2014).

Race, Class, and Unsafe Abortion in Brazil

As discussed at the beginning of this chapter, Dilma Rousseff issued a provisional measure, MP 557, in late December 2011 calling for the creation of the National System of Registration, Tracking and Follow-up of Pregnant and Puerperal Women for the Prevention of Maternal Mortality. The measure also would have granted rights to unborn fetuses, which feminist health activists argued was unconstitutional. Although the Congress never passed MP 557, some Brazilian health advocates argued that it raised issues that remained unresolved more than a year after it was introduced (Costa and Bieber 2012).

Provisional Measure 557 is a glaring example of a breakdown in the Brazilian state's recognition of the importance of civil society participation in health policy development and implementation. Although the provisional measure expired before being passed in Congress, it raised a number of troubling questions about state surveillance of pregnant women, issues of privacy, and the abuse of executive power in creating new health policies that uniquely impact women. When the experiences of African-descendant women (*pretas* and *pardas*) are considered in light of this provisional measure, further complications arise because MP 557 did not adequately address the epidemic of maternal mortality within this population (Adesse and Monteiro 2007; Leme 2009; Martins 2006). In addition, poor African-descendant women were more likely to fall under the provisions of MP 557, due to their lower socioeconomic status, and thus be under increased state surveillance and potential criminalization when suspected of having an induced abortion.

Rates of unsafe abortion in Brazil have been shaped by regional, racial, and class dynamics. A 2007 study in Brazil found that annual rates of unsafe abortion were markedly higher in the country's northern and northeastern regions. While the range of unsafe abortion was between 20.4 and 45.2 per 1,000 women in northern and northeastern states such as Bahia, Pernambuco, Ceará, and Pará, the rates were lower than 20.4 per 1,000 women in southeastern Brazil for females between ten and forty-nine years of age (Adesse and Monteiro 2007). Similar rates were found for adolescent females between fifteen and nineteen years of age. These data highlight the greater vulnerability of females residing in less developed regions of the country to unsafe abortions. In addition, given the high concentration of people of African descent in the Brazilian northeast, many of these women fall into this category. Adesse and Monteiro's (2007) study found a high index of maternal death owing to unsafe abortion. Post-abortion curettage, which removes tissue remaining in the uterus, was also found to be the second-most sought after procedure for in-patient healthcare services in the Brazilian north and northeast. Nationwide, from 2002 and 2004, the rate of maternal mortality was found to be 77.9 deaths/100,00 live births for *preta* women and 38.2 deaths/100,000 live births for *branca* women. From 2002 to 2004, the nationwide rate of mortality owing to abortion was found to be 5.2 deaths/100,000 live births for *parda* women, 9.4 deaths/100,000 live births for *preta* women, and 3.2 deaths/100,000 live births for *branca* women. This amounted to a relative risk of death owing to abortion that was 3.0 times greater for *pretas* than for *brancas* (Adesse and Monteiro 2007). Galli (2011) has also noted that low-income African-descendant women with minimal education and limited access to family-planning services are more likely to die or suffer complications from unsafe abortions. In Salvador, Bahia, a city that has a majority African-descendant population, abortions have been the leading cause of maternal death for several decades (Galli 2011).

In February 2012 the Articulation of Black Brazilian Women's Organizations (*Articulação de Organizações de Mulheres Negras Brasileiras*, AMNB), a Brazilian network of black women's organizations and activists, posted a response to Dilma Rousseff's Provisional Measure of December 2011 (MP 557) on the Web site of Geledés (a leading black women's NGO based in São Paulo).[10] The AMNB statement highlighted the fact that, although maternal mortality was avoidable in most cases, it constituted a grave public health problem. The statement also pointed to the disproportionate rates of maternal mortality among black women, as compared to white women, and underscored the role that racism and institutional violence play in perpetuating a cycle of "neglect, negligence, [and] lack of access to services and information" regarding the lives and health of black women (Articulação de Organizações de Mulheres Negras Brasileiras 2012). The statement eloquently described the impact maternal mortality had on black women, noting: "For us, black women, maternal mortality is lived dramatically. Because we have around us a community that we sustain economically and emotionally, death becomes a tragedy of a broad spectrum" (Articulação de Organizações de Mulheres Negras Brasileiras 2012).

While the AMNB statement affirmed black women activists' interest in having the government institute measures that address racism and institutional violence, it also criticized MP 557 for failing to provide the tools needed for the public health system (SUS) to fulfill its role in preserving the lives and health of black women and prevent deaths owing to preventable causes. The AMNB statement also outlined five ways MP 557 reflects "misunderstandings and traps": First, it was issued without consultation or dialogue with interested parties, black women and their organizations in particular, which meant that the principles of democracy and civil society participation that had been established by social movements for decades were disregarded. The statement points out that the same error was committed in issuing the decree creating the Rede Cegonha, which according to the statement "demonstrated a grave democratic deficit and a great contradiction in the government of the first woman to occupy the presidency of the republic in Brazil" (Articulação de Organizações de Mulheres Negras Brasileiras 2012). Second, the content of MP 557 failed to consider two important national conferences, the National Health Conference and the National Conference for Women's Policies (both of which occurred in 2011). MP 557 also failed to consider the role of the National Health Council as a "privileged interlocutor and agency of deliberation about health in Brazil" (Articulação de Organizações de Mulheres Negras Brasileiras 2012). Third, MP 557 did not guarantee the expansion of the Health Network of the SUS (*Rede de Saúde*) with comprehensiveness and efficiency. Fourth, MP 557 and the Rede Cegonha did not propose explicit measures that permit institutional violence and institutional racism to be confronted and curbed as recommended in the National Health Policy for the Integral Health of the Black Population.[11] Fifth, MP 557 exposed the health of Brazilian women to disputes and the interests of the ultraconservative minority forces present in the society and the parliament. The statement concludes by affirming that while the AMNB opposed MP 557, it was willing to contribute to the debate and construction of instruments that supported health promotion and preserving the lives of women, especially, black Brazilian women.

President Dilma Rousseff's decision to issue MP 557 highlights the precarious state of women's health policy in Brazil by the early 2010s and the ongoing struggle to have the state recognize women's health needs and reproductive rights. Although feminist health activists, including many black women, had mobilized to promote gender health equity and increased attention to women's health needs for several decades by the time MP 557 was issued, the gains made were fragile and subject to being reversed, if not completely dismantled.[12]

During the 2014 presidential election, the issue of abortion came to the fore of public debate because of the widely publicized deaths of two young white women, Jandira Magdalena dos Santos Cruz and Elizângela Barbosa, who died as a result of complications from abortions carried out in clandestine clinics in the city of Rio de Janeiro. The death of Jandira Magdalena highlighted the unsafe conditions many Brazilian women face when they undergo an abortion procedure. Magdalena went missing after undergoing an abortion, presumably one that had been botched. Her body was later found in the trunk of a car after being incinerated and having her teeth and fingers removed in an attempt to conceal her identity. Although Magdalena's and Barbosa's deaths provoked a public outcry and extensive media discussion of abortion, none of the major presidential candidates took the issue on. This was particularly surprising considering that two women, Marina Silva and Dilma Rousseff, were frontrunners in the election. As Sonia Corrêa has noted: "no manifestation of public concern and regret was heard from authorities at federal, state and municipal levels and much less from candidates in the presidential race. The state's response to these evitable [avoidable] loss of lives was limited to police action aimed at chasing those directly involved in the deaths and closing remaining clandestine clinics in the metropolitan region of Rio" (Corrêa 2014b). Both presidential candidates' silence on the issue of abortion likely was due to fear of the high political cost that could accompany a position critical about abortion, and highlights the ways in which discussing abortion as a public health issue was censored by conservative political and religious forces in Brazil by 2014.

While the deaths of Jandira Magdalena and Elizângela Barbosa led to police action against clandestine abortion clinics, politicians, especially presidential candidates, failed to use them as an opportunity to address the high rates of unsafe abortion in Brazil. It is also important to note that the deaths of black women owing to abortion have rarely, if ever, been the subject of news stories or investigative journalism in the nation. Despite the lack of sustained discussion of unsafe abortion as a public health problem, data point to high rates of clandestine abortions in Brazil. The 2010 National Abortion Survey highlights the frequency of abortion there. According to the survey, in urban areas, 15 percent of women interviewed had undergone an illegal abortion. In addition, the survey found that one out of five Brazilian women terminated a pregnancy before age forty (Diniz and Medeiros 2010). Moreover, in 2013, 205,000 Brazilian women were hospitalized in the public health system for attempting to terminate a pregnancy (Mariz et al. 2014). A study conducted by the State University of Rio de Janeiro (UERJ) also found that there were 865,000 illegal abortions in the country the same year (Mariz et al. 2014).

The high rate of illegal and unsafe abortions in Brazil contrasts sharply with official laws and policies that fail to acknowledge the frequency of the procedure, as well as its public health consequences. Bonnie Shepard's (2000) work examines reproductive rights policies in Latin America and calls attention to the "double discourse system" that operates in the region. According to Shepard, this system "maintains the status quo in repressive or negligent public policies while expanding private sexual and reproductive choices behind the scenes" (2000, 111). In Brazil, as in many other Latin American countries, official denial of the prevalence of abortion, and public discourses that emphasize conservative values has forced the practice behind closed doors, which has deadly consequences for many women, particularly young women, poor women, racially marginalized women, and single women (Shepard 2000). High rates of unsafe abortion also violate human rights norms about reproductive rights as articulated in international instruments, such as the Programme of Action from the 1994 International Conference on Population and Development (Shepard 2000).

Conclusion

Since the mid-1980s, ongoing challenges with respect to women's reproductive rights in Brazil demonstrate the tenacity of conservative and regressive beliefs about women's health and sexuality and their impact on policy formulation and implementation. As noted in this chapter, views of women as reproducers and a strong emphasis on their maternal roles gained prominence in the 2010s, despite decades-long feminist activism that challenged these ideas. Policies proposed by President Dilma Rousseff, most notably MP 557 and Rede Cegonha, reflect this shift and also reveal the growing influence of conservative religious and political forces in Brazil. In addition, it is important to note that policies that take a more progressive approach to women's reproductive rights have been put on paper but rarely have been fully implemented, thus reflecting the Brazilian notion of not "leaving paper" (não sair do papel).

Sonia Corrêa, a prominent Brazilian feminist and sexuality rights activist and researcher, has described efforts to achieve human rights in the areas of sexuality and reproduction in Brazil as a "winding road" (2014a, 234). According to Corrêa:

> A compelling lesson from this winding road is that legal and policy reform, though indispensable, is wholly insufficient. History in Brazil and elsewhere shows that realizing human rights in the realm of sexuality requires unending struggles within the social fabric itself. Progress also depends, importantly, on dialogues and solidarity among the various constituencies advocating for sexual freedom and non-discrimination, and on sustained work to overcome class, race and other social hierarchies and inequalities that intersect with sexuality and human rights. [2014a, 234–35]

The existence of a strong feminist health movement and active civil society mobilization around health access did not translate into significant health gains for many Brazilian women by the mid-2010s. Brazil's regressive reproductive health policies became starkly apparent with the outbreak of the Zika virus in late 2015 and 2016. The emergence of the Zika virus highlighted the "tragic failures of reproductive health and rights policies in Latin America" (Roa 2016, 843). During January 2016, in response to the spread of the virus and a rising number of cases of microcephaly, in which infants are born with small heads and brains and experience severe cognitive and health disabilities, health ministers from several Latin American countries made public recommendations that women and couples postpone pregnancy for six months to two years (Roa 2016). However, as Mónica Roa has noted, "These recommendations seemed out of place in view of the fact that 56% of pregnancies in the region are unintended" (2016, 843). Official government responses to the Zika virus in the Latin American region also reflect the deep entrenchment of conservative beliefs related to contraception and abortion. With respect to abortion, seven of the last remaining countries in the world where there are bans on abortion under all circumstances are located in Latin America and the Caribbean. Legal abortion upon request during the first trimester is only available in Cuba, Mexico City, and Uruguay. The remaining countries in the region criminalize abortion, allowing few exceptions for the procedure (Anderson 2016).

When women of African descent are included in discussions and analyses of women's health and reproductive rights in Brazil, the picture becomes even more bleak considering African-descendant women's reliance on the country's public health system, the SUS, further increases their vulnerability to precarious health services and a public health system that has been substantially weakened by neoliberal economic reforms in recent decades. Subsequent chapters of this book examine both advances and challenges with respect to achieving health equity in Brazil, by addressing the relationship among gender, race, and class in the development and implementation of health policies, and the importance of adopting an intersectional approach to ensure that such policies address the health needs of African-descendant women.

Black Women's Health Activism and the Development of Intersectional Health Policy

> We consider health to be a strategic area from the point of view of organizing the black population. We believe that when we speak about health we are not speaking only about things, about wealth, about the objects that a person does or does not have . . . when we speak about health we are speaking about inequalities that are inscribed, that are crystallized on the very bodies and minds of people.
>
> —Edna Roland, São Paulo[1]

> I understand that we are doing the work of an ant, the work of an ant in the sense that we bring a woman here, begin work, begin a dialogue about empowerment . . . and this is our ant's work to get there and make an ant hill.
>
> —Staff member, Maria Mulher, Porto Alegre

The first epigraph above is from an interview I conducted with Edna Roland in December 1994. This was my first visit to Brazil and occurred at the beginning of my training as a Ph.D. student in anthropology. At the time, Roland was the director of the health program at Geledés, a leading black women's non-governmental organization in São Paulo. I met Roland when I visited the offices of Geledés in the hopes of gaining a better understanding of issues related to black Brazilian women's reproductive health and black women's activism in this area. During my visit, I was able to speak with Roland about the work that she and other members of the organization were doing to bring visibility to health issues affecting black women. The health department of Geledés had organized a seminar on the reproductive rights of black women earlier in the year in preparation for the 1994 International Conference on Population and Development (ICPD). At the time, they were part of a small group of black women activists who were attempting to call attention to racial and gender health disparities in Brazil, especially as they affected black women. This was largely a taboo topic at the time and one that was largely invisible within the medical community, as well as among health researchers.

During my first trip to São Paulo, I also met Dr. Fátima Oliveira, a well-known black feminist, women's health activist, and author, and visited CEBRAP (*Centro Brasileiro de Analise e Planejamento*), a leading progressive think tank in Brazil. When I visited CEBRAP, I had an opportunity to speak with Dr. Elza Berquó, a renowned Brazilian demographer who conducted pioneering research on race and reproductive health. During the 1990s, Dr. Berquó led a research group at CEBRAP focusing on black women's reproductive health. This research group was comprised of several black women researchers, including Fátima Oliveira, which was a rarity at the time. Although I was initially interested in researching black women's reproductive health as a graduate student, I soon discovered that it would be extremely difficult to do research in an area for which reliable data and an established tradition of research did not exist.

This chapter examines black women's activism related to health and explores how black women activists have sought to develop intersectional perspectives on health that call attention to the (simultaneous) role of gender, race, class, and other forms of social identity and experience in shaping health and wellness. The analysis focuses on black women's organizations and black women's activism at the local and national level, and their transnational activism, particularly in relation to the 2001 World Conference Against Racism. My analysis highlights the central role activists in the black women's movement have played in developing intersectional approaches to health in Brazil that emphasize the interconnected nature of racial, gender, and class inequalities in shaping health and illness.

Black Women's Organizations and Black Women's Health

Black women have been at the forefront of efforts to call attention to the impact of racial discrimination and social exclusion on the health status of Afro-Brazilians. Black women's health activism in Brazil initially stemmed from concerns about the reproductive rights of Afro-Brazilian women and later began to address a broader range of health issues, both for black women and the black community more generally. Examples of early health-related campaigns that had major involvement from black women, as well as "mixed" organizations of women and men, include the *"Não Matem Nossas Crianças"* (Don't Kill Our Children) campaign in 1989, which denounced the extermination of black children and youths by paramilitary groups and state forces in urban centers throughout the country (Lopes and Werneck n.d.). As Fernanda Lopes and Jurema Werneck have noted, this "campaign had international repercussions, creating broad mobilization and having a strong influence" on the process of creating the Statute of the Child and the Adolescent in 1990 (n.d., 10).

The founding of autonomous black women's organizations in Brazil during the late 1980s and 1990s led to the articulation of an intersectional perspective on women's health issues, particularly reproductive health, that emphasized the impact of race, gender, and class on black women's health and well-being. Table 2.1 profiles five black women's non-governmental organizations (NGOs) that were formed in the cities of Porto Alegre, São Paulo, and Rio de Janeiro during the late 1980s and 1990s.[2] All of these organizations have been at the forefront of efforts to address the health needs of black Brazilian women.[3] It should be noted that these organizations are located in either southern or southeastern Brazil. These regions of the country have historically had a higher concentration of black women's NGOs. The smaller size of the black population in the Brazilian south and southeast led to a strong tradition of political activism, particularly through black newspapers and organizations, such as the *Frente Negra Brasileira* and the *Teatro Experimental do Negro,* dating back to the early twentieth century (Alberto 2011). Black women's organizations founded in this region have likely developed for similar reasons, particularly because racial discrimination is often felt more acutely and a black/white divide is often more pronounced in areas that have smaller black populations (Alberto 2011, Butler 1998).[4]

Maria Mulher is one of the oldest black women's NGOs in Brazil. Founded in the southern Brazilian city of Porto Alegre, Rio Grande do Sul in 1987, Maria Mulher developed several innovative programs focusing on the relationship between violence and HIV infection among low-income black women, as well as providing psychological and economic assistance to HIV-positive women. Maria Mulher works directly with low-income communities located in the *periferia* (periphery) of Porto Alegre in addition to being engaged in activism and policy development at the local and national level. Geledés was founded in the city of São Paulo in 1988 and is one of the best-known black women's organizations in Brazil. The health department at Geledés was created in 1991. During the early 1990s, department staff there developed several pioneering health programs focused on black women's reproductive and mental health. It also produced important dossiers on black women's health that were some of the area's first publications. In 1991, Geledés published two dossiers focusing on health. The first was titled "Mulher Negra e Saúde" (Black Woman and Health) and the second "Esterilização: Impunidade ou Regulamentação" (Sterilization: Impunity or Regulamentation). These publications were important means of documenting black women's health concerns and initiating discussions about these issues. This was both significant and rare given the lack of research in this area at the time. In 1993, Geledés organized the National Seminar on the Reproductive Rights and Policies of Black Women, in preparation for the International Conference on Population and Delevopment (ICPD) held in Cairo the following year.

Sonia Santos (2012) has noted that there were members of Geledés, as well as some black movement activists and sectors of the mainstream feminist movement, who criticized the organization for promoting discussions of female sterilization in Brazil. While male members of the black movement often called for black women to reproduce and bear children in ways that did not emphasize women's reproductive autonomy, members of Geledés in São Paulo and some members of the MNU (Unified Black Movement, *Movimento Negro Unificado*) in Belo Horizonte argued that the issue of reproductive rights should be analyzed based on the "needs and desires of black women" (Damasco et al. 2012, 136). As has been noted for the United States, concerns about population control and genocide have often been used within black communities to challenge women's reproductive autonomy (Nelson 2003; Roberts 1997). Such concerns have made it difficult for black women to prioritize their health needs or have them recognized within the larger black community.

Criola, a black women's NGO founded in Rio de Janeiro in 1992, has also played a major role in bringing greater visibility to the health concerns of black women. Criola's health program has focused on promoting the inclusion of black women's health concerns under the rubric of women's health and focusing greater attention on the specific health needs of black women. During the 1990s, the organization trained dozens of Afro-Brazilian adolescent girls and women to disseminate health information in their communities and workplaces. Criola has also developed initiatives to support the mental and physical health of Afro-Brazilian women through self-help groups and the *Jornada Omowalê*, which integrates traditional Afro-Brazilian medicine with scientific and medical knowledge related to women's health. In 2006, Criola began to organize training seminars for health professionals to raise awareness of the racial/ ethnic dimensions of health and illness. Criola has also been instrumental in producing books, pamphlets, and other publications related to black women's health and health policies for the black population.

The *Associação Cultural de Mulheres Negras* (Black Women's Cultural Association, ACMUN) was formed in Porto Alegre, Rio Grande do Sul, in 1994. ACMUN has developed several important health research and intervention programs, with a particular focus on HIV/AIDS prevention. Members of AC-MUN have also undertaken important research projects focusing on HIV/AIDS and other health issues that disproportionately affect the black population (Santos 2008). These studies have documented the health status of black communities in Rio Grande do Sul and other states in southern Brazil. This is particularly important, considering that the black population is relatively small in this region of the country and has traditionally been less visible than in other areas of Brazil.

In 1997, Edna Roland and several members of the health department left Geledés to form Fala Preta. This São Paulo–based NGO focused on health issues, particularly reproductive health and sexually transmitted infections (STIs) and HIV prevention for adolescent girls and women. Its programs and activities targeted low-income communities living on the periphery of the city of

Table 2.1. Black Women's Organizations Founded in the 1980s and 1990s

Organization Name	Location	Year Founded	Health-Related Initiatives and Programs
Maria Mulher	Porto Alegre (RS)	1987	Violence and women's health, HIV/AIDS prevention, psychological and economic assistance for HIV-positive women. Research on domestic violence and health issues; sexuality education for youth.
Geledés	São Paulo (SP)	1988	STD prevention, reproductive health, mental health. Organized 1993 National Seminar on Reproductive Rights and Policies of Black Women. Produced publications on black women's health during 1990s.[1]
Criola	Rio de Janeiro (RJ)	1992	Reproductive health, health promotion in local communities, HIV/AIDS prevention, publications (magazine, books), training seminars for health professionals.
Associação Cultural de Mulheres Negras (ACMUN)	Porto Alegre (RS)	1994	HIV/AIDS prevention, research on HIV/AIDS and other health issues.
Fala Preta!	São Paulo (SP)	1997	Reproductive health, STD prevention, HIV/AIDS, sickle cell anemia.

RJ = Rio de Janeiro; RS = Rio Grande do Sul; SP = São Paulo

1. The health department of Geledés was responsible for health-related programs and initiatives until the late 1990s. Geledés discontinued most of its health-related work when members of the health department left to form Fala Preta in 1997.

São Paulo, as well as those in rural areas and *quilombos,* including communities in other states. Members of Fala Preta developed projects such as *Salva-vidas* (Life Savers), which provided capacity building for adolescent girls and women related to health and reproductive rights, with an emphasis on AIDS and other STIs (Silva and Figueiredo 2005). A project known as *Bando* (band) also focused on the formation of community agents with training in reproductive health. Through Bando, members of Fala Preta sought to develop "multiplying" activities that would reduce rates of HIV infection, as well as other STIs, and lessen the impact of HIV on poor, black communities (Silva and Figueiredo 2005).

Intersectional Approaches to Health

By developing intersectional approaches to health, activists in the black women's movement have called attention to the ways in which race and gender shape African-descendant women's experiences with regard to health and illness, particularly in relation to health concerns that affect black women in disproportionate numbers, such as fibroid tumors, sterilization, and maternal mortality. In their work with local communities, government officials, and policymakers, activists in the black women's movement have utilized an intersectional perspective that emphasizes racism, sexism, and classism as interlocking forms of domination that have material consequences in terms of health and wellness. As longtime health activist and black feminist Edna Roland argued during the Global Forum of ECO 1992, the United Nations Conference on Population and Development:

> Whoever has lived historically the experience of being merchandise knows that control over the body is an essential part of our liberation and self-determination. . . . However, we are not only our bodies, but also our relationships with the community of the past and the community of the future. [Cited in Corrêa 1993, 7]

Activists in black women's organizations have promoted greater awareness of the specificities of black women's health experiences by calling attention to the ways in which racial, gender, and class dynamics shape patterns of illness and wellness in Brazil, as well as access to quality health care. Black women health activists have also argued that race plays a major role in worsening the health status of black women when compared to white women. It is important to recognize that while the terms "intersectional" and "intersectionality" have not always been used by activists in the black women's movement, the political praxis of activists reflects an intersectional view of race, gender, class, and sexuality that posits them as mutually constituted and inseparable determinants of black women's social identities and social experiences. This perspective reflects an attempt to develop a more integrated and holistic perspective on health that resonates with conceptualizations of intersectionality that emphasize gender, race, and class as interlocking forms of identity and domination that have been articulated by black feminists in the United States since the late twentieth century.[5] Moreover, while many activists in Brazil's black women's movement are familiar with the work of U.S. black feminists such as Kimberlé Crenshaw, Patricia Hill Collins, and bell hooks, they have also developed contextually specific conceptualizations of intersectionality in response to the needs and experiences of local Afro-Brazilian communities and Afro-Brazilian women.

One of the key differences in the conceptualizations of intersectionality that have been developed by black feminists in Brazil and the United States is the relative emphasis placed on race and class. Because the significance of race and racial inequality has often been overlooked and elided in Brazil, black Brazilian feminists have worked to call attention to the role of race and racism in the experiences of black women in the country. In the U.S. context, the lack of discussion of class has worked in similar ways, although black feminists in the United States have emphasized the role of capitalism and class exploitation in black women's experiences, to varying degrees.[6] The concept of intersectionality is particularly relevant to the health needs of Afro-Brazilian women, because it provides a means of addressing the interlocking nature of racial, gender, and class inequalities. While the political praxis of many black women activists and organizations has reflected an intersectional understanding of gender, race, class, and sexuality, as well as other axes of identity for more than two decades, the translation of these perspectives and forms of praxis in other sectors of Brazilian society has happened more slowly.

Longtime black Brazilian feminist health activist and author Fátima Oliveira has advocated use of an intersectional approach to health in Brazil, stating that it is "unacceptable, on the basis of being antiscientific, to not perceive the interpenetration of the variables sex/gender, race/ethnicity, and social class as informing the process of health/illness" (2002, 31). The conceptualization of intersectionality offered by Fernanda Lopes and Jurema Werneck, two leading black women health activists and researchers, further elucidates the relationship between social inequalities and public policies, with regard to health as well as other areas. According to Lopes and Werneck:

> Utilization of the concept of intersectionality allows one to give visibility to differences—inequalities and privileges—between population groups and within different populations. In this way, it makes the elaboration of

proposals oriented toward the *vivências* (lived experiences) and necessities of specific groups possible. Being able to provide adequate responses also allows for the confrontation of inequalities that are established on the general plane of society as well as within groups, further allowing for better *resolutividade* (resoluteness) of actions and programs, efficiency and efficacy in the execution, monitoring and evaluation of public policies. [n.d., 18–19]

Black Women, Sterilization, and Reproductive Rights

As discussed in chapter 1, Brazilian feminists held deep concerns about population-control policies that targeted women in the country during the 1970s and 1980s. While black women's criticisms of population control policies and the practice of female sterilization addressed the issue of women's reproductive rights, they also highlighted the racial dimensions of such policies. In particular, black feminists argued that population-control policies had the black population as their primary target (Damasco et al. 2012). Indeed, practices such as sterilization and the issue of reproductive rights more generally have often taken on more coercive dimensions for women of African descent, as has been documented for countries such as the United States (Kluchin 2009; Roberts 1997; Schoen 2005). However, in the Brazilian case, the lack of racially specific health data and research on racial disparities in health has led to a limited amount of empirical evidence to prove when reproductive rights violations have occurred against black women.

Racially motivated population-control policies became a major concern for black women activists in the state of São Paulo during the early 1980s. In 1982, a plan to limit reproduction in the *parda* (brown) and *negra* (black) segments of the state's population designed by members of the state government of Governor Paulo Maluf came to light. A document written by economist Benedito Pio da Silva titled *O Censo de 1980 no Brasil e no Estado de São Paulo e Suas Curiosidades e Preoccupações* outlined concerns about the growth of the *parda* and *negra* populations based on data from the 1980 census (Damasco et al. 2012). The text was originally intended as an internal government document officials would use to debate the issue of population growth in these populations and its potential electoral consequences by the year 2000. Portions of the text became public during a speech by state deputy Luiz Carlos Santos in August 1982. In his speech, Santos stated that the document's author, Benedito Pio da Silva, proposed population control in the *parda* and *negra* populations through sterilizations that could be carried out by the organization Pró-Família (Damasco et al. 2012).

Politicians who were linked to the *Partido dos Trabalhadores* (Worker's Party, PT) and black activists requested copies of the speech made by Santos in order to organize protests against the document and the study on which it was based. The controversy sparked by the release of the document led to Benedito Pio da Silva leaving the state government and shelving of the proposal to control the growth of the *parda* and *negra* populations. The proposals for population control were widely criticized by leading newspapers, including *O Estado de São Paulo, Folha de São Paulo,* and *Jornal da Tarde* (Damasco et al. 2012). In addition, the explicitly anti-natalist tone of the proposals helped to support claims that black feminists were making at the time regarding race and reproductive health (Damasco et al. 2012).

Due to the efforts of black women activists, by the early 1990s, the impact of female sterilization on black women had become a frequently discussed issue among researchers, activists, and politicians. As mentioned at the beginning of this chapter, the National Campaign against the Sterilization of Black Women, which was launched in November 1990 by Jurema Werneck, a medical doctor and subsequent founder of the black women's NGO Criola, was an important moment of mobilization focusing on black women's reproductive rights. Black women affiliated with CEAP (the Center for the Articulation of Marginalized Populations, Centro de Articulação de Populações Marginalizadas), a nongovernmental organization in Rio de Janeiro, developed the campaign to place pressure on the government to punish sterilization as a form of genocide and also to end mass sterilizations (Damasco et al. 2012).

On November 20, 1991, a date that black activists recognize as the National Day of Black Consciousness,[7] Federal Deputy Benedita da Silva and Senator Eduardo Suplicy presented a proposal to constitute a Parliamentary Inquiry Commission (CPMI) to investigate the practice of female sterilization in Brazil and determine whether the practice represented eugenic or racist policies (Damasco et al. 2012; Santos 2012). As the first black woman to serve in Brazil's Congress and later in the Senate, and also as someone who had undergone an involuntary sterilization procedure, da Silva was able to bring a personally informed perspective to this investigation by Brazil's House of Representatives.[8]

Federal Law 9.263, the Law of Family Planning, passed in 1996 after six years of debate in the National Congress (Santos 2012). This law established various activities related to fertility regulation and limited the number of offspring women, men, or couples could have. The measure also placed restrictions on sterilization, with voluntary sterilization only being allowed in two situations: (1) for women and men above twenty-five years of age or with at least two living children; and (2) when a future conception poses a risk to the life of the mother as confirmed by the written and signed testimony of two medical doctors. The law forbade the practice of surgical sterilization for women during childbirth or abortion, except in cases of proven necessity, such as when women have previously had multiple cesarean sections. In addition, the law called for the use of reversible methods, such as tubal ligation, and required that the express consent of both partners be given when a woman sought sterilization. Passage of this law demonstrates the impact of black women's activism around forced sterilization, as well as the impact of Benedita da Silva's efforts to bring visibility to this issue. Ultimately, the political pressure placed on the state resulted in a law that helped protect the reproductive rights of all Brazilian women, regardless of racial or ethnic background.

Black Women's Transnational Policy Activism

Black Brazilian women's activism during the conference processes for the International Conference on Population and Development (ICPD) in 1994 and the U.N. World Conference on Women in 1995 provided an opportunity for them to articulate an intersectional perspective on questions of race, gender, class, and sexuality in transnational arenas. In preparation for ICPD, black women produced the *Declaração de Itapecerica da Serra das Mulheres Negras Brasileiras* (Itapecerica da Serra Declaration of Brazilian Black Women) during the National Seminar on Reproductive Rights and Policies of Black Women, which was organized by Geledés. Importantly, this document provided an alternative view of development and population policy from the perspective of black women (Caldwell 2007). Black women also participated in the *Encontro Nacional Mulher e População, Nossos Direitos Para Cairo* (National Encounter Women and Population, Our Rights for Cairo), which took place in 1994 in preparation for the ICPD, and contributed to the *Carta de Brasília* (Letter from Brasília), which was produced during this national encounter.

During the preparatory process for Beijing, black women's demands became central features of "national and regional movement and government debates about women's rights and gender policy" (Alvarez 2000, 45). Targeted funds from agencies and inter-governmental organizations (IGOs) enabled some black women activists to participate in government seminars held to prepare the governments' report to the U.N. and to play a leadership role in the women's movement coalition that was formed to influence the Beijing process (Alvarez 2000). Black women also played leadership roles in the Mar del Plata Non-Governmental Forum, which was part of the Beijing preparatory process, by bringing together black women activists from eight Latin American countries during a three-day session. In addition, the Economic Commission for Latin America and the Caribbean (ECLAC) Platform for Action incorporated several of the demands that were part of the Proposal of Latin American and Caribbean Black Women for Beijing.

Sueli Carneiro, a leading figure in the black women's movement and the longtime coordinator of Geledés, has argued that black women understood that the "Beijing Conference should definitely place on the agenda the fact that racism is a form of violence and violation of women's rights. We argued that racism makes the exercise of citizenship unviable . . ." (2000b, 250). The Beijing Platform and Plan of Action included the terms *race* and *ethnicity*, marking an important shift in the recognition of racism within an official United Nations document. In addition, Nilza Iraci, the communications director of Geledés, has noted that black women from the Global North and Global South forming a lobby in alliance with white feminists during the Beijing conference was even more important than the inclusion of race in documents from the conference (Carneiro 2000b).

Black Brazilian women's increasing involvement with transnational policy advocacy during the 1990s was part of a larger trend within Latin American women's movements and women's movements globally. Sonia Alvarez has argued that Latin American women's movements involvement in transnational activism during the 1990s was an outgrowth of regional networks and connections that activists formed beginning in the early 1980s (Alvarez 2000). Regionwide feminist organizing that took place around the U.N. conferences held in Rio, Vienna, Cairo, and Beijing was also important during the 1980s and 1990s. These conferences enabled Latin American feminists to mobilize at the regional level and develop a shared agenda for women's rights.

Alvarez's (2000) conceptualization of the transnationalization of Latin American women's movements is useful in understanding how these movements have negotiated the dynamics of local and transnational organizing since the early 1990s. Alvarez has used the term *transnationalization* to refer to:

> local movement actors' deployment of discursive frames and organizational and political practices that are inspired, (re)affirmed, or reinforced—though not necessarily caused—by their engagement with other actors beyond national borders through a wide range of transnational contacts, discussions, transactions, and networks, both virtual and "real." [2000, 30]

In a discussion of "transnationalism reversed" in Venezuela, Elisabeth Friedman has pointed to the importance of examining the impact of transnational organizing on local women's movements in light of political and social dynamics within specific countries, and within the context of specific time periods. In addition, Friedman has noted that the impact of transnational activities can be quite varied. As she has written:

> Although not ultimately determinative of national dynamics, they provide opportunities for the development of national movements and may also be used in ways that exacerbate tensions in national organizing, such as their manipulation by particular leaders to the detriment of the movement as a whole, the introduction of foreign agendas that may or may not be relevant to national concerns, and the unequal distribution of increased external support. [Friedman 1999, 359]

Below I examine many of the issues and tensions identified by Alvarez and Friedman in light of black Brazilian women's organizing for the III World Conference against Racism.

Black Women's Mobilization for The III World Conference against Racism

During the early 2000s, black Brazilian women's involvement in transnational activism centered on the conference process for the III United Nations World Conference against Racism, Xenophobia and Related Forms of Intolerance (WCAR), which was held in Durban, South Africa, from August 28 to September 8, 2001. By broadening the antiracist agenda to include "related forms of intolerance," which opened space for discussion of gender, this U.N. conference provided an important and rare opportunity for both antiracist activists and feminists of color from different geographic regions to network and develop a global antiracist agenda.[9] Black Brazilian women activists played key roles in the preparatory process for the WCAR and during the conference proceedings. Their involvement in the national and regional preparatory processes for the WCAR and subsequent participation in the conference provided an important means of articulating a black feminist perspective on issues such as health, labor, and development. Black women's participation in the WCAR and the previous U.N. world conferences greatly increased the visibility and concerns of activists in the black women's movement and provided a mechanism for them to pressure the Brazilian government to address racial and gender disparities in the country.

By 2000 dozens of black women's organizations existed in various states throughout Brazil. Members of these organizations highlighted the intersection of race and gender and the specificities of black women's experiences during events organized by black movement entities during the preparatory process for the Durban conference. By this time a number of activists in the black women's movement had become familiar with the policy advocacy process as a result of their participation in previous United Nations conferences.[10] These activists were thus poised to play a leading role in shaping the agenda for black movement organizations from Brazil for the conference.

The preparatory process for the WCAR allowed activists in the black women's movement to engage in alliance building and negotiation with a number of different sectors of Brazilian society, as well as with transnational actors. Black women's concerns were also given greater visibility by two leading Brazilian women's organizations during the preparatory process. During 2001 the *Articulação de Mulheres Brasileiras* (Articulation of Brazilian Women, AMB) produced a lengthy publication focusing on black women (Articulação de Mulheres Brasileiras 2001). The *RedeSaúde* also published a special 2001 issue of its journal on the health of the black population in Brazil. These publications provide evidence of the increasing recognition of issues that disproportionately and uniquely affect black women within the larger women's movement in Brazil (Oliveira 2002). They were also important means of further legitimizing black women's concerns by providing the endorsement of the larger women's movement. By publishing materials on black women, the AMB and *RedeSaúde* also demonstrated their increased level of solidarity with black women and the antiracist struggle.[11]

It is important to view the positive changes with respect to alliance building with the AMB and RedeSaúde as the fruit of black women's longstanding efforts to sensitize their white counterparts in the women's movement to the intersectional nature of racial and gender discrimination. An example of this can be seen in the fact that Fátima Oliveira, a prominent and well-respected activist in the black movement, black women's movement, and larger women's movement, served as the executive secretary of RedeSaúde during the preparatory process for the WCAR. In this role, Oliveira was able to function as an effective liaison between the black women's movement and the larger women's movement. It is also worth noting that, despite the visible solidarity that the AMB and RedeSaúde offered to the black women's movement, such solidarity was not extended by all women's organizations in Brazil. The most glaring example of this is that the *Conselho Nacional de Direitos da Mulher* (National Council for Women's Rights, CNDM) did not support black women's efforts during the preparatory process for the WCAR.[12] This lack of support was especially surprising given the fact that six black women served on the council at the time ("Uma Oportunidade Ímpar na Luta Contra o Racismo").

The *Articulação de Organizações de Mulheres Negras Brasileiras* (Articulation of Black Brazilian Women's Organizations, AMNB) was formed during the preparatory process for the III World Conference against Racism. Formation of this network was an important step in the process of consolidating a collective political voice for black women at the national level.[13] The AMNB held a national meeting in September 2000, at which time the executive secretariat was charged with producing "a document that would gather in one place all current and relevant information and proposals for the struggle of black women as they lobby on public policy" (Articulação de Organizações de Mulheres Negras Brasileiras 2001, 7). The document *Nós, Mulheres Negras* (*We, Brazilian Black Women*) was subsequently published by the AMNB and endorsed by thirty entities representing the country's black movement and black women's movement.[14]

We, Brazilian Black Women is an important source for understanding the aspirations and objectives of activists in the black women's movement, particularly as they relate to health policy development. This report also merits special discussion because it offers the most comprehensive analysis of black women's status found in any document published by the black women's movement prior to that point. A wide range of issues relevant to black women's experiences are covered in the fifty-two-page report, including health, life expectancy, employment, education, violence, sexuality, and the media. The document also contains proposals in all of these areas and discusses their significance in light of international treaties, United Nations declarations, and domestic policy. The level of detail found in this document and its engagement with substantive policy issues underscore its significance as a policy text that sought to frame black women's issues in ways that would resonate with officials from Brazil and other countries present at the Durban conference. Copies of the report were presented to governmental and non-governmental representatives for all of the countries participating in the conference. To facilitate access to the report by non-Portuguese speakers, translations were provided in English and Spanish. Activists in the black women's movement saw the provision of the report in multiple languages as a way "to bring visibility to the situation of black women."[15]

In a compelling discussion of the importance of developing a "racial/ethnic perspective on health," the Durban report notes:

> From infancy to adulthood, "premature death" from preventable causes, including a higher rate of maternal and infant mortality, is a reality for the

black population in Brazil. The blatant lack of concern for diseases that occur more frequently in the black population—such as high blood pressure, sickle-cell anemia, type 2 diabetes, and uterine fibroid cysts—has strong, negative repercussions for the reproductive health of black women and provides evidence of how racism is entrenched and institutionalized in health care delivery and research, as well as in the educational apparatus, notably in the training of health care professionals. [Articulação de Organizações de Mulheres Negras Brasileiras 2001, 23]

By providing statistical evidence of black women's unfavorable status within Brazilian society, the Durban document sought to challenge the Brazilian government's historical silence about the discrimination experienced by them. As Nilza Iraci, the communications director for Geledés, noted in a July 2001 newspaper interview,

Whenever we go abroad, we hear that racial democracy exists and that in our country there is not racism. When we bring up the reality of black women, there is always a suspicion that we are exaggerating the facts. With this document we are showing that we are not working with a "victimization" [mentality], but with data that reflects reality. [Almeida 2001]

Iraci's comments underscore the importance of having empirical data on racial inequalities for use in the struggle against racism in Brazil. As noted earlier, the infrequent collection of data by race in Brazil has largely been shaped by beliefs that the country is a racial democracy and, as a result, does not need to collect data in government documents such as the national census. In their efforts to document and challenge racial health disparities in Brazil, activists in the black women's movement have had to contend with the lack of racially specific health data and color-blind approaches to health.

The Durban report reflects black women activists' understandings of the significance of the U.N. process for policy development and the promotion of progressive cultural change at the national level.[16] Activists in the black women's movement hoped that their documentation of black women's status would be useful in their efforts to prompt the Brazilian government to align its discourse and practice, particularly with regard to racism, and to recognize the plight of black women within international arenas. Activists viewed the Durban document as a tool that could be used by the official delegation to the World Conference against Racism and members of Brazilian civil society in their negotiations for specific public policies, at the local, state, and national level (Almeida 2001).

The Durban report provides insight into black women activists' views of the significance of the U.N. conference process for policy development and the promotion of progressive political and cultural change at the domestic level. Activists hoped that the data provided in the report would demonstrate the impact of racial and gender inequalities on black women and strengthen their efforts to promote initiatives and policies designed to combat such inequalities. Given the paucity of statistical data on race and racial inequalities in Brazil at that time, particularly as they related to black women, activists viewed the report as a vital tool in their efforts to pressure the Brazilian government to take a proactive stance in the struggles against racism and sexism. Activists also viewed the Durban report as an instrument that could be used to negotiate specific public policies at the local, state, and national level.[17]

Despite their sober assessment of the limitations of the U.N. conference process, activists in the black women's movement viewed the WCAR as a unique and important opportunity to advance the struggles against racism and sexism in their country. Indeed, some activists believed that the preparatory process was more important than the conference itself. When I interviewed her in 2007, Nilza Iraci expressed her view that the conference preparatory process provided an opportunity for mobilization, political intervention, and capacity building for black women activists that would not have been possible otherwise.[18]

Organizations such as Geledés focused on capacity building (*capacitação*) for black women activists during the conference preparatory process in Brazil. Members of Geledés previously had participated in U.N. conferences, such as the 1994 World Population Conference and 1995 World Conference on Women, and had become familiar with the U.N. conference process. In her role at Geledés, Nilza Iraci maximized the opportunity presented by the WCAR to improve the advocacy skills of other black women.[19] Geledés provided training for black women in the areas of advocacy and the media, as well in how to intervene in the official conference process and the parallel process. In so doing, Iraci and other members of Geledés utilized the preparatory process for the WCAR as a means to strengthen the movement and increase its effectiveness.

The approach described above was important strategically because activists utilized transnational activism to strengthen the black women's movement, rather than allow it to weaken their efforts or distract from important concerns. The formation of the Network of Black Brazilian Women's NGOs for the III Conference was also important in this regard, as it served to consolidate the black women's movement at the national level. This consolidation was an important shift away from the lack of consensus regarding national-level organizing that characterized discussions within the black women's movement during the 1990s (Caldwell 2007; Roland 2000). Moreover, following the WCAR, activists in the black women's movement decided to continue the network, shortening the name to the Articulation of Black Brazilian Women's Organizations (*Articulação de Organizações de Mulheres Negras Brasileiras*, AMNB).[20]

Black activists in Brazil and other Latin American countries used mobilization for the III World Conference against Racism (WCAR) to increase efforts to challenge racism and influence state policy in the region (Dzidzienyo 2005; Mullings 2004; Telles 2004; Turner 2002; Davis et al. 2012). The conference preparatory process was an important turning point in racial dynamics in various countries and was vital to the consolidation of a collective Afro–Latin American voice and agenda on racism in the region (Turner 2002). Given the prevalence of racial democracy ideologies and the official denial of racism in many Latin American countries, both the preparatory process and the WCAR were used by antiracist activists as an opportunity to develop mechanisms to challenge racism and racial inequality.

During the conference preparatory process, Latin American governments officially recognized the existence of racism in the region, which was a major breakthrough in efforts to challenge the invisibility of Afro–Latin Americans and denial of racism regionwide (Dulitzky 2005). In addition, the Inter-American Democratic Charter, adopted by the Organization of American States General Assembly in Lima, Peru on September 11, 2001, established that "The elimination of all forms of discrimination, especially gender, ethnic and race discrimination, as well as diverse forms of intolerance, the promotion and protection of human rights of indigenous peoples and migrants, and respect for ethnic, cultural and religious diversity in the Americas contribute to strengthening democracy and citizen participation" (cited in Dulitzky 2005, 53).

Black Brazilian women played a vital role in regional efforts to organize Afro–Latin Americans during the preparatory process for the WCAR. They were important contributors to the regional conference of the Americas, which was held in Santiago, Chile in December 2000. Chile was chosen as the site of this regional conference after Brazil refused to host it. Black women comprised the majority of the Brazilian delegation to the Santiago Conference, with 120 members of the black women's movement attending, including a busload of young women.[21]

During the regional preparatory conference, black Brazilian women argued for the importance of utilizing the term *afro-descendente* to identify and describe African-descendant populations in the region.[22] The term *afro-descendente* (Afro-descendant) was adopted and used in the Santiago Declaration and later adopted in the Official Declaration and Plan of Action for the Durban conference. Since 2000, the term *afro-descendente* has also been adopted by many Afro–Latin American activists as a replacement for the Spanish and Portuguese term *negro* (black), and has increasingly been used in government documents in the region. This terminological shift was important given traditions of racial/color self-identification in the Latin American region and the tendency for many Afro–Latin Americans to identify with color categories, such as moreno or mulatto, rather than as negro/a. Use of the term *afro-descendente* also offered another self-identification option that did not carry the stigma often associated with blackness, and self-identification as "negro/a," as well as the possibility for individuals to recognize their African ancestry without excluding or denying their other ancestry (indigenous, European, Asian, and so forth).

Black Brazilian women's contributions to the Santiago Conference were also evident in the emphasis placed on health and the use of the category "victims of aggravated or multiple discrimination" in the Santiago Declaration and Plan of Action. During the Santiago Conference, Fátima Oliveira, a medical doctor and longtime participant in the black women's movement, argued for the importance of developing policies to address racial inequities in health.[23] Oliveira's interventions during the Santiago conference were strengthened by her expertise in women's health and racial/ethnic health and led to increasing participation by the Pan-American Health Organization (PAHO) during the conference preparatory process ("A Unique Opportunity to Fight against Racism").[24] The Santiago Declaration and Plan of Action also recognized women, children, and other individuals affected by HIV/AIDS and persons living in poverty as "victims of aggravated or multiple discrimination." The use of this terminology reflected the inclusion of "related forms of intolerance" in the agenda for the WCAR and created space for the discussion of intersecting forms of oppression, including racism, sexism, and economic exploitation.[25]

Black women's mobilization during the preparatory process for the WCAR placed them at the forefront of organizing efforts and enabled them to make important contributions to the official conference, as well as the parallel conference and NGO forum. Brazil had one of the largest, if not the largest, civil society delegation at the WCAR. Black women also succeeded in becoming part of the official delegation from Brazil. During the conference, Geledés provided informational materials to the official Brazilian delegation and also published a daily bulletin, which provided updates from the conference for conference participants and nonparticipants alike. The impact of black women on the

WCAR was also demonstrated by Edna Roland's selection as the special rapporteur during the conference. In this capacity, Roland served in the second highest position during the conference, giving greater visibility to the black women's movement in Brazil. The contributions of black women from Brazil and other areas of the African diaspora were recognized when Mary Robinson, then–United Nations High Commissioner for Human Rights and the Secretary General of the World Conference against Racism, made a declaration that "black women made the difference" during the conference (Werneck 2003, 11).

Maylei Blackwell and Nadine Naber's (2002) observations about the implications of the U.N. World Conference against Racism for transnational feminist practices are relevant to examining the efforts of black women activists in Brazil. Blackwell and Naber argue that the struggles waged over "language, histories, and discourses" during the conference played an important role in establishing international norms to which states are held accountable, creating dialogue about shared oppressions in an international context and broadening the definition of racism to include an intersectional analysis of multiple forms of oppression (2002, 245). While recognizing the gains made during the WCAR, Blackwell and Naber also argue that transnational organizing is only effective when activists are able to "bring it home." As they note, "The usefulness of the Declaration and Plan of Action is not that we leave them behind as empty words but that we use them in our daily struggles against racism and its complex intersections" (2002, 239).

Black Women's Activism and the Acquisition of Social and Political Capital

In recent decades, black women activists have made a significant impact on public policy and civic culture in Brazil, with their efforts being recognized nationally and internationally. Increasing public recognition of the contributions of black women's organizations was demonstrated when the Brazilian Ministry of Justice awarded the National Human Rights Prize to Geledés in December 1996, which was conferred by President Fernando Henrique Cardoso. In December 1998, French Prime Minister Lionel Jospin bestowed a human rights award on Geledés in recognition of the fiftieth anniversary of the Universal Declaration of Human Rights. Maria Mulher was selected by the United Nations to receive the World Citizenship Prize in 2001. Maria Mulher was also recognized by the *Red de Salud de Las Mujeres Latinoamericanas y del Caribe* (Latin American and Caribbean Women's Health Network, RSMLAC) in 2003 for its violence-prevention programs. Also during 2003, Brazilian president Luiz

Inácio "Lula" da Silva appointed longtime black feminist Matilde Ribeiro to direct the newly created Special Secretariat for the Promotion of Racial Equality Policies (*Secretaria Especial de Promoção de Políticas de Igualdade Racial,* SEP-PIR). Ribeiro's appointment provided evidence of the increasing recognition of the contributions of black women activists, particularly by leftist politicians such as Lula. In 2010 Luiza Bairros, another longtime feminist and activist in the black movement, was selected by Lula to lead SEPPIR.[26]

Public recognition of activists in the black women's movement by Brazilian heads of state and members of the international community has been important on a symbolic level, because it involves the acknowledgment, and thus the legitimization, of black women's roles as political actors and engaged members of civil society. By conferring political capital on the black women's movement, public recognition has increased the legitimacy of black women's effort to combat racism and sexism and shape public policy. Black women's transnational activism and advocacy, particularly in relation to U.N. world conferences, have been an important means of increasing the social and political capital of individual activists, individual black women's organizations, and the black women's movement as a whole. However, it is important to note that the process of acquiring greater social and political capital by black women is not without its problems or asymmetries. A potential downside of transnational activism and advocacy lies in the fact that individuals and organizations that have already acquired substantial social and political capital tend to be favored in these arenas. As a result, relatively well-established and well-funded organizations such as Geledés and Criola are often at an advantage in terms of their ability to participate and contribute to transnational activism and advocacy. Moreover, organizations that are less well established and that have fewer resources may be at a disadvantage when they attempt to engage in transnational activism.[27]

Conclusion

By examining black women's activism within non-governmental organizations and transnational forms of mobilization, this chapter provides insight into the important role black women have played in creating health policies that are discussed in chapter 3. While scholars and commentators often refer to the "black movement" in general terms, and its interaction with the Brazilian state related to policy issues, particularly since 2001, the gendered dynamics of this interaction are often overlooked. This has had the effect of erasing the central role that black women have played, both as individuals and as members of organizations, in creating a foundation for civil society engagement with the state around issues of racial equity and racial equality and racial health equity in particular.

Chapter 3 examines the development of health policies for the black population in recent decades. However, it is important to see changes in the discussion and implementation of racially conscious health policies within the Brazilian government, at the federal, state, and local level, as the fruit of long-fought struggles by black activists, particularly black women activists. While the presidential administrations of Cardoso and Lula promoted more open discussion of race and racism in Brazil, this shift did not result simply from the goodwill of political leaders; instead it was the result of decades-long efforts by black activists. The development of public policies to address racial inequities in health, education, and employment following the III U.N. World Conference against Racism in 2001 also demonstrates the impact of black activists' transnational organizing on policy development at the domestic level, further underscoring the importance of external pressure in promoting state action to combat racism.

Activists in the black women's movement have highlighted the need for non-universalist public policies that address racial, gender, *and* class inequalities—a need that is made all the more critical by Brazil's ongoing process of democratization, which involves not only access to formal citizenship rights but also the creation of discursive and political space for marginalized groups to assert identities and interests that differ from the norm. Ultimately, black women's efforts to promote the development of non-universalist health policies underscore the importance of activists, scholars, and the Brazilian state reconceptualizing health disparities in ways that acknowledge the interrelationship among racial, gender, and socioeconomic inequalities and developing intersectional approaches to challenge them.

Mapping the Development of Health Policies for the Black Population

From the Centenary of Abolition to the Statute of Racial Equality

"The authorities do not care [about sickle cell disease] because it is a black thing."

—Sickle cell anemia activist from Rio de Janeiro

The preceding statement was made by a sickle cell anemia activist during a November 2010 seminar on black women and health organized by the *Rede de Mulheres Negras do Paraná*. This woman was joined by two other panelists who shared personal stories related to sickle cell disease, which is known as *anemia falciforme* or *doença falciforme* in Brazil. One panelist was a teenager who spoke about the health and physical challenges she faced, and the other was the mother of a young boy suffering from sickle cell disease. Hearing these women share their personal stories put a human face on sickle cell disease and deeply moved many members of the audience, including myself. It was particularly striking that all three of the speakers were African-descendant women, two of whom had faced tremendous difficulties in their attempts either to receive treatment or to have a loved one treated for sickle cell disease.

During the session, speakers described challenges such as dealing with health professionals who were poorly informed about sickle cell disease and thus unable to properly treat them and who, in some cases, prescribed the wrong medications. One described her experiences by using the Portuguese term *descaso*, which conveyed a sense of neglect, indifference, and carelessness, on the part of the public health system. While the mother of the young sickle cell patient pointed out that 2010 marked the one-hundredth anniversary of the discovery of the hemoglobin S gene, which causes sickle cell disease,[1] she also mentioned that there had been both "*avanços*" and "*retrocessos*," or advances and setbacks, over the years. She also challenged the notion that this anniversary should be universally celebrated, stating, "we don't have anything to celebrate. We want respect and government responsibility."

Sickle cell anemia provides an important and useful entry point for examining health policies for the black population in Brazil. As an illness often characterized as primarily affecting people of African descent, sickle cell anemia represents an important discursive and political site, in which ideas and policies related to race, inequality, and state action have been developed and contested in recent decades. In addition, while the disease is one of several health conditions that disproportionately affect Afro-Brazilians, it has figured prominently in efforts to bring greater visibility to racial health equity issues in Brazil. Sickle cell anemia was an important focus of black health activists in the 1990s as they sought to make demands on the state for greater attention and services focused on the health needs of the black population. The condition also served as an important symbol of racialized health disparities, because it has often been viewed as a disease that disproportionately affects people of African descent, both in Brazil and in other countries (Rouse 2009; Tapper 1999; Wailoo 2001). Though black activists in Brazil have fought for more than two decades for the development of policies to diagnose and treat sickle cell anemia, such policies have been criticized by some scholars for promoting outdated, biologically based notions of race (Fry 2005; Laguardia 2007).

Although racial dynamics in Brazil have often been compared to the those of the United States, given both countries' histories of slavery and large African-descendant populations, it is important to note that, unlike the United States, Brazil does not have a long tradition of research or policies focusing on racial or ethnic health disparities. Despite having the second-largest African-descendant population in the world, policies to address health issues that disproportionately affect Afro-Brazilians were not developed in earnest until the early twenty-first century. In addition, accurately assessing which health conditions affect Afro-Brazilians and gaining an understanding of the extent to which racial/ethnic health disparities might exist have been major challenges because, traditionally, health data by race either has not been collected or has been collected inconsistently in Brazil.

Official denial of race as a salient category of social identity and social experience enabled the Brazilian state to forgo the collection of racial data in the national census and government records for much of the twentieth century (Nobles 2000; Telles 2004). Furthermore, until 1996, Brazil lacked an official policy that would permit the collection of health data by race. Prior to the development of this policy, it was extremely difficult to ascertain the health status of Brazilians of African ancestry. In many ways, the lack of racially specific health data has been consistent with official representations of Brazil as a racial democracy, or a society in which racism is considered to be virtually, if not completely, nonexistent. Official views of Brazil as a nonracist society and the Brazilian state's traditional reluctance to admit to the existence of racism have led to a color-blind approach to health that historically has overlooked the specific health needs and challenges of Afro-Brazilians. However, research has shown that maternal mortality and health conditions such as fibroid tumors, hypertension, type II diabetes, and sickle cell anemia affect Afro-Brazilians in disproportionate numbers (Batista et al. 2013; Fundação Nacional de Saúde 2005; Lopes 2005).

The lack of health data by race in Brazil has made the task of documenting and addressing health disparities an extremely arduous one. Given the lack of empirical evidence of racial health disparities, it has also been very difficult for health activists and researchers to provide proof of the need to develop specific health policies for the African-descendent population. Although black activists, particularly black women, have been at the forefront of efforts to address racial health disparities, shifts in government policy with regard to health did not begin to take place until the early 2000s, largely owing to the efficacy of black movement organizing for the United Nations–sponsored III World Conference against Racism, Racial Discrimination, Xenophobia, and Related Forms of Intolerance, which was held in Durban, South Africa in 2001.

This chapter examines the development of state policies focusing on the health of the black population in Brazil and analyzes them in the context of political shifts and changes over a nearly twenty-five-year period, beginning in 1988, a year that marked the one-hundredth anniversary of Brazilian abolition and the promulgation of a new democratic constitution. During the mid to late 1980s, as Brazil emerged from the military dictatorship, black movement activism began to increase and critiques of racial inequalities and racism began to be articulated more forcefully (Hanchard 1994). Given Brazil's longstanding image as a society in which race and skin color hold little importance as a basis of social division and discrimination, this chapter explores how the relationship between race and health and the health status of Afro-Brazilians have been conceptualized in recent decades. The analysis is guided by the following questions: How have health policies for the black population developed at the federal level and within the context of Brazil's Unified Health System (SUS) from the late 1980s to the early 2010s? How have advocates and critics of race-conscious health policies conceptualized the relationship between race and health? How does the development of health policies for the black population and other race-conscious public policies, such as affirmative action, since the early 2000s provide insight into changing state discourses and practices related to race and racism?

Federal Policy Initiatives on the Black Population and Racism, 1988 to 2000

Black activists began to engage with the state in new ways during the democratic transition as Brazil returned to civilian rule during the mid to late 1980s. The constitutional process was an important moment of antiracist mobilization that led to the inclusion of racism in the 1988 constitution as a crime without a statute of limitations and for which bail cannot be posted. The new constitution significantly strengthened previous antiracist federal legislation, such as the Afonso Arinas law, which was passed in 1951. However, problems persisted in the enforcement of the antiracist provisions of the constitution, and few cases of racial discrimination were taken before the courts during the 1990s and early 2000s (Hernandez 2013).

Establishment of the Palmares Cultural Foundation (*Fundação Cultural Palmares*) within the federal government in 1988 signaled growing recognition of racial issues and the cultural specificities of the African-descendant population by the Brazilian state after the military dictatorship. On the federal level, the Palmares Cultural Foundation symbolized "the inauguration of a new phase in the treatment of the racial question," as well as the growing legitimacy that began to be accorded to discussions of racism (Jaccoud 2009, 26). However, it is also important to note that while the foundation was a federal organ, it was linked to the Ministry of Culture and had a primarily cultural emphasis (Telles 2004). The foundation derived its name from Palmares, a *quilombo* that was a renowned federation of runaway slave communities that existed in northeastern Brazil during the seventeenth century; it was also the largest and longest-lasting *quilombo* in the Americas.

During the 1990s, one of the Palmares Foundation's main objectives was to identify *quilombo* communities, which consisted of both urban and rural communities either established by escaped slaves between the 1500s and 1800s or were predominantly African-descendant. The foundation also worked to demarcate and title *quilombo* lands and was in charge of policy directed toward the black population. Some scholars have noted that, over the years, the foundation's effectiveness became limited because of its cultural emphasis and lack of necessary resources to adequately fulfill its objectives (Jaccoud 2009; Telles 2004). In addition, during the 1980s, a split within the black movement existed regarding the cultural versus political orientation of the movement, which led some activists to feel that an exclusive emphasis on culture did not adequately address the needs of the black population in other areas, such as education, work, and health (Hanchard 1994; Telles 2004).

Another key moment related to black movement mobilization and state action on racial issues occurred during and after the *Marcha Zumbi dos Palmares Contra o Racismo, Pela Cidadnia e a Vida* (Zumbi dos Palmares March against Racism, for Citizenship and Life), which took place on November 20, 1995. This date marked the three-hundredth anniversary of the death of Zumbi, the renowned leader of the *quilombo* of Palmares. During a speech on November 20, 1995, the National Day of Black Consciousness and the date of the march, Fernando Henrique Cardoso became the first Brazilian president to officially recognize the existence of racism in the country. On this date, President Cardoso also formed an Interministerial Working Group with the goal of developing "valorization" policies for the black population (*Grupo de Trabalho Interministerial com a finalidade de desenvolver políticas de valorização da População Negra*, GTI). This federal-level working group investigated the feasibility of compensatory policies, such as affirmative action, as a way to address racism and racial inequality in the country.

A marked change in state discourse on racial issues was evident during both terms of President Cardoso (1995–1998 and 1999–2002). This shift came largely in response to issues raised by black activists, particularly in relation to mobilization for the Zumbi March. Beginning in the early 1990s, a series of government policies were developed establishing guidelines for early detection of sickle cell anemia and other blood disorders in infants. Drawing on the recommendations of the GTI formed by Cardoso, in 1996 the Brazilian Ministry of Health elaborated the Sickle Cell Anemia Program (*Programa de Anemia Falciforme,* or PAF). Programs and actions at the national, state, and municipal level focusing on sickle cell anemia were also launched in 1996. The national Sickle Cell Anemia Program focused on the reduction of morbidity and mortality stemming from sickle cell anemia and improving the quality of life of those living with the disease, as well as disseminating information relevant to the illness (Jaccoud 2009). However, by the end of 2002, PAF had only been implemented in a few states and municipalities in Brazil.

Another important outcome of the Cardoso administration's response to black activists' demands during the 1995 Zumbi March was the increased contemplation and discussion of affirmative action policies. During 1996, an international seminar called Multiculturalism and Racism: The Role of Affirmative Action in Contemporary Democratic States (*Multiculturalismo e Racismo o papel de ações afirmativas nos estados democráticos contemporaneos*) was organized by the Department of Human Rights, which fell under the purview of the Secretariat for the Rights of Citizenship (*Secretaria dos Direitos da Cidadania*). The conference served as an important marker in the national debate about affirmative action policies and their applicability in Brazil (Souza 1997). Leading Brazilian and U.S. scholars gave presentations on topics such as racial inequality, democracy, human rights, multiculturalism, and affirmative action. President Cardoso also participated in the conference and made an opening speech describing his views of racial prejudice, racism, and affirmative action. Cardoso's background as a sociologist who studied racial issues in Brazil early in his career and participated in the landmark 1950s United Nations Educational, Scientific, and Cultural Organization (UNESCO) study on racism in Brazil likely influenced his understanding of the importance of addressing racial discrimination and inequality in the country (Hernandez 2013; Telles 2004).

Establishment of the National Human Rights Program on May 13, 1996 (the 108th anniversary of abolition) by Presidential Decree 1.904 was another important part of the Cardoso administration's response to concerns articulated by black activists during and after the Zumbi March. In particular, this decree presented proposals for affirmative action that were in line with demands made by black movement activists at the march. The program proposed affirmative action programs and efforts to increase university access for Afro-Brazilians. The Human Rights Plan of 1996 also recommended that the Brazilian Institute of Geography and Statistics move from a color-based system of classification in the census to one based on two racial categories, *branco* (white) and *negro* (black). This plan marked the first time that racial groups were officially recognized as targets of state policy in Brazil (Reichmann 1999). An important health and research-related development also took place in 1996 when data on skin color and race, known in Portuguese as the *quesito cor,* was included in declarations of live births and deaths, in the national system for live births (SINASC) and national mortality data (SIM), as well as for human research subjects. This was a significant development, because data on births and deaths would now be available by skin color, thus facilitating researchers' efforts to document and examine the epidemiologic profile of the black population.

Post-Durban Policy Shifts in Brazil

Following the III World Conference against Racism, Xenophobia and Related Forms of Intolerance, one of the most noteworthy, and in many ways unexpected, developments in Brazil was the increasing discussion and implementation of race-conscious public policies, particularly affirmative action policies in government employment and university admissions. Although affirmative action was officially placed on the federal government's agenda, at least as a discussion item, after the 1995 Zumbi March, policies in this area were not implemented until after the III World Conference against Racism took place. As Edward Telles has noted, "large-scale affirmative-action programs were, prior to the Durban conference, merely plans" (2004, 71).

When examining shifts in state policy on race and racial discrimination in Brazil after the Durban conference, it is important to recognize the role that political dynamics at the national level played in creating openings for black activists to interface with the Brazilian state in the development of public policies. As noted above, beginning in the mid-1990s, the greater openness toward discussion of racial issues displayed by Cardoso's administration played a significant role in promoting state action to combat racism.[2] Mala Htun (2004) has argued that the unprecedented move to develop race-specific public policies during the late 1990s and early 2000s owed to three key factors: political action by black activists and the effectiveness of a race-based "issue network,"[3] presidential initiatives by Fernando Henrique Cardoso, and the impact of the Durban conference.

Public policy developments following the 2001 World Conference against Racism (WCAR) were a watershed in the evolution of the antiracist struggle in Brazil. As a number of scholars have observed, marked changes in official government discourse and policy development related to racial issues took place after the Durban Conference (Dzidzienyo 2005; Htun 2004; Jaccoud 2009; Martins et al. 2004; Telles 2004). An important shift in official government discourse on race occurred when President Cardoso's administration admitted to the existence of racism in Brazil in a 2001 report to the Convention on the Elimination of All Forms of Racial Discrimination (CERD), which monitors governmental compliance with the International Convention to Eliminate All Forms of Racial Discrimination (ICERD), making Cardoso's administration the first to officially acknowledge racism in a document produced by Brazil's federal government. Prior to this, the federal government had long denied the existence of racism in the country and officially promoted the country's national image as a racial democracy (Dulitzky 2005; Telles 2004). In fact, official denial of racism was central to government policy throughout the twentieth century, particularly during the military dictatorship of 1964 to 1985.

As noted in chapter 2, black activists in Brazil and other areas of Latin America seized the opportunity presented by the Durban conference process to dialogue with state representatives and articulate antidiscriminatory and race-conscious policy demands. In Brazil, the preparatory process provided an opportunity for black activists to directly engage with the state, rather than having the Palmares Cultural Foundation act as a channel (Telles 2004). This was an important development, which led to increased interaction between the black movement and the Brazilian state during the early 2000s.

A number of important affirmative action and antidiscrimination programs were instituted at the federal, state, and local level beginning in 2001. In most cases, these policies focused on the establishment of quotas for the black population, in employment and university admissions. President Cardoso also made a formal gesture of support for affirmative action by signing a Presidential Decree on May 13, 2002, the 114th anniversary of Brazilian abolition, which instituted a national affirmative action program in the Brazilian public administration.

The development of affirmative action programs and policies challenged Brazil's longstanding image as a society in which racial divisions and racialized forms of inequality did not exist. Affirmative action policies also underscored the state's role and duty to ensure racial equality and justice. Through the adoption of specific, non-universalist policies, the Brazilian state acknowledged the need for differentiated policies for racial groups that had received historically unequal and discriminatory treatment.[4]

During the first and second administrations of President Luiz Inácio Lula da Silva (2003–2006 and 2007–2010) there was an increasing emphasis on policies and measures to combat racial discrimination, including affirmative action programs. Federal law 10.639 of 2003 focused on diversifying the school curriculum by mandating the teaching of African and Afro-Brazilian history. Moreover, the slogan of Lula's administration, "*Um País de Todos*" (A Country of All), reflected the government's emphasis on and commitment to create a country that was more inclusive, at least symbolically. The creation of the *Secretaria Especial de Promoção de Políticas da Igualdade Racial* (Special Secretariat for the Promotion of Racial Equality Policies, SEPPIR), a cabinet-level federal secretariat, in March 2003 by President Lula signaled his administration's efforts to address racial problems in Brazil during his first term in office. In addition to focusing on issues affecting the black population, SEPPIR's mandate also focused on underrepresented ethnic and racial groups such as Jews, Roma, and the Arab population in Brazil. Because the *Fundação Nacional do Índio* (National Indian Foundation, or FUNAI) already focused on indigenous communities in Brazil, these communities were not included in SEPPIR's mandate.[5] During the installation ceremony for SEPPIR, President Lula recognized the existence of racism in Brazil. By doing so, he followed President Cardoso's lead, becoming the second president in Brazilian history publicly to challenge the longstanding belief that Brazil was a nonracist society.

While the creation of SEPPIR was an important milestone in state acknowledgment of racial inequalities and the need to take proactive measures to combat them, it is also important to note that the creation of SEPPIR came in response to black activists' demands, and was not simply an expression of goodwill or progressive political ideology on the part of Lula. Black activists placed pressure on Lula to establish governmental mechanisms to challenge racism during the 2002 presidential election and once he was in office. Moreover, unlike the *Secretaria Especial para a Promoção de Politicas para a Mulher* (Special Secretariat for Women's Policies, SPM), which was created in January 2003, SEPPIR was created two months later. Some observers have argued that the relatively late creation of SEPPIR indicated that the Lula administration lacked a strong commitment to an antiracist agenda (Santos et al. 2011). Even within this context, it is an undeniable fact that Lula's government demonstrated a higher level of engagement with black activists, and civil society in general, than any previous presidential administration. As a leftist and the first Brazilian president not of an elite background, Lula's election represented a break with historical patterns of elite domination of politics. In addition, a large number of black activists were active in the Worker's Party (PT), Lula's political party, since its founding in the late 1970s, which further strengthened ties between the black movement and the Lula administration.[6]

The establishment of SEPPIR made Brazil the first country in the world to have a cabinet-level government unit that focused on achieving racial equality. In so doing, Brazil fulfilled one of the major objectives of the Plan of Action from the Durban conference, which was the creation of governmental organizations to combat racism. SEPPIR was charged with promoting racial equality policies at the municipal, state, and local level for the purpose of incorporating the struggle against racial discrimination and racism into all spheres of government. SEPPIR's primary objective was to focus on the development and implementation of public policies, such as affirmative action and health policies for the black population, in conjunction with federal ministries, such as the Ministry of Education and the Ministry of Health. The notion of "transversalization" (*transversalização*), or the creation of transversal policies, was central to SEPPIR's approach to working with other government ministries and units. Transversalization, or the development of crosscutting policies within the apparatus of the federal government, has been described by a SEPPIR publication as the "perspective of incorporating ethnic-racial equity into the diverse initiatives of the Brazilian state" (Secretaria de Promoção da Igualdade Racial 2005, 10).

By transversalizing policies on racial equality during this time period, SEPPIR sought to make race-conscious policies an integral part of all sectors of the federal government. As one staff member noted when I visited SEPPIR's office in Brasília in 2007, the staff was working so that SEPPIR would no longer be needed. The notion of working oneself out of a job was consistent with SEPPIR's commitment to combating racial equality on a permanent basis. It should also be noted that SEPPIR's mandate was broader than that of the Palmares Cultural Foundation, which preceded it, and was not solely focused on Afro-Brazilian culture.

Beginning in 2004, SEPPIR defined its priorities with a focus in three key areas: (1) supporting *quilombos* and other traditional communities, including indigenous communities and gypsies; (2) promoting the development and implementation of affirmative action policies; and (3) exchanges and international relations. In addition, SEPPIR's approach to affirmative action was not limited to education. It also addressed issues related to development, work, and income; health and quality of life; and culture, organization, and diversity. This broad approach enabled SEPPIR to support efforts to develop policies focusing on racial equity in the health sector. Through promoting a more expansive definition of affirmative action, SEPPIR's activities underscored how health policies for the black population could contribute to the larger struggle to ensure racial equality and equity in Brazil.

Sickle Cell Anemia, Race, and Health in Brazil

In addition to the 1996 passage of the Sickle Cell Anemia Program, PAF, there were important policy developments related to sickle cell anemia during the early 2000s. In June 2001, Portaria 822 established the National Sickle Cell Anemia Neo-Natal Triage Program, which tested newborns for sickle cell anemia in the hospitals where they were born. However, some researchers have argued that the promulgation of Portaria[7] 822 on June 6, 2001 impeded the implementation of PAF, because the aspects of PAF that focused on diagnosing sickle cell anemia were covered by it; however, other aspects of care related to the disease did not receive special attention (Jaccoud 2009). In 2005, a federal regulation was passed calling for establishment of the National Sickle Cell Anemia Program within the SUS. The following year, the *Política Nacional de Atenção Integral às Pessoas com Doença Falciforme* (National Policy for Integral Attention to People with Sickle Cell Anemia) was launched. This policy established regulations for the National Neonatal Triage Program, also known at the *Teste de Pezinho*, or little foot test, in the public health system. The program focused on the identification, quantification, and medical accompaniment of infant cases of sickle cell anemia, as well as the planning and organization of the Network of Integral Attention to Individuals with Sickle Cell Anemia (Jesus 2010, 286). By the end of 2010, fifteen states were doing neonatal tests to detect the sickle cell trait; however eleven states still did not do the tests at that time (Jesus 2010).

Sickle cell anemia is the most common monogenetic hereditary illness in Brazil, occurring primarily among the African-descendant population (Cançado and Jesus 2007). The distribution of the hemoglobin S gene in the country has been found to be extremely heterogeneous, depending on the racial/ethnic composition of a region. Higher prevalence of the hemoglobin S gene has been found in the North and Northeast regions of Brazil (6 percent to 10 percent), while the prevalence is lower in the South and Southeast (2 percent to 3 percent) (Cançado and Jesus 2007, 204). The prevalence of the hemoglobin S gene within the general population is approximately 4 percent on average, with a range between 2 percent and 8 percent. Within the Afro-descendant population, the range of prevalence is 6 percent and 10 percent. In the state of Bahia, which has a large Afro-descendent population, the ratio of individuals with the hemoglobin S gene is 1:650, while states with smaller Afro-descendant populations, such as São Paulo and Rio Grande do Sul, have ratios of 1:4,000 and 1:10,000, respectively. In 2010, authorities estimated that 200,000 infants are born annually with the disease in Brazil, and the total number of individuals with the hemoglobin S gene were estimated to be approximately 7,200,000 (Jesus 2010).

Because sickle cell anemia is a genetic illness, policies for the disease have raised interesting and important questions about race, heredity, and health in Brazil, particularly since racial intermixture and blurred racial boundaries have traditionally been emphasized in official discourses. While, as shown in the statistics mentioned above, sickle cell rates are typically higher within the Afro-descendant population, efforts have been made to universalize access to sickle cell anemia testing and treatment for the Brazilian population. As a result, these services are offered to all Brazilian citizens, regardless of race or ethnicity. This is most evident in the *teste de pezinho* (little foot test), which is administered to newborns throughout the country to test for the sickle cell anemia gene. Indeed, given the high degree of racial intermixture in Brazil, it has been important to offer this sickle cell anemia test to a wide cross-section of the population, regardless of an individual's phenotypical appearance. This means that testing is encouraged and done for infants of visible African ancestry and those whose parents are known to have African ancestry, as well as for infants of visible European ancestry.

In July 2011, when I interviewed Luis Eduardo Batista, the former Coordinator of the Technical Area of the Health of the Black Population for the State of São Paulo and later a researcher at the São Paulo State Health Institute (*Instituto de Saúde*) whose work focuses on the health of the black population, he highlighted some of the policy complexities for sickle cell anemia. In response to being asked whether linking sickle cell anemia to the black population would reinforce biological notions of racial difference, Batista stated, "We do not want to biologize health. This is not the issue. So much so that we point out, even when we discuss the policy for sickle cell anemia, we are not going to talk about it as a biological issue. We are saying that it is prevalent in the black population and that it is a neglected illness because it is prevalent in poor segments [of society]." Batista's comments suggest that he was advocating for the de-linking for biology, race, and illness in discussions of sickle cell anemia. In doing so, he was also challenging the notion that sickle cell anemia was a racial illness. When asked whether he believed sickle cell anemia was also neglected because of its association with the black population, Batista responded by stating, "Speaking of this also. How is this population that is predominantly poor and that is black that has this profile and so forth is not looked at in terms of specific problems, its priority problems." Though Batista was reluctant to cast sickle cell anemia as a "black" disease, his comments highlight the ways in which it was often neglected owing to the income level and background of the people it tended to affect the most. This is a perspective I often heard voiced by activists and health professionals who focused on sickle cell anemia in their political and professional work.

Luis Eduardo Batista also pointed out gaps that existed in providing services for children diagnosed with having sickle cell anemia during the early 2010s. He explained that, following administration of the *teste de pezinho* in the state of São Paulo, parents of children with the illness would receive a letter telling them to seek out a hematologist. However, as Batista noted, "the state of São Paulo does not have a hematologist on every corner." He also mentioned that there were few reference centers or services for sickle cell patients in the state's public health system. According to Batista, approximately one in every three thousand babies in the state of São Paulo was born with sickle cell anemia; however, little to no health services or follow-up were provided to infants who tested positive. Batista highlighted the fact that 30 percent of children with sickle cell anemia were left without care or follow-up medical attention, which had a negative impact on the children's quality of life, as well as on their families. Batista's comments echoed the reflections of the panelists mentioned at the beginning of the chapter, who pointed out the neglect of sickle cell patients within the public health system. Batista noted that his own and his colleagues' approach is not to biologize illnesses that are prevalent in the black population, such as sickle cell anemia and hypertension. Instead, he argued, "We want to think how this chain within the health system, what this omission of the state, what role this social exclusion of a social group ends up bringing about in policies that make an illness invisible."

Broadening the Scope of Health Policies for the Black Population

As noted at the beginning of this chapter, sickle cell anemia was an important focus of black health activism during early stages of black health movement and before race-conscious health policies became more commonly accepted. However, in my conversations with activists and during health seminars and conferences I attended in the late 2000s and early 2010s, it was common to hear people say that sickle cell anemia was not the only issue that needed to be focused on. These comments seemed to reflect an attempt to broaden the conversation about the health of the black population and avoid a single-illness focus.

During the early 2000s, there was growing recognition of the health needs of Afro-Brazilians, particularly within federal government agencies and with respect to federal policies. During 2003, more than seventy items regarding the health of the black population were deliberated and approved during the 12th National Health Conference (Werneck 2010). This was an unprecedented development that took place at the premiere national-level gathering of government representatives, healthcare professionals, and members of civil society. In November 2003, a Term of Commitment was signed between SEPPIR and the Ministry of Health calling for mutual collaboration between the two units to develop a health policy for the black population. In early 2004 this collaboration resulted in the creation of the *Comitê Técnico de Saúde da População Negra*, which was comprised of representatives of nearly all of the secretariats and

Ministry of Health departments, as well as members of civil society whose work focused on the health of the black population. In August 2004, the committee was reformulated and comprised of representatives from different areas of the Ministry of Health, SEPPIR, and the National Council of State and Municipal Health Secretariats. The committee's tasks focused on promoting measures to: reduce morbidity and premature death in the black population; consolidate the National Sickle Cell Anemia Program; widen the black population's access to the SUS, Brazil's public health system; and develop actions to promote health in *quilombo* communities and capacity-building of health professionals in matters related to the health of the black population (Jaccoud 2009).

In 2004, a visible emphasis on the health of the black population began to surface within the Ministry of Health and other federal agencies. During 2004, officials formed a Technical Committee on the Health of the Black Population within the Ministry of Health. The same year, the Brazilian Ministry of Health developed a National Health Plan (*Plano Nacional de Saúde: um pacto pela saude no Brasil*), which made Brazil the first country in the world to call for the inclusion of racial/ethnic information in all health records. The National Health Plan also included specific provisions that addressed the health status of black and indigenous women. The Ministry of Health's co-sponsorship of the First National Seminar on the Health of the Black Population in August 2004 was another important step marking high-level Brazilian federal government discussions of the racial dimensions of health after the Durban conference. This seminar was followed by a regional workshop for Latin American and Caribbean nations on ethnic equality in health, held in Brasília, Brazil in December 2004. The workshop was sponsored by the Brazilian Ministry of Health, Ministry of Foreign Affairs, and SEPPIR and organized by the Office of the U.N. High Commissioner for Human Rights and the Pan-American Health Organization. In addition, during 2004, the Integrated Affirmative Action Program for Blacks was launched by the Ministry of Health's internationally recognized National STD/AIDS Program. This initiative signaled growing recognition of the need to examine the HIV-prevention needs of the African-descendant population in Brazil within the National STD/AIDS Program.

During 2005, the I National Conference for the Promotion of Racial Equality (I *Conferencia Nacional de Promoção da Igualdade Racial*) included important debates and discussions about health (Werneck 2010). This same year, the National STD/AIDS Program launched a strategic plan called "HIV/AIDS e Racismo" (HIV/AIDS and Racism: Brazil Has to Learn to Live without Prejudice), and for the second time, the health of the black population was included in the National Health Plan. During 2005, the Brazilian Ministry of Health also released the first publication focusing on the health of the black population, *Saúde da População Negra no Brasil: contribuições para a promoção da equidade.* This collection of essays was published by FUNASA, the *Fundação Nacional de Saúde* (National Health Foundation), which is part of the Ministry of Health, and resulted from a technical and financial collaboration between the World Bank, FUNASA, and the Health Component of the Program to Combat Institutional Racism in Brazil (PCRI), a program funded by the British Department for International Development (DFID).[8] In the book's preface, the president of FUNASA, Valdi Camarcio Bezerra, noted that it "represented a mark for health in Brazil, symbolizing, within the scope of the Ministry of Health, the beginning of the challenge of implementing a policy of health promotion that takes into account ethnic-racial differences and diversity" (Fundação Nacional de Saúde 2005).

On October 27, 2005 the black movement commemorated the first National Day of Mobilization in Support of the Health of the Black Population (*Dia Nacional de Mobilização Pró-Saúde da População Negra*). In 2006, the black movement gained representation on the National Health Council for the first time, with a mandate from 2007 to 2009. This proved an important development given the National Health Council's role as the entity charged with citizen control of health by members of civil society at the federal level. As part of the democratization process, the practice of citizen control became an important way for members of civil society to provide input and oversight in the development of health policies and budgeting for the public health sector (Avrtizer 2009). Federal law number 8.142 of 1990 instituted national health conferences and health councils as ways to guarantee community participation in the operation of the SUS. Citizen control is exercised by members of civil society through health councils and health conferences that operate at the municipal, state, and federal levels. These entities provide a mechanism for citizen input into policy making and budgeting, and are a means of holding the state accountable for ensuring access and quality in health care. Gaining representation on the National Health Council was a means to facilitate and ensure input into the health-policy-making process by black health activists.

On October 27, 2006, the National Day of Mobilization in Support of the Health of the Black Population, then–Minister of Health, José Agenor Álvares da Silva, publicly recognized the existence of institutional racism in the Unified

Health System (SUS) and stated his commitment to challenge it. The increasing recognition and discussion of institutional racism in the health sector was an important development at both the federal and municipal levels during this time, particularly in cities such as Recife and Salvador, owing to initiatives sponsored by the Program to Combat Institutional Racism (PCRI).[9] This program was instrumental in promoting discussions of institutional racism in the public health sector and in pushing for a shift to viewing racism as being a systemic and pervasive aspect of Brazilian society (Bastos and Bittencourt 2010; CRI 2006; Lopez 2012).

Perhaps the greatest single outcome of efforts to acknowledge and address the health needs of the Afro-Brazilian population was the development of the *Política Nacional de Saúde Integral da População Negra* (National Policy for the Integral Health of the Black Population, PNSIPN), also known as *Portaria 992* (Ministério da Saúde 2009). This policy earned approval by the National Health Council in 2006 and was officially promulgated by the Brazilian Ministry of Health on May 13, 2009 (the 121st anniversary of Brazilian abolition). It was also included as part of the Statute of Racial Equality (Law 12.288) signed into law by President Lula in July 2010.[10] The PNSIPN was the first federal policy in Brazilian history focusing on the health of the black population. The PNSIPN was designed to promote health equity and address racial health disparities that disproportionately impact Brazil's African-descendant population.

The text of the PNSIPN states that the policy's general objective is to "Promote the comprehensive health of the black population, prioritizing the reduction of ethnic-racial inequalities, combating racism and discrimination in the institutions and services of SUS" (Ministério da Saúde 2009). The policy contains seven general directives: (I) include the themes of Racism and the Health of the Black Population in the formation and permanent education of health workers and in the exercise of citizen control in health; (II) expand and strengthen the participation of the Black Social Movement in citizen control of health policies; (III) encourage the production of scientific and technological knowledge about the health of the black population; (IV) promote the recognition of popular health knowledge and practices, including those preserved by African-based religions; (V) implement the process of monitoring and evaluating actions pertinent to combating racism and the reduction of ethnic-racial inequalities in the health sector in the distinct government spheres; and (VI) develop information, communication, and educational processes that deconstruct stigmas and prejudices, strengthen a positive black identity and contribute to the reduction of vulnerabilities (Ministério da Saúde 2009).

Table 3.1. Timeline of Key Developments Related to the Health of Black Population

2001	Creation of Program to Combat Institutional Racism (PCRI)
2003	SEPPIR Signs Term of Commitment with Brazilian Ministry of Health
2004	Formation of Technical Committee on Health of the Black Population in Brazilian Ministry of Health
2004	First National Seminar on the Health of the Black Population, organized by Brazilian Ministry of Health
2004	Inclusion of Health of Black Population in National Health Plan, *Plano Nacional de Saúde: um pacto pela saúde no Brasil,* which also called for race/color to be included in all health records
2004	Creation of Brasil Afroatitude Program focusing on Black Population and AIDS, National STD/AIDS Program, Ministry of Health
2006	Launch of National Policy for Integral Attention to People with Sickle Cell Anemia and Other Blood Diseases
2006	Black Movement Gains Representation on National Health Council for First Time (2007–2009)
2006	Minister of Health Recognizes Existence of Institutional Racism in Unified Health System (SUS)
2006	National Health Council Unanimously Approves Creation of National Policy for Integral Health of the Black Population (PNSIPN)
2007	13th National Health Conference Reinforces Importance of PNSIPN for Ensuring Equity in the SUS
2008	National Health Council Creates Intersectoral Commission on Health of Black Population
2009	Approval of PNSIPN by Tripartite Intersectoral Commission which oversees health policy at municipal, state, and federal levels
2009	PNSIPN Becomes Official with Publication of Portaria 992 in the *Diário Oficial da União*
2010	National Council of Municipal Health Secretaries Publicly Affirms Commitment to Health Equity and Disseminates PNSIPN at XXVI National Congress
2010	PNSIPN included in text of Statute of Racial Equality (Law 12.288) signed into law by President Lula

Adapted from Werneck (2010)

The Black Movement and Health Activism

While activism by black health activists has been mentioned throughout this chapter, it is important to highlight strategies and perspectives developed by health activists who have called attention to racial health disparities in Brazil, as well as challenges and critiques activists have faced. Though health was made a right of every Brazilian citizen in the 1988 Constitution, some health activists and researchers have highlighted the shortcomings of universalist approaches to health that fail to take into account racial/ethnic and socioeconomic differentials in access to health care, as well as structural conditions that lead to worse health outcomes for racially marginalized groups (Lopes 2005; Fundação Nacional de Saúde 2005). In calling for specific health policies for the black population, black health activists have challenged Brazilian tenets of universalism and color blindness that fail to recognize racial and racialized differences and disparities within the broader population. These are particularly salient arguments considering that Brazil's public health system, SUS, is a form of socialized health care intended to meet the health needs of the entire population, regardless of income level. However, as some black activists have noted, the socialist principles undergirding SUS have often failed to recognize the role of racial dynamics in shaping access to health and health care (Cruz et al. 2008).

As discussed in chapter 2, black women activists and black women's organizations were instrumental in calling for the development of health policies for the black population from the mid to late 1980s onward. Activists such as Fátima Oliveira, Jurema Werneck, Edna Roland, and Fernanda Lopes have been at the forefront of efforts to develop policies focusing on the health of the black population, and black women in particular, for several decades. In addition, black women's organizations such as Maria Mulher, ACMUN, and Criola have done important health-related work in local communities, nationally, and transnationally. While individual black women's organizations have been instrumental in developing a policy agenda for the health of the black population, the formation of networks such as the Articulation of Black Brazilian Women's Organizations (AMNB) enabled black women activists to mobilize and articulate a policy agenda for a number of important issues, including health, at the national level.

Moreover, several national activist networks focusing on the health of the black population were created during the early 2000s. *Rede Lai Lai Apejo*[11]— *Aids e População Negra* (Lai Lai Apejo Network)—was formed in 2002 with a focus on HIV/AIDS in the black population. This network was an outgrowth of the Lai Lai Apejo conferences that were organized by the black women's NGO ACMUN/*Associação Cultural de Mulheres Negras*. A national network focusing on Afro-Brazilian religions and health, the *Rede Nacional de Religiões Afrobrasileiras e Saúde*, was formed in 2003. Two national networks with an emphasis on the citizen control of health for the black population, the *Rede Nacional de Controle Social e Saúde da População Negra* and *Sapatá*, which focuses on health promotion and citizen control for black lesbians, were launched in 2007 and 2008, respectively (Werneck 2010).

The aforementioned networks provided an opportunity for black health activists to communicate, collaborate, and mobilize at a national level. Their formation also increased activists' ability to place pressure on the Brazilian state regarding health issues affecting the black population. As noted earlier, beginning in 2007, the black movement gained formal representation on the National Health Council, which was an important mark of legitimacy for the movement's health interventions and increased activists' access to decision making and policy development arenas within the state.[12] The first two black movement representatives on the National Health Council were Fernanda Lopes (2007 to 2009) and Jurema Werneck (2010 to 2012), leading black women health activists and researchers. In December 2009, Werneck was elected president of the National Health Council and served as the General Coordinator of the 14th National Health Conference, which was held in 2011. These developments highlighted the growing recognition of black activists' contributions to health policy and citizen control of health, particularly those of black women.

"Dangerous Divisions": Scholarly Critiques of Race-Conscious Public Policies

During the early 2000s, legal developments related to affirmative action and racial equality increased public discussion of the pros and cons of race-conscious public policies and state action to combat racial discrimination. Examining broader debates about state action to combat racial equality is essential to understanding how ideas about race, racism, and racial equality circulated and were strategically employed by opponents of affirmative action during this time period. Two important laws, The Statute of Racial Equality and the Law of Quotas, were proposed within the Brazilian Congress during the early 2000s, and sparked heated controversies within the media and political arena about appropriate measures to acknowledge and address racial inequalities in the country.

The development of affirmative action policies and health policies focusing on the black population sparked intense debates about their legitimacy and appropriateness in Brazil, particularly within academic circles and in the national media. A major argument used by critics of race-conscious health policies is that they perpetuate biological notions of race and promote the racialization of Brazilian society. In addition, opponents of affirmative action policies argued that the high degree of racial intermixture in Brazil would make identification of "black" candidates for affirmative action nearly impossible (Santos 2006). Opponents of these policies have also charged that Brazil would become racialized and thus racially polarized along the lines of the United States owing to the enactment of affirmative action policies and health policies for the black population (Fry 2007; Fry et al. 2007a, 2007b).

In 2004, a prominent group of Brazilian-based scholars began publishing newspaper op-ed pieces and articles in scholarly publications that critiqued health policies for the black population, as well as affirmative action policies (Fry and Maggie 2004; Maggie 2005a, 2005b; Maio and Monteiro 2005; Monteiro 2004). This group included prominent anthropologists, such as Peter Fry, Yvonne Maggie, and Ricardo Ventura, as well as leading public health researchers, such as Marcos Chor Maio and Simone Monteiro. Prior to developing critiques of public policies for the black population, several of these scholars had conducted research on race and Afro-Brazilian culture, and in some cases on indigenous communities, so their critiques of affirmative action policies were a surprising departure from the acknowledgement of racism characterizing much of their previous work. In addition, prior to publicly critiquing affirmative action policies and health policies for the black population, some of these scholars previously had rather close ties to black movement organizations. Though these scholars often made criticisms of race-conscious policies individually, in the form of scholarly articles as well as newspaper articles, editorials, and political manifestos, jointly authored criticisms also appeared in scholarly articles. This group of scholars argued that, in asserting the importance of racially specific health policies, black activists were "racializing" the field of health and promoting biologically-based notions of race (Fry et al. 2007a, 2007b, 2007c).

An important example of critiques of race-conscious policies undertaken by Yvonne Maggie, Peter Fry, and their collaborators was a co-edited volume titled *Divisões Perigosas: Políticas raciais no Brasil Contemporâneo* ("Dangerous Divisions: Racial Policies in Contemporary Brazil"), which was published in 2007. The book contains more than forty essays that critique race-conscious policies in Brazil. It also contains a 2006 manifesto against the Statute of Racial Equality and the Law of Quotas, two legislative initiatives proposed in the Brazilian Congress during the early 2000s.[13] Yvonne Maggie, an established and well-respected anthropologist, played a leading role in generating the 2006 manifesto, which these scholars presented to the president of the Brazilian Chamber of Deputies. She also led efforts for a second manifesto against the Statute of Racial Equality and the Law of Quotas that was presented to the Brazilian Chamber of Deputies in 2008.

The 2006 manifesto, *"Todos têm direitos iguais na República Democrática"* (Everyone Has Equal Rights in the Democratic Republic), argued that the Statute of Racial Equality would implant an official racial classification of Brazilian citizens and that, if approved along with the Law of Quotas, "the Brazilian nation would come to define the rights of people based on the tone of their skin, by 'race'" ("Carta Pública" 2007, 345). The manifesto further stated that "history had already painfully condemned these attempts" ("Carta Pública" 2007, 345). One of the main criticisms of race-conscious laws made in the manifesto was that they would entrench racialized notions of identity and difference. According to the manifesto, "Policies directed toward strict 'racial' groups in the name of social justice do not eliminate racism and can, in fact, produce the opposite effect, giving legal support to the concept of race and facilitating the deepening of conflict and intolerance" ("Carta Pública" 2007, 346). In contrast to race-conscious policies, signers of the manifesto argued that "The widely recognized truth is that the main way to combat social exclusion is the construction of quality universal public services in the sectors of education, health, and social welfare, especially in job creation" ("Carta Pública" 2007, 346).

As noted above, opponents of race-conscious policies, such as the supporters of the 2006 manifesto, argued they would increase racial divisions and racial animus in Brazil. These sentiments were repeated in the introduction to the book *Divisões Perigosas*, in which the editors refer to the supporters of race-conscious policies as "reeducators," stating:

> The 'reeducators' want to impinge fixed racial identities on people and, being, unable to convince them to abdicate the fluid perceptions that inhabit the national imaginary, they try to use the power of the State to 'rectify' society. The offering of 'racial' privileges in higher education and the job market is part of this operation, which also includes the racialization of health and a version of Brazilian history as being driven by 'racial conflict.' Race is in everything—that is the banner they hold up. [Fry et al. 2007c, 21–22]

Though not explicitly referenced in this passage, black activists are invoked by these scholars through use of the term "reeducators." Fry et al. imply that members of Brazil's black movement advocate the misuse of statistical data for "racial" purposes, with the goal of installing a racist policy regime in Brazil. However, the authors fail to fully explain why the use of race and race-conscious policies is a bad idea; instead, they appear to make a series of assumptions based on their view that invoking race in the public sphere and in policy development will serve to create racialized forms of discourse and praxis that had not previously existed in Brazil. In addition, the state is portrayed as being at the whim of the "reeducators"—in line with the authors' negative view of the close interaction between the state and civil society during Cardoso's and Lula's administrations.

There is ample evidence to disprove the notion that black activists were racializing the field of health in Brazil, particularly because this presupposes that the arena of health was racially neutral prior to the implementation of race-conscious health policies. A number of scholars, particularly historians, have shown how racialist and racist thought informed medical discourse and practice in Brazil during the nineteenth and twentieth centuries, particularly through the promotion of scientific racism and eugenics (Fonseca Sobrinho 1993; Peard 1999; Sheppard 2001; Stepan 1991). These interventions offer powerful reminders of the ways in which popular and official notions of race and racial difference have shaped health and health care in Brazil, and help dispel the belief that Brazilian health care or medical practices have historically been race-neutral or nonracialized. In addition, as chapter 4 will discuss, epidemiological data and scholarly research have increasingly highlighted practices of racial discrimination and racially inequitable treatment in Brazil's health sector.

The development of race-conscious health policies for the black population demonstrates the ways in which antiracist mobilization by black activists began to impact the health sector, including the Ministry of Health, by the mid and late 2000s. These efforts took place within a larger discursive and policy environment in which there were heated debates about the appropriateness of creating public policies that explicitly acknowledged and took race and racism into account. During the 2000s, the Statute of Racial Equality and the Law of Quotas, which was later titled the Law of Quotas for Higher Education, generated a great deal of controversy, although both pieces of legislation were eventually passed.[14] In addition, although efforts to develop legislation to challenge racism and promote equity were successful in some respects, the final outcomes did not always fully reflect the antiracist principles and ideals that led to the creation of laws such as the Statute of Racial Equality. In many cases, opponents of both affirmative action and health policies for the black population were also able to draw upon their considerable social and economic capital and connections to promote their critiques of race-conscious policies in the media, as well as in academic publications.[15] Moreover, the impact of scholarly critiques of race-conscious policies often extended beyond academic circles and influenced how conservative politicians altered legislation such as the Statute of Racial Equality.

Some critics of race-conscious policy approaches have argued that affirmative action and health policies for the black population constituted potentially dangerous approaches, because they would ultimately reinscribe biological and pseudo-scientific notions of racial difference. Similar concerns have been articulated about the use of race in medicine and scientific research in the United States. However, in the U.S. context, there has been greater recognition of the need to focus on how structural forms of discrimination and inequality, as well as larger social dynamics, shape health (Smedley et al. 2003). Legal scholar Dorothy Roberts has asserted that, rather than focusing on the relationship between race and biology, U.S. researchers should give greater regard to how systemic inequalities lead to different health outcomes for different populations (Roberts 2011). This perspective has been absent from most critiques of health policies for the black population in Brazil. In addition, as I discuss below, explicit references to racism as a social determinant of health were omitted from the final version of the Statute of Racial Equality, thus making it more difficult to address the impact of social factors on health disparities between individuals of different racial/ethnic backgrounds.

The Statute of Racial Equality

The Statute of Racial Equality was a key piece of legislation developed during the 2000s to address racial discrimination and racial inequalities in Brazil. Examining the approval process for the statute highlights both the successes and challenges that have been associated with the development of antiracist legislation and race-conscious policies in Brazil. Paulo Paim, an Afro-Brazilian politician and former parliamentary deputy, presented the statute to the Brazilian Chamber of Deputies on June 7, 2000 as Project of Law 3.198/2000. Senator Paim, of the southern Brazilian state of Rio Grande do Sul, was one of a handful of Afro-Brazilian politicians serving in the Congress or Senate at the time. Santos et al. (2011) have argued that, by proposing the statute, Senator Paim was seeking to formalize rights that the black population did not have. Though the statute was eventually approved by the Brazilian Congress and Senate, it went through an extremely long and arduous approval process, and was signed into law by President Lula on July 20, 2010, ten years after originally being proposed by Senator Paim.[16]

The Statute of Racial Equality was approved in the Brazilian Congress on November 9, 2005. Following this initial five-year period, the statute became subject to broader public debates and opposition to affirmative action policies, although it was not solely focused on affirmative action. Heated discussions and objections to affirmative action policies and legislation such as the Statute of Racial Equality and the Law of Quotas regularly appeared in the Brazilian media, particularly in leading newspapers such as *O Globo,* the *Folha de São Paulo,* and *O Estado de São Paulo* (Santos et al. 2011). In addition to publishing articles that had an anti–affirmative action bias, these newspapers also regularly published editorials that criticized race-based affirmative action in employment and university admissions and called for social quotas, which would be based on social class, rather than race.

The group of scholars previously discussed who opposed affirmative action and other race-conscious public policies actively lobbied against the Statute of Racial Equality and the Law of Quotas. The previously mentioned 2006 manifesto, "Everyone has Equal Rights in the Democratic Republic," was signed by 114 prominent scholars, union members, artists, politicians, and other professionals and expressed their opposition to the passage of the Law of Quotas and the Statute of Racial Equality. While this manifesto received considerable media coverage, far less attention was given to a manifesto submitted to the Brazilian Congress in favor of the Law of Quotas and the Statute of Racial Equality in July 2006. A total of 330 people, including prominent scholars and activists, signed the second manifesto. Sixty additional people were listed as supporters. In April 2008, Yvonne Maggie returned to Brasília with a new manifesto against quotas for black students entitled, "One Hundred and Thirteen Anti-Racist Citizens Against Racial Laws." This manifesto was presented to the president of the Federal Supreme Court. Supporters of affirmative action responded to this action by submitting a pro–affirmative action manifesto signed by 640 people to the Supreme Court president on May 13, 2008. This date held important symbolic meaning, because it marked the anniversary of the abolition of slavery in Brazil. This manifesto was entitled "120 Years of Struggle for Race Equality in Brazil: A Manifesto in Defense of Justice and the Constitutionality of Quotas."

Submission of the anti– and pro–affirmative action manifestos to the Brazilian Chamber of Deputies in 2006 and 2008 captured the heated public controversy over race-conscious policies during this period. In their analysis of the approval process for the Statute of Racial Equality, Santos et al. (2011) highlight the ways in which Brazilian politicians began to adopt discursive strategies developed by Fry, Maggie, and their collaborators to challenge race-conscious public policies. In particular, politicians increasingly used the notion of "racialization" in their arguments against the statute.[17] In doing so, these individuals articulated a belief that approval of the statute would lead to racial divisions that had not previously existed in Brazil.

Between the time the Congress approved the statute in November 2005 and signed it into law in July 2010, it underwent major revisions reflecting the views of opponents of affirmative action, both inside and outside the political arena. Demóstenes Torres, a conservative senator from the state of Goiás, assumed the role of rapporteur during the final approval process. He also oversaw modifications to the text that significantly weakened the statute's impact once signed into law. At the time, Torres was a senator for the *Partido Democratas* (Democratic Party, DEMS), a center-right political party that was one of the chief opponents of affirmative action policies.[18] The removal of most explicit references to race, racism, and racial discrimination in the text was one of the most significant changes made. Terms such as "racial discrimination," "ethnic-racial intolerance," "racial inequality," "race," and "racism," were replaced with the terms "ethnic equality" and "ethnic rights" (Santos et al. 2011). Moreover, while most explicit references to race and racism were removed, some terms remained, which created conceptual inconsistences in the statute's final version (Santos et al. 2011).

Chapter 8 of the statute, which called for the establishment of a quota system, was completely removed during the revision process. Mechanisms calling for state action to promote the inclusion of blacks in various sectors of society were also removed from final version. Specifically, those relating to the inclusion of blacks in the job market and in public universities and technical schools through the quota system were stricken. This resulted in substantively weaker provisions for achieving racial equality in the statute's final version. Given the major alterations made to the statute, many black activists viewed it as far less powerful and effective than they had hoped. In fact, Federal Deputy Luiz Alberto remarked on the measure, stating that it was "an accord against the black population" (Santos et al. 2011, 53).

Although the Statute of Racial Equality made the National Policy for the Integral Health of the Black Population (PNSIPN) law, several provisions related to the health of the black population were removed from the final version. An earlier draft of the statute called for inclusion of the concept of racism as a social determinant of health; however this was omitted from the final version. In his role as rapporteur for the statute's approval process, Demóstenes Torres argued that illnesses that were believed to be more prevalent in the black population would not be included in the statute, since the genetic basis of these illnesses was still questioned by medicine (Jeronimo 2010; Pagano 2014). In doing so, Torres appears to have been challenging a biologically-based view of health. However, he did not advocate a social determinant approach to health, as was found in an earlier draft of the statute. Ultimately, neither approach to health was dominant in the final version of the statute.

In addition to the changes discussed above, the health-related provisions found in Articles 9 and 10 that were part of the version of the statute approved by Congress as Project of Law 6.264/2005, were taken out of the final iteration. Article 9 called for the three spheres of the Brazilian government—municipal, state, and federal—to implement a plan for the execution of national policies for the health of the black population. It also called for them "to establish strategies, indicators, and goals that will orient intervention in the Unified Health System (SUS) . . . in the process of confronting health inequities and inequalities with a focus on an ethnic-racial approach" (cited in Santos et al. 2011, 67). Removal of this article significantly weakened the ability of health activists and health advocates to call for implementation of the PNSIPN and also decreased government accountability in this area. In addition, Article 10 called for health priorities to be set in the following areas: (1) reducing maternal mortality among black women; (2) reducing mortality among black infants, adolescents, youths, and adults; (3) reducing violent deaths among black youths; (4) early diagnosis and comprehensive attention to persons with sickle cell anemia and other blood diseases; and (5) widening coverage focusing on the health of the black population, while retaining cultures and ways and knowing (Santos et al. 2011). The removal of this article significantly weakened the statute's ability to ensure that the state would be held accountable for its efforts to combat racial health disparities and practices that result in higher rates of violence and mortality among the black population.

Conclusion

This review and analysis of the period from 1988 to 2010 highlights both tremendous progress and ongoing challenges in the quest to ensure racial health equity in Brazil. Gains that were made in the development of health policies for the black population largely owed to political openings provided by the Cardoso and Lula administrations with regard to state acknowledgement of racism and the development of policies and programs to combat it. Black activists and health researchers used these openings to promote discussion, research, and policy development focusing on the health of the black population. Black activists also effectively used transnational mobilization, particularly in relation to the Durban conference, and worked with international donors and institutions, including United Nations agencies such as the U.N. Population Fund (UNFPA) and the U.N. Development Programme (UNDP), the British Department for International Development (DFID) and the Pan-American Health Organization (PAHO), to consolidate a policy agenda for the health of the black population. However, while tremendous gains were made with respect to the development of health policies for the black population during the early 2000s, obtaining governmental funding for these policies and achieving full implementation at the federal, state, and municipal level are major challenges yet to be resolved. Moreover, how prominently gender and the health needs of black women will be incorporated into these policies remains an open question, particularly because this would require an intersectional perspective that addresses the ways in which gender, race, class, and other forms of identity shape experiences and expressions of health and wellness.

4

Strategies to Challenge
Institutional Racism and Color
Blindness in the Health Sector

In Brazil, the ideology of racial democracy has had a material impact on government data collection practices and state policies with regard to race and health.
As noted in chapter 3, historically, the lack of health data by race fostered a
color-blind approach to health, which perpetuated the belief that racial health
disparities did not exist in Brazil. The specific health needs of Afro-Brazilians remained invisible during the latter decades of the twentieth century, despite the
existence of the SUS, a universal public health system which, in theory, provided
health care to all Brazilian citizens. In fact, one could argue that the universalist
tenets undergirding the SUS appeared to reduce the need to develop targeted
health policies for vulnerable groups. In addition, until the early 2000s, official views of Brazil as a nonracist society and the Brazilian state's longstanding
denial of the existence of racism led to a color-blind approach to health that
failed to address the specific health needs and challenges of Afro-Brazilians.
However, as has been acknowledged in a growing body of public policies and
research studies, Afro-Brazilians have been subjected to racialized forms of
treatment within the public health system that underscore the ways in which
race pervades and is manifested in the health-care sector (Batista et al. 2012;
Fundação Nacional de Saúde 2005; Kalckmann et al. 2007, 2010; Lopes 2005).

This chapter examines some of the key issues and challenges related to the
effective implementation of health policies for the black population in Brazil.
The analysis centers on the development of initiatives to combat institutional

racism in the health sector, in cities such as Salvador, Bahia, as well as on the complexities of fully and consistently implementing collection of the *quesito cor* (color/race data) in epidemiological records and health research. These two issues highlight the racial implications of health policies for the black population and the impact that beliefs that racism is either nonexistent in Brazil or confined to individual prejudice have had on possibilities for effective health policy implementation. Efforts to address institutional racism in the health sector and to encourage collection of the *quesito cor* also underscore the relationship between race and biopolitics in twenty-first-century Brazil and the potential limits of the universalist principles on which Brazil's public health system, the SUS, were founded.

By analyzing initiatives related to institutional racism and the collection of color/race data, this chapter seeks to elucidate the ways in which discourses on race, racism, and racial identity have taken shape in the Brazilian health sector since the early 2000s. I begin with a discussion of the concept of institutional racism and how it informed programmatic initiatives in cities such as Salvador and Recife during the early and mid-2000s. I also interrogate the ways in which Salvador's national and international image as the most "black" city in Brazil obscures racial health disparities and social factors that create health inequities for the black population. Later sections of this chapter analyze the collection of the *quesito cor* in health services in the state of São Paulo and the ways in which these efforts have sought to challenge color blindness in the health sector and disrupt traditional racial etiquette, both of which deny the significance of race and racism in health care and in Brazilian society more broadly. The analysis offered in this chapter has important implications for understanding the discursive and institutional environment in which health policies for the black population have been developed and implemented, as well as ongoing challenges in this area.

Operationalizing the Concept of Institutional Racism

Beginning in the mid-2000s, there was increasing discussion of institutional racism within the health sector in Brazil. The concept of institutional racism is particularly important in the Brazilian context given the historical absence of de jure or legalized segregation and racial discrimination in the country (Hernandez 2013). During 2001, the Program to Combat Institutional Racism (PCRI) was created in Brazil as a means of contributing to development policies and poverty reduction by confronting racial discrimination in institutional settings.

The PCRI was developed during the preparatory process for the 2001 World Conference against Racism. The program was established under the supervision of the Brazilian Agency of Cooperation (*Agência Brasileira de Cooperação, ABC*), which is part of the Ministry of External Relations, in partnership with the Ministry of Health, the Federal Public Ministry, the Secretariat for the Promotion of Racial Equality Policies (*Secretaria para a Promoção de Políticas de Igualdade Racial*, SEPPIR), the United Nations Development Program (UNDP), the Pan-American Health Organization (PAHO), and the British Government's Department for International Development (DFID). Both the DFID and the UNDP recognized the possibilities presented by the preparatory process for the 2001 World Conference against Racism as an opportunity to promote discussion of racism in Brazil (Instituto AMMA Psique e Negritude n.d.). The PCRI was developed to address the inertia and lack of continuity in government efforts to challenge racial discrimination by focusing on the ways in which racism was embedded in the culture of Brazilian public institutions. The PCRI also supported civil society organizations and networks focused on institutional racism, particularly with respect to health, in "augmenting their participation in formulating and monitoring public policies in search of equity" (Lopes and Quintiliano 2007, 12). This support helped strengthen the effectiveness and reach of activist networks focused on the health of the black population, such as the *Rede Nacional de Religiões Afro-Brasileiras e Saúde* (National Network of Afro-Brazilian Religions and Health) and the *Rede Lai Lai Apejo*, which is the black women's NGO, ACMUN, formed.

The PCRI adopted a working definition of institutional racism that drew upon the transnational experiences of black communities in the United States and Great Britain. This definition was based on the conceptualization of institutional racism that Stokely Carmichael and Charles Hamilton, black nationalists from the United States, used in their pioneering 1967 book, *Black Power: The Politics of Liberation in America*, as well as British views of institutional racism that grew out of the 1993 murder of Steven Lawrence, a black British young man, in London. The PCRI defined institutional racism as:

> the failure of institutions and organizations to provide a professional and adequate service to people due to their color, culture, racial or ethnic origin. It is manifested in discriminatory norms, practices and behaviors adopted in the everyday work routine, which result from ignorance, lack of attention, prejudice or racist stereotypes. In whatever case, institutional racism always places people from racially or ethnically discriminated groups in a situation of disadvantage in access to the benefits generated by the State and by other institutions and organizations. [CRI 2006, 17]

In addition, the PCRI described the characteristics of institutional racism in the following terms:

> They can be seen or detected in practices that are consolidated in everyday life, processes, attitudes and behaviors that contribute to discrimination through prejudice, ignorance, lack of attention and racist stereotypes that prejudge groups. [CRI 2006, 98]

While the first definition of institutional racism cited above served as a guidepost for the PCRI's priorities and activities, it also became a commonly used conceptualization of institutional racism that began to be used by activists, government agencies, and researchers in Brazil. The conceptual definition of institutional racism developed by the PCRI was envisioned as a tool that could be used by representatives from the government, the private sector, and civil society in efforts "to combat and prevent discriminatory practices resulting from racism in the areas of health, education, culture, human rights and access to justice, public administration, among others" (CRI 2006, 21). Although the PCRI had a somewhat broad mandate, its activities focused on health in Brazil. *Instituto AMMA-Psique e Negritude*, a São Paulo–based NGO primarily comprised of black female psychologists that focuses on racial issues, was a key partner in the PCRI.

It is worth noting that, by addressing systemic and structural forms of racial discrimination, the concept of institutional racism broke with the longstanding tradition of focusing on individual prejudice in Brazil. It also challenged the belief that racism could not exist in Brazil because the country did not have a history of legalized segregation and discrimination.[1] As a publication produced by organizations associated with the PCRI notes, despite the differences between the British and Brazilian contexts, adoption of the concept of institutional racism was useful because racism had been historically denied in Brazil (CRI 2006). In addition, the concept of institutional racism allowed for discussion of racist practices whether they were conscious and intentional or not (CRI 2006).

The PCRI focused on two dimensions of analysis, which were viewed as being interdependent and correlated: (1) interpersonal relations and (2) political-programmatic issues. The first dimension addressed relationships between public administrators (*gestores*) and workers and between workers and service users, that is, citizens/clients who used municipal services. The PRCI's activities related to this dimension focused on the deconstruction of discriminatory beliefs that were held by individuals. This was typically done by having municipal employees and administrators participate in workshops in which they discussed topics such as social representations and imagery, and how racism is learned. The second dimension of analysis addressed multiple political and programmatic issues, including the production and dissemination of information regarding inequalities related to birth, illness, and death; investment in specific actions and programs to identify discriminatory practices; and possibilities for elaborating and implementing nondiscriminatory mechanisms and strategies (CRI 2006). The program focused on identifying practices of institutional racism within municipal governments and developing strategies to combat them. Workshops were held with public employees and administrators as a means to train them to perceive instances of racism within governmental practices and actions.

The PCRI was implemented in the municipal governments of Salvador, Bahia, and Recife, Pernambuco, two capital cities located in the Brazilian Northeast. In Recife, the PCRI was coordinated by the Directorate of Racial Equality (*Diretoria de Igualdade Racial, DIR*), which was under the purview of the Secretariat for Human Rights and Citizen Security (*Secretaria de Direitos Humanos e Segurança Cidadã*), beginning in 2005. The PCRI's activities were focused in the areas of education, health, work, culture, legislation, and justice (Lopes and Quintiliano 2007). During 2005, implementation of the PCRI resulted in the Working Group on Sickle Cell Anemia in Recife becoming a Working Group on the Health of the Black Population. A municipal unit focusing on the black population more generally (*Gerencia Operacional de Atenção à População Negra*) was also formed in 2006. Its primary activity was the formulation of a Municipal Policy for the Health of the Black Population, which was approved by Recife's Municipal Health Council in October 2006. The Municipal Health Secretariat also began to focus on collecting and registering health data by race/color (*quesito cor*) and producing official statistics based on disaggregated race/color data (Lopes and Quintiliano 2007).

The PCRI was officially launched in Salvador in April 2005 as a partnership between the municipal government (*prefeitura*) of Salvador and the DFID, with the UNDP serving as an implementing agency. The program was also coordinated by the Municipal Secretariat for Reparation (*Secretaria Municipal de Reparação*) in Salvador. The PCRI in Salvador focused on actions in line with the United Nations' Millennium Development Goals and projects in the areas of poverty reduction, governance, and environment, with the following objectives: (1) contribute to challenging the notion of a racial democracy existing in Brazil, and that poverty was solely a result of economic inequality; (2) promote racial equity by combating institutional racism; (3) support the integration of efforts to combat institutional racism at the municipal level, in Bahia; and (4) focus health activities and conduct a case study about how institutional racism can be approached in a sectorial ministry, in order to allow for the necessary linkages between federal policy and its execution on the state and municipal level (Bastos and Bittencourt 2010, 180).

In 2005, the First Workshop to Combat Institutional Racism was organized by the PCRI and the Municipal Health Secretariat of Salvador (SMS). The workshop provided a basis for analyzing racism in the Municipal Health Secretariat and resulted in three strategic actions being identified: promoting respect for diversity in work relations and in the attention given to users; giving visibility to the need to prevent and combat institutional racism in the Municipal Health Secretariat (SMS); and guaranteeing the institutionalization of actions focusing on the black population and combating and preventing institutional racism (Bastos and Bittencourt 2010). The programmatic priorities and strategies of the PCRI in Salvador highlight the importance of identifying and proactively challenging racism in a city renowned for being the most black city in Brazil, and thus may be assumed to be free of racial discrimination.

Over the course of the PCRI's activities in Salvador, close to seven hundred health professionals were trained to identify, combat, and prevent institutional racism (Lopes and Quintiliano 2007). The PCRI's emphasis on providing trainings for public employees underscores the need to educate Brazilian citizens about what racism is and how institutional racism, in particular, operates. Through its workshops in the city of Salvador the PCRI provided a space in which municipal employees could learn and think about both everyday practices of racism and more systemic forms of racial discrimination and differential treatment. Workshops touched on both conscious and unconscious attitudes and behaviors. According to a PCRI publication, they were:

> constructed in order to encourage attention to the participants' perception based on memories, ideas, information and content that allowed for the identification of racial prejudices that inhabited the social imaginary and that contained within themselves stereotypes, impulses or desires, not always conscious, that are responsible for discriminatory attitudes. [CRI 2006, 24]

Following the official launch of the PCRI in April 2005, a workshop held in July 2005 was one of the first steps in implementing the program. The workshop, *I Oficina de Identificação de Abordagem do Racismo*, was used as a way to initiate a discussion about institutional racism within Salvador's Municipal Health Secretariat and included participation by coordinators, subcoordinators, and technical assistants from the secretariat (Bastos and Bittencourt 2010). The workshop used the previously mentioned definition of institutional racism as a basis for reflecting on everyday professional situations that could be seen as instances of institutionalized racial discrimination. A second workshop was held in August 2006, and that same year the Working Group on the Health of the Black Population (GTSPN) became a unit within the Municipal Health Secretariat known as the Office for Promoting Racial Equity in Health (*Assessoria de Promoção da Equidade Racial em Saúde,* ASPERS). Formation of ASPERS was supported by the National PCRI and UNDP, both of which provided conceptual and financial support for efforts to institutionalize a focus on the health of the black population within Salvador's Municipal Health Secretariat (Bastos and Bittencourt 2010). ASPERS was designed to promote racial equity in health through transversal or cross-cutting efforts that would involve multiple sectors of the municipal government, as well as articulation with the health districts and health professionals within each district known as Focal Points (*Pontos Focais*).

As part of the implementation of the PCRI within Salvador's municipal health system, Focal Points were utilized as a way to link individual health districts with the citywide effort to address institutional racism within the health sector. One to two individuals were chosen as Focal Points within each health district, beginning in 2005. The Focal Points were volunteers who served as a link between the Working Group on the Health of the Black Population (GTSPN) and the health units and sectors of the Municipal Health Secretariat. To become a Focal Point, health professionals had to demonstrate that they could identify with the theme of institutional racism and were sensitive to the complexities associated with the health of the black population. The Focal Points also disseminated information about the health of the black population and the PCRI focusing on health, as well as SUS programs such as *Humaniza SUS* (which focused on the humanization of health services), and mobilized their peers for campaigns focused on combating racism and promoting ethnic, religious, and sexual diversity both inside and outside of the health sector (Bastos and Bittencourt 2010). The Focal Points have been described as "producers of a new way of doing things (*novo fazer*) that, in addition to questioning institutional racism, question their own condition in the world, as well as the need to develop new abilities based on their own practices as a health professional" (Bastos and Bittencourt 2010, 183).

In 2006, district centers or nuclei (*núcleos distritais*) focusing on the health of the black population were formed within Salvador's municipal health system (Bastos and Bittencourt 2010). This initiative was sponsored by the municipal Working Group on the Health of the Black Population (GTSPN) and ASPERS, the newly formed unit within the Municipal Health Secretariat focusing on racial equity in health, in partnership with the National PCRI, and the Center for Afro-Brazilian Studies (CEAFRO) of the Federal University of Bahia; it was financed by UNDP.

Ten district-based workshops were held in 2006 to provide training for health professionals in ways to combat institutional racism. Eloísa Bastos and Liliane

Bittencourt were involved with the workshops as staff of ASPERS and have noted that "These workshops offered a unique space to express the ways that racism and discrimination impacted and impact, personally and professionally, each of the participants" (2010, 181). Bastos and Bittencourt also state that many health professionals did not initially make connections between everyday experiences of racism and the concept of institutional racism and, at first, categorically denied that there was racism within their workplaces. However, as time passed, the participants began to make connections between symbolic and everyday forms of discrimination and institutional racism. The initial workshops were followed by others, which received support from the federal Ministry of Health, and addressed various topics through a racial lens, including sexism, machismo, xenophobia, homophobia, and lesbophobia (Bastos and Bittencourt 2010).

Racial Health Disparities in a "Black" City?

Launch of the PCRI in Salvador highlighted the social, economic, and political complexities that characterize this predominantly African-descendant city. According to the 2010 census, the black (*preto* and *pardo*) population made up 80 percent of Salvador's total population ("Salvador é Capital Mais Negro do País"). Owing to the high percentage of Afro-Brazilians who reside in Salvador and the visibility of Afro-Brazilian cultural practices, Salvador has become a popular destination for African-based cultural tourism for visitors from Europe and the United States, particularly U.S. African Americans (Paschel 2009; Pinho 2008). By highlighting and acknowledging the existence of institutional racism within municipal government agencies and institutions, the PCRI challenged Salvador's longstanding image as a carefree tourist destination. This is particularly important given Salvador's international reputation as a city thriving with Afro-Brazilian culture, including the Yoruba-based religion of Candomblé, the Afro-Brazilian martial art *capoeira* and carnival groups such as *Ilê Aiyê* and *Olodum* (Pinho 2010). Consequently, the city of Salvador may appear to be a site in which racial disparities and inequalities are not a problem.

Until recently, a good deal of scholarly research tended to focus on cultural dynamics in Salvador, rather than on issues of racial inequality or discrimination. However, a growing body of scholarship has highlighted persistent socioeconomic divisions, discriminatory urbanization policies, and systemic violence against Afro-Brazilian communities in Salvador (Perry 2013; Smith 2013, 2016). Moreover, despite the fact that blacks comprise the majority of Salvador's population, they experience pervasive forms of social, economic, and political marginalization and disenfranchisement that have important implications for health and health-care access. A 2006 report on the health of the black population in Salvador found much higher rates of maternal and infant mortality among black women, when compared to white women (Prefeitura Municipal de Salvador 2006). The report also called for health professionals to collect data on patients' race and skin color, a practice discussed in detail later in this chapter.

Practices of violence in and against black communities in Salvador are significant social determinants of health, wellness, and mortality in these communities. High rates of violence and police homicides can also be viewed as public health issues that lead to shortened life expectancies in the black community, particularly among young black men (Smith 2016). Troubling practices of violence are perpetrated by state authorities in black communities in Salvador on an everyday basis, as well as during special events such as Carnaval, as documented in the *Observatório da Discriminação Racial, da Violéncia Contra a Mulher e LGBT* (Observatory on Racial Discrimination, Violence against Women and LGBT) (Secretaria Municipal de Reparação 2012a).

Salvador became the first city in Brazil to have a Program to Combat Institutional Racism as part of the municipal government. The PCRI's work was later continued by the Municipal Secretariat for Reparation (*Secretaria Municipal de Reparação,* SEMUR), and combating institutional racism in the health sector was included as a priority area in the *Plano Municipal de Políticas de Promoção de Igualdade Racial* (Municipal Plan for Policies to Promote Racial Equality) for 2013 to 2016 (Secretaria Municipal de Reparação 2012b). As noted earlier, ASPERS (*Assessoria de Promoção da Equidade Racial em Saúde*) was formed within Salvador's Municipal Health Secretariat in 2006 as an outgrowth of the PCRI's efforts and was intended to address racial health inequities in the city. During my interviews and conversations with current and former staff of ASPERS in 2011 and 2012, challenges the office faced in its efforts to improve health outcomes for the black population received frequent mention. Administrative instability within the Municipal Health Secretariat of Salvador was a major obstacle to ensuring continuity in initiatives that ASPERS developed, as well as solidifying the office's legitimacy within the municipal government. Between the time ASPERS was established in 2006 and 2012, several different people served as municipal secretary of health in Salvador, which created a good deal of institutional instability. In fact, two former staff of ASPERS mentioned that there were five different municipal secretaries of health between 2005 and 2009; however, it was difficult for me to verify this number.

Institutional instability within the Municipal Health Secretariat made it more difficult to sustain efforts to address racial health disparities in Salvador, particularly considering that each new health secretary would have to be convinced of the need to have an office such as ASPERS, as well as support its work institutionally. When I visited the ASPERS office in June 2011, it was located in the basement of a building that housed several units of the Municipal Health Secretariat. When I returned in June 2012, the office had moved to an upper floor of another building. The director of ASPERS expressed her belief that this move was a demonstration of the higher level of regard granted to the unit at that time. This also seemed to be a reflection of the administrative priorities of the Municipal Health Secretary.[2] This example demonstrates how the status of ASPERS and the health of the black population of Salvador more generally could receive greater or lesser priority depending on the political and philosophical orientation of current municipal administrators. Because the Municipal Health Secretary is appointed by the mayor of Salvador, this role is also determined by the political orientation of the larger municipal administration at any given time. Political instabilities and administrative changes at both the municipal and state levels are important factors to consider when examining the effectiveness of units created to focus on the health of the black population, as well as the effectiveness of the implementation of the PNSIPN at these levels.

Using the *Quesito Cor* to Challenge Color Blindness in the Health Sector

While I was conducting research in the city of Porto Alegre in 2009, one of the activists in a black women's organization that I knew shared her thoughts about some of the problems that existed surrounding collection of data on race and skin color in health records. She described a personal experience of being seen by a health professional and having them record her race as "white" in her health records. She was angry that this had been done, particularly because she self-identified as *negra* despite her light skin tone. In addition, as both a nurse and a health activist, she was acutely aware of the importance of recording the race/skin color of patients to obtain data on potential racial health disparities. Unlike many patients who might not be aware that health professionals should include the race/skin color of patients in their health records, she also knew that patients should be asked how they self-identified with respect to race/skin color. In the example described above, had this been done, this activist's race/skin color would have been recorded as black, rather than white.

The experience described above highlights several issues related to the collection of health data by race, especially with respect to health professionals recording the race/skin color of patients without consulting the patients. This practice opens the possibility for health professionals to record a race/skin color for patients that might differ from how patients self-identify, which might potentially lead to identification discordance. Given the historical tendency to privilege lighter color classifications for self-identification, as well as identification of others, in Brazil heteroclassification by health professionals might also potentially lead to them recording a lighter skin color for patients than they might choose for themselves.[3]

Encouraging collection and registration of the *quesito cor* in health records was an integral part of the PCRI's activities in Recife and Salvador (Lopes and Quintiliano 2007). This was important because, until the mid-1990s, health data was not collected by race/color in Brazil. The lack of race/color data in health records was in line with the absence of data on race in official records, such as the national census. During the twentieth century, race was included as a category in the Brazilian census on an inconsistent basis (Nobles 2000). Additionally, data on race was collected inconsistently in the 1950 and 1960 national censuses. The 1950 census also allowed self-classification for the first time based on four options: *preto* (black), *pardo* (brown), *amarelo* (yellow), and *branco* (white) (Telles 2014). No racial data was collected in the 1970 census, at the height of the military dictatorship. A limited amount of racial data was collected and tabulated for the 1980 census, largely due to demands from black activists. Racial data was collected and tabulated to a greater extent than in the past in the 1991 census.[4] Beginning in 2000, race/color data was regularly collected and tabulated for the national census.

Examining the history of race/color data collection in the Brazilian census is essential for understanding the logic that has undergirded other forms of data collection, including those in the health sector. The absence of data on race was used to support Brazil's image as a racial democracy and was also in line with censorship of open discussion of race and racism during the military dictatorship. In Brazil, the ideology of color blindness, while seemingly antiracist, has contributed to the invisibility of the black population in the health sector and the denial of their specific needs and experiences.

Fátima Oliveira, an Afro-Brazilian physician and longtime activist in the black women's movement, black movement, and women's movement, has long argued for the importance of collecting health data by race/color in Brazil. As she has observed:

> The *quesito cor,* or racial identification, is an important and indispensable item in health services, in terms of diagnosis and prognosis, and in prevention

and dignified care, most of all for illnesses that are considered to be racial/ethnic. It allows us to make an epidemiological (diagnostic) of the situation of racial or ethnic groups. . . . It demonstrates how and of what causes, for example, the black population becomes ill and dies. The *quesito cor,* in the case of Brazil, is absolutely necessary in the present, and its meaning is strategic and immeasurable. [Oliveira 2002, 212–13]

Oliveira has been a forceful advocate for the development of specific health policies for Afro-Brazilians. She has also critiqued the lack of racially based health data in Brazil and argued that the lack of research on the health status of nonwhite populations prevents the development of generalizable conclusions. As she notes, "There are no data, so it is not possible to generalize. Generalizing is not possible, since there are no data. But leaving this vicious circle requires responding, sincerely, to the question: why aren't data produced?" (2003, 32).

Recognizing the ways in which official data collection methods used by the Brazilian government have perpetuated the statistical invisibility of the Afro-Brazilian population is important for understanding and addressing challenges to meeting this population's health needs. There has been a tendency to focus on class rather than race in health research in Brazil, so collection of health data by race or including race/skin color in health records historically has not been prioritized within the public health system. In addition, because the emphasis on universality as a guiding principle for the SUS was a byproduct of leftist ideology, there has traditionally been more of an emphasis on addressing class or socioeconomic disparities in health and health access, rather than ones based on race. When combined with cultural factors that minimize and downplay the significance of race as a factor in creating social divisions and inequalities, the emphasis on universality has led to the invisibility of racial health inequalities in health statistics and epidemiological data.

In the city of São Paulo, black movement organizations, including black women's organizations such as Geledés, actively organized around the issue of health and collection of the *quesito cor* during the 1980s. Their efforts began to bear fruit when the Municipal Health Secretary of São Paulo, Dr. Eduardo Jorge, signed *Portaria* number 696 in 1990. This measure called for the introduction of the *quesito cor* in the municipal information system, making São Paulo the first city in Brazil to have health data disaggregated by skin color (Oliveira 2002). In addition, during May 1990, a seminar on the health of the black population titled "O Quadro Negro da Saúde" was held to sensitize health professionals about the importance of collecting health data by race and to define the form of collection (Oliveira 2002). During the seminar, participants decided that collection of the *quesito cor* would be based on self-classification by patient-respondents and would follow the census classifications for race/skin color designated by the Brazilian census bureau IBGE (*Instituto Brasileiro de Geografia e Estatística*): *branco, pardo, preto, amarelo,* and *indígena*.[5]

In 1992, a municipal decree, *Portaria* number 429, instituted a Working Group to plan, implement, and monitor activities related to *Portaria* number 696 in the city of São Paulo. This working group included representatives of black movement organizations such as the *Coordenadoria Especial do Negro* (CONE), *Soweto—Organização Negra,* and *Geledés—Instituto da Mulher Negra,* as well as staff from various centers and units in the Municipal Health Secretariat (Oliveira 2001). These pioneering efforts to collect the *quesito cor* launched a debate regarding the importance of race/color data in health records through-out the country, eventually obligating the federal Ministry of Health to take action.

In March 1996, the Ministry of Health decided that the *quesito cor* would be included in declarations of live birth declarations (SINASC), as well as in national mortality data (SIM) and data on human research subjects. In 2001, data on race/color was included in SINAN (*Sistema de Informação de Agravos de Notificação*), a system that tracks illnesses that states are required to report. As a result of inclusion of race/color data in these systems, information on births and deaths was made available by skin color, thus facilitating researchers' efforts to document and analyze the epidemiologic profile of the Afro-Brazilian population. Collection of race/color data for SINASC and SIM was scheduled to begin in 1997. However, in a review of health policies for the black population conducted in the early 2000s, Fátima Oliveira found a lack of compliance with these measures, including by the Ministry of Health, and noted the ministry's failure to demand compliance by parties that undertook research it sponsored (Oliveira 2003).

In 2003, a Technical Area for the Health of the Black Population (*Área Técnica de Saúde da População Negra*) was established within the São Paulo state health secretariat, making it one of the first states to develop initiatives focus-ing on the health of the black population. Luis Eduardo Batista served as the coordinator for the technical area for the Health of the Black Population from 2003 to 2010. When I interviewed Batista in June 2011, he described two periods of work in this area under his leadership.[6] The first period took place from 2003 to 2007 and focused on developing activities, such as seminars on the health of the black population and what Batista described as "*trabalho de sensibilização,*" which can be translated as "sensibility or awareness-raising work." The second period ran from 2007 to 2010 and focused on making the health of the black population a focus within the policies of the SUS. Statewide seminars on the health of the black population were held beginning in 2004, with approximately six hundred people attending each. Smaller seminars for health professionals were also held. Establishment of the *Comitê Técnico de Saúde da População Negra* (Technical Committee for the Health of the Black Population) in 2006 also made São Paulo the first state to have a committee of this type (Batista and Monteiro 2010). The committee was also a partner with the UNDP in the PCRI. It was comprised of representatives from all of the departments of the state health secretariat, the state health council, the State Council for the Participation and Development of the Black Community, the University of São Paulo, the University of Campinas, and the State University of São Paulo, as well as the research center, CEBRAP, and black movement organizations ("São Paulo Cria Comitê de Saúde da População Negra").

In 2003, the Epidemiological Bulletin for the State Program for STDs/AIDS in the state of São Paulo included the theme "Color/Race and Mortality." This publication discussed the absence of "questions of race-ethnicity in institutional actions and their impact on the vulnerability of the black population, which lead many times to illness and death, in a higher proportion than the white population" (Giovanetti et al. 2007, 165). During 2004 the State Coordination for STDs/AIDS for the State of São Paulo launched a pilot program to implement use of the *quesito cor* in data collection methods for the STDs/AIDS program (Dias et al. 2009). The project, hereafter referred to as the *quesito cor* project, was initiated by a working group on ethnicity and race called the *Grupo de Trabalho Etnias* within the Division of Prevention of the Reference and Training Center for STDs/AIDS for the state of São Paulo. It was coordinated by the research organization CEERT (*Centro de Estudos das Relações de Trabalho e Desigualdade*), in partnership with the United Nations Development Program (UNDP) and the United Nations Program on AIDS (UNAIDS). The goals of the *quesito cor* project were to: (1) inform the professionals of the state and municipal coordinators STD/AIDS programs about the different dimensions of implementation of the *quesito cor* in the forms and documents used for specialized health services; and (2) develop a pilot project in the state of São Paulo that sought to form health multipliers (*multiplicadores de saúde*) capable of driving all phases of the project: implantation, implementation, monitoring, and evaluation of the process and the results (Giovanetti et al. 2007). The project took place in thirty municipalities throughout the state of São Paulo that were prioritized by the state STD/AIDS services.[7]

The *quesito cor* project involved multiple methods of reaching health professionals, researchers, and users of the health system, including a mini-course for health professionals and researchers, publications on race relations and health and about the project, and workshops for raising awareness, monitoring, and evaluation (Souza et al. 2005). Approximately one hundred health professionals, representatives from specialized health services, reference centers, testing centers, technical schools, hospitals, ambulatory care centers, and health secretariats participated in these activities in twenty-one municipalities throughout the state of São Paulo during 2004 (Giovanetti et al. 2007; Souza et al. 2005). Similar to the trainings offered as part of the Program to Combat Institutional Racism (PCRI), trainings for the pilot program for collection of the *quesito cor* involved discussions of the ideas of prejudice, racism, and discrimination, film screenings were also used as a way to raise awareness of racial issues. Staff from CEERT led the trainings and invited participants to describe their professional background as well as their color/race. According to Giovanetti et al., "This moment was particularly important for understanding the personal and cultural difficulties of dealing with questions related to color/race in our society, permeated by beliefs and prejudices rooted in our collective unconscious" (2007, 167).

Three workshops were held for health professionals during the pilot project. The State STDs/AIDS Program subsequently made a commitment to continue the process and made it part of the activities of the *Núcleo de Populações Mais Vulneráveis* (Center for Prevention among the Most Vulnerable Populations). As a result, by November 2006, four additional workshops were held for the institutions that participated in the pilot project (Giovanetti et al. 2007). In addition, during 2006, the Reference and Training Center for STDs/AIDS (*Centro de Referência e Treinamento em DST/Aids,* CRT-DST/Aids) formed a new partnership with the NGO *Instituto AMMA-Psique e Negritude.* This new partnership resulted in implementation of the *quesito cor* in thirteen new municipalities in the state of São Paulo (Giovanetti et al. 2007). The preliminary approval of the National Policy for the Integral Health of the Black Population (*Política Nacional de Saúde Integral da População Negra,* PNSIPN) by the National Health Council in 2006 also reinvigorated the debate about the importance of collecting the *quesito cor* (Dias et al. 2009). A proposal to include the *quesito cor* in all documents and forms, as well as in the information systems for the SUS, was approved by the Comissão Intergestores Bipartite (CIB) of the state of São Paulo in August 2007 (Batista and Monteiro 2010). The Ministry of Health issued a *portaria* in December 2007 calling for the inclusion of race/

color in the ambulatory care and hospital information systems (Batista and Monteiro 2010).

Assessing the Effectiveness of Color/Race Data Collection

As noted above, the state of São Paulo was at the forefront of efforts to collect the *quesito cor*, particularly in STD/AIDS services, nationwide. Between 1988 and 2002, the Reference and Training Center for STDs/AIDS in the state of São Paulo collected information on the color/race of service users using a system of heteroclassification, which permitted health professionals to classify a patient's race/color identity. In 2002, patient registration records were updated and questions regarding race/color began to be answered based on self-classification by patients themselves. Giovanetti et al. (2007) found that the proportion of *brancos* fell from 84 percent to 66 percent and the proportion of *negros,* combining *pardos* and *pretos,* increased from 14 percent to 30 percent when self-classification of race/color was used as opposed to heteroclassification. These authors also note that health professionals at the center were surprised by the changes in race/color classification that took place when patients were able to identify their color, as opposed to having a health professional do it for them. According to Giovanetti et al., the fact that fewer people self-identified as white than was expected "demystified the belief, that was mentioned by some [health professionals] during the trainings that preto and pardo individuals, especially the latter, tended to self-classify as branco" (2007, 165).

As part of the pilot project that was launched in 2004 in the STD/AIDS services in the state of São Paulo discussed above, a questionnaire was distributed to care centers in various municipalities, including specialized ambulatory services, testing centers, basic health units (*Unidades Básicas de Saúde,* UBS), and hospitals. Giovanetti et al. (2007) found that 15 percent of the services used the *quesito cor* in all of their forms, 48 percent used it in some, and 37 percent did not include this information. In 37 percent of the institutions that collected the *quesito cor,* the color of the patient was defined by the staff and in 22 percent it was defined by the patient. In the remaining institutions the *quesito cor* was collected based on heteroclassification (by the staff) in some cases and self-classification in others, depending on the situation.

Questionnaire respondents noted the difficulty of classifying users into just one category (Giovanetti et al. 2007). Several respondents stated that they asked patients how they self-classified when they were in doubt, and there were also cases of discordance between health professionals and patients regarding how a patient should be classified. As Giovanetti et al. note, "The major part of people who responded to the questionnaire felt that the information is important, but delicate" (2007, 166). They also found that analysis of the questionnaires indicated that more actions were needed to clarify why the *quesito cor* was needed, as well as to train health professionals to collect it without making value judgments about the merits of color/race data.

The process of reclassifying health records by race/skin color in the state of São Paulo impacted the indigenous population as well as the black population. According to Luis Eduardo Batista, "When we began to do it [data collection] by self-declaration, if before we had discovered two indigenous people [by heteroclassification], by self-declaration there were twenty indigenous people with AIDS in the state of São Paulo. . . . And no AIDS-related activity focusing on the indigenous community existed." Though Barbosa's comments likely do not reflect actual numbers of AIDS cases in São Paulo, they highlight the extent of potential undercounting when health records are based on heteroclassification of skin color. Barbosa also noted that, in the case of the indigenous population, individuals who lived in cities needed to be counted in addition to those living in *aldeias,* or traditional indigenous communities. Failing to account for urban indigenous populations was another way to severely underestimate the size of this group and its representation among individuals with AIDS, which had important policy implications.

The question of heteroclassification versus self-classification of race/color in health records is particularly important given Brazil's long history of race mixing, as well as wide potential differences in how individuals classify their race/color and how others might perceive them.[8] The delicate nature of asking about the race/color of an individual in Brazilian health-care settings is closely linked to racial etiquette and social norms that have historically discouraged open discussion of race and skin color, particularly as they relate to African-descendant individuals. Antiblack discourses in Brazil also have discouraged self-identification and identification of others as *negro/a* and promoted the commonsense belief that overt discussions of blackness and African ancestry are impolite (Caldwell 2007; Racusen 2012; Sheriff 2001; Twine 1998).

Historically, a strong emphasis on racial intermixture/miscegenation in Brazil has often led health professionals to question the utility of and need for collecting health data by race/color. Such questioning has centered on the notion that it would be difficult to identify individuals based on race/skin color in a society that is largely racially mixed. This notion has often been used to challenge affirmative action policies in higher education and is consistent with Brazil's longstanding image as a racial democracy (Santos 2006). Anthropologist João Vargas's (2005) conceptualization of the "hyperconsciousness/negation of race dialectic" is useful in understanding how race, and silences around it, functions in Brazil, including in health-care settings. As Vargas argues:

> By silencing the relevance of race in social relations, the hyperconsciousness/ negation of race dialectic obscures the role race plays in determining one's position in the historical structures of power and resources. . . . On the other hand, the hyperconsciousness/negation of race dynamic confronts the myth of racial democracy inasmuch as it reveals how Brazilians are acutely aware of racial differences and utilize those to (often tacitly) justify, think about, and enforce behavior and social inequalities. [2005, 446]

In addition, Vargas argues the hyperconsciousness/negation of race dialectic points to deeply racialized understandings of the social world, despite longstanding claims that race and skin color do not matter in Brazil.

Unlearning Racial Etiquette in Health Care

The *quesito cor* project that took place in STDs/AIDS services throughout the state of São Paulo during the early 2000s and similar efforts in cities such as Salvador have sought to inform the public and health professionals about the importance of collecting health data by race/color. For many health professionals, the training process regarding collection of the *quesito cor* centered on unlearning and challenging the belief that asking about patients' race/color was a racial offense or an act of racism.

Collection of the *quesito cor* called upon health professionals and service users to break with traditional racial etiquette that discouraged open discussion of racial identity and race. As noted below, agreement had to be achieved from both health professionals and service users regarding collection of the *quesito cor*. This meant that health professionals had to be willing to ask questions about color and service users had to be willing to answer them. In this way, the process was dialogical and required consciousness or awareness raising for all parties involved.

In 2009, the Reference and Training Center for STDs/AIDS in the state of São Paulo released a book-length publication, *Perguntar Não Ofende. Qual é Sua Raça/Etnia? Responder Ajuda a Prevenir* (Asking the Question Does not Offend. What is Your Color or Race/Ethnicity? Responding Helps to Prevent) (Dias et al.

2009). This publication contains four sections and an appendix that provided additional informational materials on issues of race and health, as well as affirmative action decrees and a list of suggested readings, films, videos, and Web sites. The sections of the publication addressed topics such as: Why Collect the Quesito Cor or Race/Ethnicity in Health; How and For What Purpose to Collect the Quesito Cor or Race/Ethnicity in Health; and How to Implement the Quesito Cor or Race/Ethnicity in Health Information Systems. This publication serves as a primer on racial disparities in socioeconomic status and health and introduces the reader to the importance of collecting health data by race/color in order to challenge such disparities. The main text provides definitions of terms such as racism and institutional racism, which are central to the publication's conceptual framework. A glossary is also provided in an appendix, which defines additional terms such as equity, whitening, race, ethnicity, and stereotype.

Perguntar Não Ofende discusses the categories used to classify race/color and ethnicity in the health system, which are based on categories used in the Brazilian census: *branca, preta, parda, amarela,* and *indígena.* The publication points out that people may not readily self-identify with these categories, considering that individuals are not exactly white or yellow. In this way, the publication highlights the constructed and imprecise nature of official race/color categories. This is particularly important because official census categories have often been critiqued for not accurately reflecting the color and racial categories used by Brazilians in their everyday lives. The color *moreno,* for example, is likely used by individuals to self-classify their color/race much more often than *pardo,* which is an official census category. Black activists have also long criticized the Brazilian Census Bureau (IBGE) for not including terms such as *negro* and *afro-descendente* (African descendant) as census categories, as well as for separating the African-descendant population into the categories of *parda* and *preta,* which creates the perception of much lower numbers than when the categories are combined.

Perguntar Não Ofende sought to address concerns that terms such as *preta* might be viewed as discriminatory, given the history of the term being used as a form of racial insult directed toward African-descendant Brazilians. As the authors note: "It is important to highlight that none of these colors is utilized, in health information, in a pejorative sense or with the intention of discriminating against any ethnic-racial group" (Dias et al. 2009, 27). In addition, the publication discusses the importance of self-classification by patients and provides suggestions for ways that providers can address concerns and feelings of discrimination that might be raised by patients when asked what their race or skin color is.

In addition to providing suggestions for ways to effectively collect the *quesito cor,* the publication also introduces readers to the concept of institutional racism. By discussing institutional racism, this publication highlights the link between programs to combat institutional racism that were discussed in the first part of this chapter and efforts to encourage collection of the *quesito cor.* Although these initiatives took place in different locations and regions of the country, they were part of a broader effort to bring attention to and challenge racial disparities in health. In addition, given the small number of researchers, activists, and health professionals/administrators who led these initiatives, a close-knit community spearheaded these efforts nationwide, despite being geographically dispersed. It is also important to note the ways in which a color-blind approach to health can perpetuate institutional racism precisely because it discourages acknowledgment or recognition of racially discriminatory practices and sanctions the structural neglect of racially marked groups in institutional settings.

The publication *Perguntar Não Ofende* outlines four phases in its recommendations for implementing the *quesito cor* in health services: institutional commitment, capacity building of professionals, awareness raising among health services users, and analysis and dissemination of data. The publication describes the second phase of capacity building among health professionals as being the most "fruitful" (Dias et al. 2009). As noted earlier, the pilot project worked with health professionals to raise awareness of delicate and complex racial issues and equip them to speak more openly with their patients about issues of racial identity and broach a subject that was often viewed as taboo and/or unnecessary. The process of capacity building also sought to make the concept of institutional racism and its role as a social determinant of health, illness, and care part of the programmatic agenda for health services (Dias et al. 2009).

The process of capacity building focused on technical training of health professionals that would equip them to effectively collect the *quesito cor;* it also sought to provide them with a different view of interethnic relations that would enable them to address issues such as health disparities and institutional racism. As the authors note:

> It is an experience in which the participants are able to come into contact with their own prejudices and, thus, unveil the beliefs and values that are rooted in the social imaginary that maintain and reproduce racism. . . . Racism, when treated as a psychosocial phenomenon, looks through its subjective dimension, which is a determinant for understanding its multiple forms

of expression and its impact on interpersonal relationships. Only by knowing the repercussion of racism within the interior of the institution, in the day-to-day lives of people and groups, does the implantation of measures to combat and prevent it become viable. [Dias et al. 2009, 39–40]

Importantly, this approach to capacity building addressed both personal and institutional dynamics and encouraged self-reflection about prejudices that professionals might hold, as well as the role of individual actors and their behaviors on the formation and perpetuation of discriminatory institutional practices and norms. The emphasis on self-reflection and thinking about individual beliefs and practices was similar to the approach used in the PCRI trainings for health professionals. In both cases, health professionals were encouraged to consider how the micro- and macro-level dynamics of race, racism, and racial identity functioned to shape the culture of health-care institutions and patient-provider interaction.

The third phase outlined in the publication, awareness raising among health services users, focused on the theme of health equity and the role of patients in improving collection of the *quesito cor*. It was believed that, just as health professionals needed to be informed of the importance of collecting the *quesito cor* and doing so based on self-classification, health service users also needed to be informed of the importance of this practice and their participation in it. Community leaders and health services users were included in training efforts, and emphasis was placed on explaining that collection of the *quesito cor* did not seek to encourage or perpetuate discrimination, rather it sought to assist in the prevention of illnesses that were prevalent in specific ethnic-racial groups. In addition, the right of citizens to receive equitable health care was emphasized. A variety of means were suggested to encourage health service users to respond to the *quesito cor,* including the use of messages on posters, billboards, pamphlets, stickers, and T-shirts, as well as through use of videos, films, newspapers, magazines, radio, and television (Dias et al. 2009).

It is useful to think of the *quesito cor* project in light of the 1991 census campaign that was undertaken by black activists (Nobles 2000). This campaign focused on encouraging Afro-Brazilians to darken, rather than lighten, their color in response to the census question regarding color. While the *quesito cor* project did not articulate an explicit goal of increasing the number of patients who were of African descent through use of self-classification, this was often the result. In addition, the *quesito cor* project was intended to encourage and promote discussion of the importance of collecting health data by color/race in order to obtain more accurate health statistics and potentially use them to improve health outcomes for the African-descendant population. Another difference between the two efforts is the fact that the *quesito cor* took place within the state government apparatus, rather than being an initiative driven by activists. This raises the question of potential implications and consequences of government involvement in racial/color consciousness raising as well as the ideal role of the government with respect to these issues.

Conclusion: Biopolitics and Color-Conscious Policies

As noted in chapter 3, race-conscious public policies became more common and prominent in Brazil following the World Conference against Racism in 2001. In light of the analysis presented in this chapter, it is interesting and important to consider how race-conscious and color-conscious policies might be similar or different. Certainly, in the Brazilian context, skin color has been important historically in terms of methods of classifying the population, as well as strategies for evading open discussion of racism, particularly given the historical and official emphasis on color in Brazil. In addition, both race consciousness and color consciousness played an important role in initiatives focused on institutional racism and the *quesito cor* during the 2000s. Raising awareness of racism and race consciousness among health professionals was an indispensable starting point for activities supported by the PCRI. Similarly, the *quesito cor* project in the state of São Paulo highlighted the importance of color consciousness by both patients and health professionals as a way to acknowledge and address how color and race might affect health outcomes for the black population.

By the late 2000s, the concept of institutional racism had become a common feature of discussions about the health of the black population in Brazil. In addition, by this time, collection of the *quesito cor* had moved into the mainstream of discussions and policies related to race in states such as São Paulo. The state of São Paulo's Health Plan for 2008 to 2011 had specific objectives for the black population, including improving the quality of information available for the *quesito cor* with respect to collection, processing, and analysis, and raising awareness regarding themes related to the health of the black population (Souza et al. 2008). This demonstrates the extent to which an emphasis on the *quesito cor* had been mainstreamed within the state-level health apparatus, rather than being confined solely to STD/AIDS services. The state of São Paulo also provided a national model for ways to address and focus on color/race in health and the health needs of the black population. In 2005 the National STD/

AIDS Program created the *Programa Estratégio de Ações Afirmativas* (Strategic Affirmative Action Program), which called for the collection of the *quesito cor* in all information systems and epidemiological records governed by the program, as well as in all of its intervention programs (Ministério da Saúde 2005).

Efforts focusing on increased collection of the *quesito cor* were undertaken in cities such as Salvador, Rio de Janeiro, Belo Horizonte, and Santo Andre as well as in cities such as Porto Alegre, where the black population is much smaller (Souza et al. 2005). Such efforts typically were initiated or advanced by black health activists and advocates, some of whom worked within municipal or state governments. Black women's organizations, such as Criola and Geledés, also played an important role in furthering this work in many Brazilian cities. The influence and support of international agencies such as the Pan-American Health Organization, DFID, UNDP, and UNFPA were also instrumental in supporting efforts to address institutional racism in Brazil. It is likely that efforts to initiate discussions of institutional racism and create initiatives in this area would not have been as successful without the support of these external, nonstate actors. The presence of state actors, particularly within municipal and state-level health secretariats who were supportive of discussions of institutional racism and the health of the black population was also vital to the success of efforts in these areas.

While this chapter analyzes developments focusing on institutional racism and the *quesito cor* as somewhat separate processes, in many ways they were interconnected, and the resonances between these areas should be carefully considered. In fact, discussions of the importance of the *quesito cor* often became part of efforts to address and challenge institutional racism in cities such as Recife (Lopes and Quintiliano 2007). In addition, discussions of institutional racism were integrated into efforts to raise awareness of the importance of collecting the *quesito cor* in the state of São Paulo.

Scholars such a Guimarães (1995, 2005) have long argued that Brazilian discourses on color are used to conceal racialist and racist beliefs and practices. Linking efforts to challenge institutional racism and efforts to increase race/color data collection highlights how official discourses and practices of color blindness can serve to uphold and perpetuate institutional forms of racial discrimination precisely because they are denied and, thus, rendered invisible. Official color blindness can also create an environment in which denial of racism flourishes (Dulitzky 2005), and in which there is both an evasion of discussions of difference and inequality and evasion of state responsibility for addressing inequality.

The *Alyne* Case

Maternal Mortality, Intersectional Discrimination, and the Human Right to Health in Brazil

In 2002, Alyne da Silva Pimentel Teixeira, a twenty-eight-year-old Afro-Brazilian woman, died following complications resulting from a stillbirth inadequately treated at a health center. A resident of the city of Belford Roxo, which is located in the metropolitan region of Rio de Janeiro, da Silva Pimentel Teixeira was twenty-seven weeks pregnant when she sought medical treatment at a health center for vomiting and strong abdominal pain. The doctor prescribed medication for nausea, B-12 vitamins, and a topical medication for a vaginal infection. Her symptoms worsened, causing her to return to the health center two days later. An ultrasound showed that the fetus was dead. Doctors induced labor, but did not perform surgery to remove the placenta until fourteen hours later. All of this was done at a private health clinic, *Casa de Saúde Nossa Senhora da Glória de Belford Roxo,* also known as *Casa de Saúde,* which was not adequately equipped or staffed for emergency obstetric procedures.[1] Following removal of the placenta, Alyne Pimentel began to hemorrhage and vomit blood, and her blood pressure dropped. The medical staff then decided to transfer her to a public hospital in the region; however, only one hospital would accept her, the *Hospital Geral de Nova Iguaçu,* and it refused to send its only ambulance in the evening to transport her. The family was also unable to obtain assistance from a private ambulance service.

Alyne Pimentel waited eight hours for an ambulance, and manifested clinical symptoms of a coma during the final two hours prior to being transported to the hospital. The health center treating her did not send her medical records to the hospital, so the hospital staff did not know her clinical state or the fact that she had recently been pregnant. When she arrived at the hospital, Alyne was hypothermic and had acute respiratory distress. Her blood pressure had dropped to zero and she had to be resuscitated. She was also placed in the hallway of the emergency room owing to the lack of an available bed, eventually staying in the hallway for twenty-one hours without receiving treatment. Alyne died the following day. Five days passed between the initial onset of Alyne Pimentel's illness and her death.

The circumstances leading to Alyne Pimentel's death highlight gross inadequacies and failures in the quality of maternity care and emergency obstetric care provided to poor, African-descendant women in Brazil. This chapter uses the circumstances surrounding her death and the subsequent legal decision as a case study to examine maternal mortality in Brazil, particularly as it affects poor, Afro-descendant women. The chapter explores the ways in which Alyne's death and the legal case that her family pursued highlight the intersectional relationship among gender, race, and class in shaping Afro-Brazilian women's vulnerability to maternal death. I analyze the racial dimensions of maternal mortality in Brazil and the legal implications of the 2011 decision made by the Committee for the Convention on the Elimination of All Forms of Discrimination against Women (CEDAW). This decision recognized the multiple forms of discrimination—racial, gender, and class-based—that led to Alyne's death and called for the Brazilian government to compensate her surviving family members. Through examination of the CEDAW Committee's decision, I highlight the potential benefits that can be gained from using a human rights approach to address intersectional discrimination in health as experienced by African-descendant women in Brazil.

Maternal Mortality in Brazil

The World Health Organization (WHO) defines maternal death as "the death of a woman while pregnant or within 42 days of termination of pregnancy, irrespective of the duration and site of the pregnancy, from any cause related to or aggravated by the pregnancy or its management but not from accidental or incidental causes."[2] This organization has estimated that 8,700 women died from complications related to pregnancy and childbirth in Brazil during 2000 (World Health Organization 2004). Brazil also accounted for more than one-third of all maternal deaths in Latin America at this time. Data from the Brazilian federal government indicates that there were more than 1,600 pregnancy-related deaths per year in Brazil between 2004 and 2012. According to government records, the number of maternal deaths fell to close to six hundred per year in 2013.[3] The maternal mortality ratio (per 100,000 live births) in Brazil was also found to be 143.2 in 1990, 73.3 in 2000, and 68.2 in 2010.[4] Data released from the World Health Organization show that the maternal mortality ratio in Brazil was 56/100,000 and was 63/100,000 for the WHO Americas region in 2011.[5]

Statistics on maternal mortality rates in Brazil are markedly unreliable and do not accurately reflect maternal mortality trends in the country. Until recently, reliable vital statistics on maternal mortality were only available for eight states (out of a total of twenty-six states plus the capital of Brasília) (Barros et al. 2010). All of these states are in the Southeast, South, and West-Central regions of the country. In addition, since 1980, a variety of different methods have been used to calculate maternal death, and the rates have likely gone up in more recent data because of audits conducted by maternal mortality committees in Brazil, which are discussed below (Barros et al. 2010). Researchers such as Barros et al. (2010) urge caution in the interpretation of data on maternal deaths, owing to differences in levels of underregistration among regions of the country and the fact that maternal mortality death committees, which investigate and attempt to develop reliable numbers on maternal deaths, are more active in some regions than others.

Underreporting and misclassification of maternal deaths have made it difficult to develop an accurate sense of how many maternal deaths occur in Brazil and also suggest that the officially reported numbers are grossly underestimated. Some experts have argued that, for every reported maternal death in Brazil, one goes unreported (Tanaka 2006). Researchers have also argued that reported rates of maternal death should be multiplied by a factor of at least 1.4 to reach a more accurate estimate (Laurenti et al. 2004). A correction factor of 1.67 has been used by the Brazilian Ministry of Health to account for subestimates of maternal deaths (Martins 2006). Underreporting of maternal deaths often occurs because health professionals may list a vague cause of death, so the deaths may be misclassified as having non-pregnancy-related causes. For example, infections or cardiac arrest may be mentioned as a cause of death, but the fact that these conditions were related to pregnancy may not be listed (Tanaka 2006).

Most maternal deaths in Brazil owe to avoidable causes. One study of reported causes of maternal death for 2007 found that hypertensive disorders of pregnancy, including eclampsia and preeclampsia, accounted for the largest single number of maternal deaths (22.6 percent), followed by sepsis and hemorrhage (Barros et al. 2010). Abortion was found to be the fourth leading cause of death; however, because abortion is illegal in Brazil, the number of maternal deaths owing to abortion was likely to have been severely underreported. Other reported causes of death included placental disorders, complications of labor, embolism, and abnormal uterine contractions.

In recent years, researchers have begun to focus on the discrimination experienced by African-descendant women during pregnancy and childbirth, which underscores the importance of acknowledging the racial, as well as gendered dimensions, of their experiences in the health-care sector. Health disparities experienced by African-descendant women, with respect to reproductive health and maternal mortality, have been acknowledged in policies such as the 2009 National Policy for Integral Attention to Women's Health (PNAISM); however, this policy also highlights the importance of further research on the health needs of African-descendant women, because research in this area is relatively new and is rarely done. Instead, research on women's health has tended to focus on class and poor or low-income women, rather than explicitly focusing on African-descendant women, and has not typically included race as a variable. In addition, inconsistent collection of the *quesito cor* (color/race data) in health records also has important implications for obtaining reliable data on maternal mortality rates among women of different groups.

Research has shown that *negra* (black) and *parda* (brown) women experience higher rates of "pilgrimage" or travel to maternity hospitals while in labor. Brazilian researchers have used the Portuguese term *peregrinação* (pilgrimage) to describe the process by which women travel to more than one maternity hospital because they are unable to receive care at a hospital when they arrive. Leal et al. (2005) found that 31.8 percent of *negras* (black women), 28.8 percent of *pardas* (brown women), and 18.5 percent of *brancas* (white women) traveled to more than one maternity hospital in the municipality of Rio de Janeiro in order to give birth. Racial disparities in access to anesthesia during childbirth were also found, with 16.4 percent of *pardas* and 21.8 percent of *negras* (the term Leal et al. used for black women) not having access to anesthesia. Nonwhite women also tend to use public health establishments and those that have agreements with the SUS (public health system) at higher rates for childbirth. In the same study, 58.9 percent of *negras* and 46.9 percent of *pardas* gave birth in public health establishments, while 43.7 percent of *brancas* did (Leal et al. 2005). According to the authors:

> Almost a third of *pardas* and *negras* did not receive attention at the first establishment they sought out and they received less anesthesia for vaginal birth. Wandering (*perambulação*) to maternity wards at the time of childbirth is one of the dimensions of a lack of a welcoming climate (*acolhimento*) in

health institutions and reflects the absence of systematic planning for birth assistance in the municipality of Rio de Janeiro, with harmful consequences for the mother and her offspring. [2005, 106]

Leal et al. (2005) also found that discrimination by health professionals based on race and educational level had a noticeable impact on the prenatal and childbirth experiences of low-income black and brown women in Rio de Janeiro. In addition, field tests of a tool created by the World Health Organization and Harvard's School of Public Health to examine maternal mortality in Brazil and two other countries between 2003 and 2006 highlighted the experiences of vulnerable groups and led to a recommendation for increased prenatal care services for black, low-income Brazilian women (Cottingham et al. 2010).

Nationwide rates of maternal mortality in Brazil were found to be higher for *preta* women in all age groups and were three times higher than those of white women in 2003 (Volochko 2010). During the same year, regional rates of maternal mortality were markedly higher for *pretas* and *pardas* than *brancas*. In the Southeastern, Southern, and West-Central regions of Brazil, rates of maternal mortality were two to three and a half times higher for *pretas* than brancas (Volochko 2010). In specific states, rates of maternal death were even higher. For example, in Alagoas, rates for *pretas* were ten times higher than for *brancas*, and rates were twenty times higher in Espírito Santo (Volochko 2010). Both states are located in the Brazilian Northeast, which has the largest concentration of African-descendants in the nation. A publication by the Brazilian Ministry of Health noted that *pardas* had the highest maternal mortality rates between 2000 and 2003 and accounted for 41.5 percent of maternal deaths in 2003. In addition, hypertensive illnesses, such as eclampsia and preeclampsia, were to found to be higher among *pardas* (35.3 percent) and *pretas* (26.7 percent) in 2003 (Ministério da Saúde 2007c). The same publication noted:

> The causes of maternal death are related to the biological predisposition that *negras* have for illnesses such as arterial hypertension; factors related to difficulty in [healthcare] access; the low quality of care they receive and the lack of actions and training for health professionals focused on the specific risks to which *mulheres negras* [black women] are exposed. [Ministério da Saúde 2007c, 11]

The relationship between clandestine abortions and maternal mortality for African-descendant women in Brazil also merits wider discussion and investigation. There was an important development in this regard in August 2011, when the Brazilian Senate sponsored a public audience to discuss the sexual and reproductive rights of women. Testimonies given during the public audience highlighted the fact that poor and black women were the most disadvantaged with respect to their ability to obtain safe abortions, which are only legally allowed in cases of rape, when pregnancy and childbirth pose a risk to the mother's life or when the fetus has been shown to have anencephaly, a serious birth defect in which a baby is born without parts of the brain and skull (Koshimizu 2011). Unsafe induced abortions have contributed to higher rates of maternal mortality for poor, black women, since their lives are placed in danger owing to their lack of access to safe and sanitary conditions in which to terminate their pregnancies, as well as their common mistreatment within the health-care system when suspected of inducing an abortion. Although abortion is illegal in most cases, middle-class white women are typically able to pay for access to safe and sanitary medical establishments in which to have abortions performed, whereas low-income black women are often subjected to precarious and unsafe conditions, which may jeopardize their lives and long-term health.

One study found that, between 1999 and 2002, the maternal mortality rate owing to abortion was 5.59 per 100,000 live births for *brancas,* 9.98 for *pardas,* and 36.23 for *pretas* (Rede Feminista de Saúde 2005). However, it should be noted that, because miscarriages are included under the category of abortion in government mortality records, all of these abortions were not induced. A 2008 study showed that the risk of maternal death owing to abortion was markedly higher for *negras* and *pardas* than for *brancas* (Monteiro et al. 2008). The risk of maternal death resulting from pregnancies that end in abortion was also found to be 2.5 times higher for black women compared to white women in this study. In addition, the same study showed that the decriminalization of abortion would permit the reduction of risks of complications and maternal mortality resulting from pregnancies that end in abortion (Monteiro et al. 2008).

Alaerte Martins, a public health professional, researcher, and executive director of the *Rede de Mulheres Negras do Paraná* (Black Women's Network of the State of Paraná), has argued that the higher rates of maternal mortality among black women are linked to racism and prejudice. According to Martins:

> Racism and prejudice are so *incrustada* (encrusted) in us that people learn to treat others in a *pacote* (bundle). This is reflected in maternal mortality, in health care. The first who are cared for are those who are equal, afterward those who are different.... Imagine in the hour of an abortion [not specified whether spontaneous or induced]. Black women are already discriminated against. In a situation of abortion, they are more discriminated against than white women. They will be the last of the last to be attended, leading to a higher risk of death. [Leme 2012]

International Norms Related to Maternal Mortality and Women's Right to Health

Since the 1980s, women's right to health has been increasingly recognized as a human right in international law and policy. As part of this evolving process, maternal mortality has been placed on the global policy agenda as an issue that affects women in gender-specific ways, and thus constitutes a violation of their human rights. The fact that most maternal deaths are preventable has increased criticisms by researchers and feminist health activists about the human rights dimensions of these deaths. The Convention on the Elimination of All Forms of Discrimination against Women (CEDAW) was ratified by the United Nations in 1979, becoming an important marker in the struggle to recognize women's right to health. Following ratification of CEDAW, discrimination against women became recognized as a violation of the principles of equality, rights, and human dignity, as well as an impediment to women's participation in society on an equal basis with men. CEDAW addresses women's health and reproductive health in paragraphs 1 and 2 of Article 12, stating:

> 1. States Parties shall take all appropriate measures to eliminate discrimination against women in the field of health care in order to ensure, on a basis of equality of men and women, access to health care services, including those related to family planning.
> 2. . . . States Parties shall ensure to women appropriate services in connection with pregnancy, confinement and the post-natal period, granting free services where necessary, as well as adequate nutrition during pregnancy and lactation.[6]

The International Safe Motherhood Conference, which took place in Nairobi, Kenya in 1987, signaled increasing global recognition of maternal mortality as a "tragedy that needed to be confronted globally" (Reis et al. 2011, 1143). Representatives of international agencies, national governments, and international non-governmental organizations attended the conference. During the proceedings, world leaders, including the director general of the WHO, Dr. Halfdan Mahler, recognized that maternal mortality was a "neglected tragedy" that resulted from the powerlessness that women experienced (Roseman 2009, 94). The International Safe Motherhood Initiative (SMI) was launched during the conference and had the goal of reducing maternal mortality by 50 percent by the year 2000. Efforts to combat maternal mortality received support at the regional level in Latin America when the Pan-American Health Organization launched the Regional Action Plan to Reduce Maternal Mortality in 1990. By this time, maternal mortality was recognized as a complex issue that resulted from social disadvantages, or what are now called social determinants of health, and one that thus required a multipronged approach (Reis et al. 2011). Various international organizations and U.N. agencies became involved in the effort to reduce global rates of maternal mortality during the late 1990s, including the World Health Organization (WHO), the United Nations Children's Emergency Fund (UNICEF), the United Nations Population Fund (UNFPA), and the World Bank.

The 1994 U.N. International Conference on Population and Development (ICPD), which was held in Cairo, Egypt, and the 1995 U.N. Conference on Women, which was held in Beijing, China, were important milestones in efforts to have women's rights recognized as human rights, particularly reproductive rights. During the ICPD feminist activists were instrumental in shifting the discourse from a Malthusian developmentalist paradigm, which emphasized competition for scarce resources and the need to control population growth, to one recognizing that "persistent inequality and discrimination against women fueled (over)population and (under)development" (Roseman 2009, 94). The ICPD served as an important turning point in global feminist health activism, because it brought human rights into discussions of reproduction and sexuality. In addition, ICPD built on the momentum of the Safe Motherhood Initiative (SMI), which did not include explicit discussion of human rights. According to Mindy Roseman,

> As if to highlight maternal health, ICPD proposed a clear goal: to cut the number of maternal deaths by half by the year 2000, and in half again by 2015—one of the few elements of ICPD directly translated into an MDG [Millennium Development Goal]. To reach that goal, governments promised in ICPD and subsequent agreements, to develop comprehensive strategies to ensure universal access to reproductive health services, with particular attention to maternal and emergency obstetric care, especially in underserved areas. [2009, 95]

As discussed in chapter 1, feminist activists in Brazil anticipated the emphasis on reproductive rights that was developed during the Cairo conference and in the Program of Action for ICPD in the development of PAISM in the 1980s; however, the program was never fully implemented.

International health and development organizations increasingly recognized the importance of reproductive rights as human rights during the mid to late 1990s. The World Health Organization, UNICEF, and UNFPA issued an important statement on maternal mortality in 1999, which declared:

The right to life is a fundamental human right, implying not only the right to protection against arbitrary execution by the state but also the obligations of governments to foster the conditions essential for life and survival. Human rights are universal and must be applied without discrimination on any grounds whatsoever, including sex. For women, human rights include access to services that will ensure safe pregnancy and childbirth (World Health Organization 1999).

The following year, in 2000, the U.N. Human Rights Committee elaborated General Comment 28 on the U.N. International Covenant on Civil and Political Rights, which addressed equality of rights between men and women. The comment requires states to provide data on birth rates and on pregnancy and childbirth-related deaths of women (Gruskin et al. 2008).

Efforts to Reduce Maternal Mortality in Brazil

In an effort to assess the number of maternal deaths that were occurring and reduce that number, maternal death committees were established in Brazil beginning in the late 1980s. Brazil, as well as other countries, followed the example set by the United States, which established the first maternal mortality committee in 1931. In Brazil, maternal mortality committees were established at the municipal level in cities throughout the state of São Paulo; committees were later established in the states of Paraná, Goiás, and Rio de Janeiro (Ministério da Saúde 2007). Between 1993 and 1996, state maternal mortality committees were established in all Brazilian states. In addition, during 1994, a National Committee to Combat Maternal Mortality was instituted, comprised of non-governmental organizations, scientific societies, the women's movement, and notable health professionals. In 2005, Brazil had 27 state committees, 172 regional committees, 748 municipal committees and 206 hospital-based committees (Ministério da Saúde 2007). During 1994, the Brazilian Ministry of Health issued *Portaria* 663 which made May 28 the National Day to Reduce Maternal Mortality (*Dia Nacional de Redução da Mortalidae Materna*), which signaled increasing governmental and public recognition of maternal deaths in the country (Martins 2006).

Maternal mortality committees conduct audits of maternal deaths by analyzing all pregnancy-related deaths that have occurred in a particular city or state and suggesting forms of intervention that can reduce such deaths. The committees have also been recognized for their importance in accompanying and evaluating policies focused on women's health (Ministério da Saúde 2007). The committees investigate deaths of pregnant women that are declared to result from pregnancy-related causes, as well as those that are declared to be non-pregnancy related. They also investigate all deaths of women of reproductive age to identify deaths that owe to pregnancy-related causes. The committees play a vital role in correcting official maternal death statistics, which often grossly underestimate the number of maternal deaths that occur. They are also involved in promoting discussions, debates, and events focused on the problem of maternal mortality and possible forms of prevention (Ministério da Saúde 2007). While maternal mortality committees exist at the municipal and state level throughout Brazil, it should be noted that these committees have functioned with varying degrees of activity and effectiveness in investigating maternal deaths. While some committees have been active, others have been dormant. By 2011, the National Committee to Combat Maternal Mortality had not met for two years (Martins 2011). In addition, the *quesito cor* has not been collected consistently for all maternal deaths. Since 1993, the city of São Paulo and state of Paraná have collected the *quesito cor*. In 2002, the Committee for Maternal Death of the state of Paraná revised its records for investigating maternal deaths and began to include age, race, and level of schooling (Martins 2006).

Reducing maternal death rates was put on the global health agenda and Brazil's national health agenda when the Millennium Development Goals were adopted in 2000. The Millennium Development Goals (MDG) were designed by the United Nations as a global antipoverty initiative and addressed the following areas: poverty and hunger (Goal 1); universal primary education (Goal 2); gender equality and women's empowerment (Goal 3); reducing child mortality (Goal 4); improving maternal health (Goal 5); combating HIV/AIDS, malaria and other diseases (Goal 6); and ensuring environmental sustainability (Goal 7). Millennium Development Goal 5 focused on reducing the maternal mortality ratio (number of maternal deaths per 100,000 live births) by 75 percent from 1990 to 2015. It also aimed to achieve universal access to reproductive health by 2015. In 1990, Brazil's adjusted maternal mortality ratio was 140 maternal deaths per 100,000 live births. The adjusted ratio factors in underreporting of maternal deaths and can range from a factor of 1.67 to a factor of 2 (Martins 2006). The adjusted ratio declined to 75/100,000 by 2007, although the MDG target was 35/100,000 by 2015 (Presidência da República 2010). Based on this trajectory, a report issued by the Brazilian government projected that the maternal ratio would fall short of the target set by the Millennium Development Goals (Presidência da República 2010).[7] However, some researchers argued that Brazil's progress toward achieving Millennium Development Goal 5 was unclear. As Barros et al. have noted, "although coverage of proven reproductive and maternal health interventions has increased, improved death reporting—a sign of improvement in Brazil's vital registration systems—may obscure any declining trends" (2010, 1887–88). Data from the World Health Organization showed that Brazil's maternal mortality ratio (maternal deaths per 100,000 live births) declined from 104 in 1990 to 44 in 2015, which was a 57.7 percent decline (World Health Organization 2015b). Based on these data, Brazil was found to be "Making Progress" toward Millennial Development Goal 5, but it still fell short of the goal of reducing maternal mortality by 75 percent (World Health Organization 2015b).

During the early 2000s, Brazil undertook a number of legal and programmatic efforts to reduce maternal mortality.[8] The Brazilian Ministry of Health issued *Portaria* number 569 in 2000, which instituted the Humanization of Pre-Natal and Birth Program (*Programa de Humanização no Pré-natal e Nascimento*). The program's main objective was to increase access and coverage for prenatal, birth, and postnatal services and improve their quality. The program addressed the right of pregnant women to know where they would give birth and have assured access to birthing facilities in an effort to minimize the need to travel to various maternity services while in labor. The program also sought to ensure the care women received during childbirth would be safe and humanized (*humanizado*) (Reis et al. 2011). The program's conceptualization of humanized care sought to address institutional practices within the public health system that led to high rates of maternal death. This approach was especially important given the history of pregnant women's poor treatment within Brazil's public health system. The Humanization of Pre-Natal and Birth Program was structured around the following principles:

a) All pregnant women have the right to have access to dignified and quality treatment during the course of pregnancy, childbirth, and the post-partum period.

b) All pregnant women have the right to know about and have access to the maternity facility where they will be assisted during childbirth.

c) All pregnant women have the right to assistance during childbirth and the post-partum period that is provided in a humanized and safe manner, in accordance with the general principles and conditions established by medical knowledge.

d) All newborns have the right to neonatal assistance in a humanized and safe manner.[9]

A National Pact for the Reduction of Maternal and Neonatal Mortality (*Pacto Nacional pela Reducao da Mortalidade Materna e Neonatal*) was launched by President Lula on March 8, 2004, International Women's Day, after being approved by the National Health Council, as well as by the Intergestorial Tripartite Commission, which represents administrators from the SUS at the municipal, state, and federal levels. The guiding principles of the pact focused on investing in the improvement of obstetric and neonatal services, and respecting the human rights of women and children (Santos and Araujo 2006; Reis et al. 2011). The pact set a goal of reducing indices of maternal and neonatal mortality by 15 percent by 2006 and by 75 percent by 2015. The second goal was consistent with Millennium Development Goal 5. Seventy-eight Brazilian municipalities were selected to receive financial support to achieve these goals. All of the municipalities had more than 100,000 inhabitants, low levels of human development, and high rates of maternal and neonatal mortality (Reis et al. 2011). A National Commission for Monitoring and Evaluating the Pact (*Comissão Nacional de Monitoramento e Availação do Pacto*) was also created in 2005. Another important policy development took place during 2004 when the National Policy for Integral Attention to Women's Health (*Política Nacional de Atenção Integral à Saúde da Mulher*) was launched. This policy focused on guaranteeing women's human rights and reducing maternal morbidity and mortality owing to preventable causes.[10] By emphasizing women's human rights, the National Pact for the Reduction of Maternal and Neonatal Mortality stood in sharp contrast to Provisional Measure 557, which was later issued by President Dilma Rousseff in 2011, as well as the maternalist emphasis of Rede Cegonha, both of which were discussed in chapter 1.

The Case of Alyne da Silva Pimentel

The death of Alyne da Silva Pimentel in 2002 highlights the precarious and unsafe health conditions that many poor, African-descendant women face in Brazil. Following Pimentel's death, the Center for Reproductive Rights, an international legal advocacy organization based in the United States, engaged in an eight-year battle on behalf of her family. Pimentel's mother was represented by the Center for Reproductive Rights and a Brazilian non-governmental organization called *Advocacia Cidadã pelos Direitos Humanos*. The Center for Reproductive Rights submitted a shadow letter[11] on the case in July 2007 to the Committee for the Convention on the Elimination of All Forms of Discrimination against Women (CEDAW) and filed a brief for the case in November 2007.[12] The *Alyne* case was eligible for review by the CEDAW Committee because Brazil became a signatory of the CEDAW in March 1981 and ratified it in 1984. In addition, as a signatory of the Optional Protocol to the CEDAW in

2001, Brazil was subject to monitoring and investigation for systematic violations of women's human rights.[13]

CEDAW is often considered by human rights experts to be an international
bill of rights for women. Sally Engle Merry has identified three key features of
CEDAW:

> It focuses on eliminating discrimination against women that violates the
> principle of equality of rights and respect for human dignity. It emphasizes
> equal rights for men and women and explicitly prohibits discrimination on
> the basis of sex. Like other human rights discourses and instruments, it is
> committed to universalism: to the idea that there are minimal standards of
> human dignity that must be protected in all societies. [2006, 74]

CEDAW is one of six U.N. conventions that have been widely ratified and
monitored by a committee, known as a treaty body. However, the committee
that monitors CEDAW has limited enforcement control or power to compel
states to comply. As Sally Engle Merry has noted, "CEDAW is a law without
sanctions" (2006, 72). Lack of compliance, as can be seen in the Alyne da Silva
Pimentel case discussed below, is a major challenge for CEDAW, as well as for
the other five U.N. conventions. Despite these challenges, scholars such as
Merry (2006) have argued that CEDAW plays an important role in fostering
cultural changes that promote gender equity within individual nation-states.

The CEDAW Committee reviewed the case *Alyne da Silva Pimentel v. Brazil*
and issued a ruling on August 10, 2011, finding that the Brazilian state violated
"the right to life enshrined in article 6 of the International Covenant on Civil
and Political Rights, the right to effective protection of women's rights, and the
right to health" under CEDAW (CEDAW 2011, 13). The Committee found that
the Brazilian government "has not ensured access to quality medical treatment
during delivery and to timely emergency obstetric care, implicating the right
to non-discrimination based on gender and race. The inability of her family to
obtain reparations from the State party violated the right to effective protection" (CEDAW 2011, 13).

The Committee's decision provided a detailed overview of points made in a
document the Brazilian government submitted regarding the case on August 13,
2008. In this document, the Brazilian government challenged its characterization by the CEDAW Committee as lacking commitment to reduce maternal
mortality and as suffering from "systemic failure to protect the basic rights of
women" as stated in the case against it (CEDAW 2011, 11). The Brazilian government's submission discussed various measures that were implemented in
the country, as well as national plans and mechanisms that were in place re-

garding women's rights, particularly women's health, sexual rights, and reproductive rights. In addition, the government's document described President
Dilma Rousseff's administration's prioritization of women's health, especially
as it relates to preventable maternal deaths, as well as the federal government's
recognition of maternal death as a human rights violation. The Committee's
decision described the Brazilian government's view of the role of discrimination in Alyne's death, stating:

> With regard to the existence of discrimination, insofar as the case involves an
> Afro-Brazilian woman from the urban periphery, the State party highlights
> the fact that the technical report prepared by the audit department of the
> health system found no evidence of discrimination. However, the State party
> does not rule out the possibility that discrimination may have contributed,
> to some extent, but not decisively, to the event. Rather, the convergence or
> association of the set of elements described may have contributed to the
> failure to provide necessary and emergency care to Ms. da Silva Pimentel
> Teixeira, resulting in her death. [CEDAW 2011, 11–12]

In its submission to the committee, the Brazilian government denied a lack
of interest or insensitivity to the importance of implementing health policies
that provide specific care for women. The Brazilian government's submission
discussed the emphasis placed on qualified and humanized obstetric care in
the National Plan for Women's Policies, particularly for Afro-Brazilian and
indigenous women, including a focus on unsafe abortions and maternal morbidity and mortality (CEDAW 2011). The Brazilian government also pointed
to the 2004 *Política Nacional de Atenção Integral à Saúde da Mulher* (National
Policy for Integral Attention to Women's Health, PNAISM) as evidence of
its commitment to guaranteeing the human rights of women and reducing
morbidity and mortality that arises from preventable causes. Moreover, the
Brazilian government pointed to the participation of various government agencies and civil society organizations in the formulation of this policy, including
the Special Secretariat for the Promotion of Racial Equality (SEPPIR), the
women's movement, the black women's movement, health systems administrators, and international cooperation agencies (CEDAW 2011). It should be
noted that in the state party submission for the case, the Brazilian government
presented itself as a beneficent authority regarding women's health, particularly
because it expressed a commitment to a comprehensive approach to women's
health, which was not restricted to sexual and reproductive rights, but offered
care focused on women's overall physical and mental well-being. Ironically,
as discussed in chapter 1, this policy approach resulted from pressure placed

on the Brazilian government by feminist health activists since the early 1980s. Ultimately, however, the existence of policies, such as the National Policy for Integral Attention to Women's Health (PNAISM), was used by the Brazilian government as evidence of its commitment to women's health, although the effective implementation of such policies has often been questioned.

The Committee criticized the Brazilian government for its "rhetorical recognition" of the problem of maternal mortality and noted that it had failed to meet its obligation to guarantee women's right to life and health (2011, 12). The Committee further noted that the "high rates of maternal mortality in the State party constitute a systematic failure to prioritize and protect women's basic human rights. The preventable maternal death of Ms. da Silva Pimentel Teixeira clearly exemplifies this failure" (2011, 12–13). Additionally, the CEDAW Committee found that state parties had a legal obligation to ensure the right to health. Its decision noted that adoption of a national health strategy was not sufficient to meet the obligations of a state party; instead, the strategy also needed to be "implemented and periodically reviewed on the basis of a participatory and transparent process" (CEDAW 2011, 14). The Committee also found that Brazil was experiencing problems in implementing the provisions of CEDAW at all levels of the federal republic in a consistent manner, owing to different degrees of political will and commitment of state and municipal authorities. These findings are important because they highlighted inadequacies in the implementation of health policies in Brazil. As the committee noted, greater civil society participation and government transparency were needed, as well as effective functioning of the country's process of decentralization at the state and municipal levels in order to ensure full implementation of such policies. In the *Alyne* decision, the committee also made an important distinction between *obligations of conduct* and *obligations of result* in realizing the right to health. According to the committee, *an obligation of conduct* involves the creation of policies designed to realize the right to health, whereas *an obligation of result* involves ensuring that those policies achieve the desired results (CEDAW 2011). These observations by the committee suggest that federal-level initiatives such as the National Pact for the Reduction of Maternal and Neonatal Mortality were not achieving the desired results, although they had been created and had admirable goals. The terms *obligation of conduct* and *obligation of result* also pointed to the need for the Brazilian state to ensure it fulfilled its responsibilities under international treaties and covenants such as CEDAW. According to the Maastricht Guidelines that were articulated in 1997 for the International Covenant on Economic, Social, and Cultural Rights, "The obligation of conduct requires action reasonably calculated to realize the enjoyment of a particular right. . . . The obligation of result requires States to achieve specific targets to satisfy a detailed substantive standard" (Yamin and Maine 1999, 446).

The CEDAW Committee stated that the "grossly negligent" health care provided to Alyne constituted a form of de facto discrimination under the Convention on the Elimination of all Forms of Discrimination against Women (CEDAW 2011, 16). According to the *Alyne* decision, the failure to provide adequate maternal health services in the city of Belford Roxo constituted a violation of the right to nondiscrimination on the basis of gender under CEDAW. The decision found the denial or neglect of health-care interventions that are only needed by women to be a form of gender discrimination. The decision also described the city of Belford Roxo as having inadequate maternal health services, which constituted a violation of the right to nondiscrimination. In addition, the decision stated that the "fact that the population of the city is largely of African descent further compounds this situation" (CEDAW 2011, 16). This terminology expanded the gender-focused definition of discrimination in CEDAW to include related forms of inequality as well as differential treatment and discrimination, such as those based on race and ethnicity. Recognizing other forms of inequality was especially significant given Alyne's background as an African-descendant woman. However, it is also important to note that this conceptualization of multiple forms of inequality and discrimination did not reflect an explicitly intersectional approach; instead, it seemed to be based on an additive or compounded model. Later in the decision, the Committee adopted a more intersectional approach, recognizing that Alyne experienced multiple forms of discrimination and arguing that she was discriminated against on the basis of sex, as well as being a woman of African descent and owing to her socioeconomic background (CEDAW 2011, 21).

The Committee sharply criticized the Brazilian government for the way in which Alyne da Silva Pimentel's death was classified as being nonmaternal. Her official cause of death was listed as being "digestive hemorrhage." However, the Committee's decision noted that medical evidence demonstrated that the death resulted directly from pregnancy-related causes and was preventable. The Committee stated that the failure to correctly register Pimentel's cause of death exemplified the widespread underreporting and misclassification of maternal deaths in Brazil. It further noted that Pimentel's cause of death statement was incomplete and insufficient according to both international and Brazilian medical standards.

The Committee's recommendations called for the Brazilian government to provide adequate reparation to Alyne's surviving mother and daughter, including adequate financial compensation commensurate with the gravity of the violations against her. This was important because Alyne was a main source of income for her family, and her husband left the family after her death. As a result, her mother was forced to raise Alyne's daughter in extremely impoverished conditions. The Committee also made six other recommendations in the following areas: ensuring women's right to safe motherhood and affordable access for all women to adequate emergency obstetric care; providing adequate professional training for health workers, especially on women's reproductive health rights; ensuring access to effective remedies in cases where women's reproductive health rights have been violated and provide training for the judiciary and for law enforcement personnel; ensuring that private health care facilities comply with relevant national and international standards on reproductive health care; ensuring that adequate sanctions are imposed on health professionals who violate women's reproductive health rights; and reducing preventable maternal deaths through the implementation of the National Pact for the Reduction of Maternal and Neonatal Mortality at state and municipal levels, including by establishing maternal mortality committees where they do not exist. This final item was related to the Committee's concluding observations for Brazil in 2007. The Brazilian government was expected to provide a written response within six months of the Committee's decision. The six recommendations outlined above point to glaring problems and omissions with respect to obstetric care in Brazil.

The Committee's decision addressed the civil claim filed by Alyne's family on February 11, 2003, three months after her death. This civil claim for material and moral damages had not been resolved by the time of the *Alyne* decision in 2011 (Cook 2013). Although the family twice filed measures to "prevent irreparable or serious harm pending a decision on the civil claim," these measures were either ignored or denied (Cook 2013, 107). The Committee found that the eight-year delay since the claim was filed was "unreasonably prolonged" and therefore constituted a violation of Article 2(c) of the CEDAW, which addresses the protection of women's rights in national courts (CEDAW 2011; Cook 2013).

The Impacts and Impasses of the *Alyne* Decision

Legal and human rights scholar Rebecca J. Cook (2013) has argued that the *Alyne* decision was a major advance in the application of human rights law to women's health, because it was the first time a United Nations human rights committee decided a maternal mortality case. According to Cook, in this instance, the Committee "identified and analyzed the discriminatory gaps in a country's health care system from the perspective of a poor, pregnant, minority woman" (Cook 2013, 108). However, Cook's use of the term "minority" requires further interrogation, given that the African-descendant population constitutes more than half the Brazilian population according to the 2010 national census. Nonetheless, despite the size of the African-descendant population, social and economic indicators routinely point to its marginalization (Beato 2004; Paixão 2003).

The fact that Alyne da Silva Pimentel was a poor, Afro-descendant woman played a central role in how she was treated in the public health system and the deplorable treatment, as well as medical neglect, that ultimately led to her death.[14] The *Alyne* decision recognized the intersectional nature of her health status and underscored the importance of eliminating intersectional discrimination in accessing maternal health services (Cook 2013). This recognition constitutes an advance in international legal and human rights discourse, because it represents a move away from viewing race, gender, sexuality, class, and other social distinctions as separate and disconnected. Alyne's horrific experiences also indicate that she was subjected to multiple, interrelated forms of discrimination, which led to treatment within the health-care system that differed significantly from that experienced by pregnant, white middle-class women, especially considering that women of higher socioeconomic levels are typically able to afford private healthcare. As a result, many of the challenges Alyne faced, such as lack of access to an ambulance and inordinately long waits, likely would have been averted by women who did not depend on the public health system.

It is noteworthy that the first maternal mortality decision by a U.N. human rights committee involved an African-descendant woman, particularly considering that the decision recognized the role of multiple, intersecting factors (in this case race and class) in shaping women's vulnerability to maternal mortality and was not solely focused on the issue of gender. By acknowledging multiple forms of discrimination, this decision opened the possibility of developing more effective ways to recognize, monitor, and address maternal mortality in Brazil as well as in other countries. In this sense, the decision broadly framed the issue of maternal mortality and was relevant to women of diverse backgrounds in multiple national contexts. The *Alyne* decision also highlighted the specific forms of discrimination that women experience owing to the physiological and biological requirements of pregnancy and childbirth, which distinguish them from men and make them physically vulnerable in gender-specific ways.

While the committee's decision was an important development in efforts to address Brazil's high maternal mortality rates, and their specific impact on

Afro-descendant women, the fact that Brazil failed to fully comply with the Committee's recommendations and indemnify Alyne's mother and daughter for her death in a timely manner highlights ongoing challenges in this area. On August 10, 2012, the one-year anniversary of the *Alyne* decision, a group of twenty-eight Brazilian civil society organizations and networks that focus on human rights, sexual and reproductive rights, and women's health, submitted a letter calling for government action on the *Alyne* case. The group sent the letter to President Dilma Rousseff and several high-ranking government officials, including the Minister for Women's Policies, the Minister of Health, the Minister of Human Rights, the director of the Department of Human Rights and Social Issues in the Foreign Affairs Office, and the Federal Attorney General for the Rights of Citizens. This letter was initiated by Beatriz Galli, who was the Special Rapporteur for Sexual and Reproductive Health of the Dhesca Platform, the Brazilian Platform on Human, Economic, Social, Cultural, and Environmental Rights.[15] As special rapporteur, Galli was charged with monitoring the Brazilian government's implementation of the CEDAW decision and receiving complaints related to sexual and reproductive health violations.

The Dhesca letter states that the Brazilian state has the obligation to accept and implement the Committee's decision, based on "the principle of good faith" that guides international relations (Dhesca 2012). In addition, the letter calls attention to the importance of the *Alyne* decision as the first case of its kind and as a milestone with regard to recognition of maternal mortality as a human rights issue. The letter also notes the symbolic importance of the decision for governments, because they would now have to stop treating maternal mortality as an inevitable fate of women for which the state had no responsibility. In addition, the Dhesca letter mentions that, despite the importance of the *Alyne* decision, until that point the Brazilian government had not taken any concrete measures to comply with or implement the recommendations made in the decision. The letter notes that the decision had an impact in Brazil as well as in other countries, because it calls for establishing human rights parameters to strengthen health systems and improve health policies and practices. As the letter states:

> The delay in complying with the decision in the *Alyne* case and for Alyne's family is unacceptable for Brazilian society and the rest of the world. The government's delay ignores the national and global scenario of maternal mortality, pointing to the neglect (*descaso*) of the lives of hundreds of women who run the risk of dying during childbirth due to preventable causes due to their situation of vulnerability, as happened with Alyne. [Dhesca 2012]

The letter closes by calling for the Brazilian government to take immediate action to implement the committee's recommendations, with priority being given to the indemnity payment to Alyne's family.

Although the Brazilian government never responded to the Dhesca letter, it is an important example of civil society mobilization and citizen control focused on women's reproductive rights and human rights. This political pressure was the outgrowth of sustained commitment by feminist health activists to see the *Alyne* decision implemented. The Dhesca Platform initiated the human rights rapporteurships in 2002 as a way to examine potential human rights violations in Brazil that members of civil society called attention to and recommend solutions for them. Beatriz Galli acted as the special rappourteur for sexual and reproductive health for the Dhesca Platform beginning in July 2012 and, in this capacity, took the lead in submitting the aforementioned letter to President Rousseff and other high-ranking officials in the federal government. The letter was part of efforts to move the Brazilian government out of a state of inertia in its response to the *Alyne* decision.

While the Brazilian government recognized human rights violations in the *Alyne* case, it had not taken concrete steps to act on the Committee's recommendations more than eighteen months after the decision, although the decision called for a response within six months. Government action became a possibility when an Interministerial Group was formed on April 15, 2013. The group was comprised of representatives from the Ministry of Health, Secretariat for Women's Policies (SPM), Secretariat for Human Rights, the Ministry of Foreign Affairs, and SEPPIR. However, there was no civil society representation in the group, nor were members of civil society, including the Dhesca Platform, notified of plans to form it.[16] The group's formation was announced in the *Diário Oficial da União*, a federal government publication that disseminates information on government decrees and policies.

In May 2013, in recognition of the tenth anniversary of Alyne da Silva Pimentel Teixeira's death, the Dhesca Platform formed a special commission to evaluate maternal mortality and maternal health services in four cities in Baixada Fluminense, the region in which Pimentel lived and died. Because Alyne traveled to a total of four different health centers and hospitals to receive treatment prior to her death, the commission visited all of these locations and reported on them. The commission was initiated by Galli, the special rapporteur, for the Dhesca Platform. The commission for the *Alyne* case found the maternal health-care situation to be at a critical level and filed a complaint with the Federal Public Prosecutor for Citizens' Rights (*Procuradoria Federal dos Direitos do Cidadão*), asking for the closing of poor-quality maternal health services in the region.

When I interviewed her in July 2013, Galli, the director of the Dhesca commission, described maternal services in the Baixada Fluminense region as "denigrating" and noted that pregnant women did not have access to life-saving care or other necessities, such as blood.[17] She also noted that institutional violence against women was crystallized in the health-care system, particularly in maternal health care. Galli described the maternity wards in the Baixada Fluminense as examples of the Netherlands and Zimbabwe existing in the same area. This description poignantly conveyed the disparities found in maternity facilities, with facilities similar to those found in a highly developed European country existing alongside those of a developing African nation. These gross disparities are also comparable to the policies of apartheid and Jim Crow found in countries such as South Africa and the United States during the twentieth century, where there existed institutional policies of separate development and inequality on the basis of race. While the more "developed" maternity facilities in the Baixada Fluminense had amenities such as massages and doulas to assist women while in labor, the less "developed" ones had serious infrastructure and building maintenance problems, including sewage run-off and chickens running in front of buildings.

The executive summary for the Dhesca Commission's report was released in early 2014 and called attention to the "precarious" infrastructure and absence of necessary equipment in the local public health hospital, *Hospital Geral de Nova Iguaçu,* and health center, *Casa de Saúde Nossa Senhora da Gloria de Belford Roxo* (Plataforma Dhesca Brasil 2014). Some of the key issues highlighted by the commission for the *Casa de Saúde Nossa Senhora da Gloria* were: (1) The high number of young people who have undergone C-sections and surgical sterilization; (2) The lack of a blood bank, intensive care unit, or efficient transportation; and (3) The lack of health-care professionals to attend to all women in childbirth in a satisfactory manner. The commission also noted the following issues for the *Hospital Geral de Nova Iguaçu:* (1) a lack of health professionals to cover the maternity ward; (2) a precarious infrastructure, with walls and ceilings infested with mold and leaks; (3) a lack of adequate bathrooms and those that meet minimal hygiene conditions in the infirmaries; (4) women in childbirth were encountered in degrading conditions, feeling pain, unassisted, waiting hours without information about their health state, and lying on gurneys that were dirty and rusted; and (5) a lack of space in the intensive care units. The Commission also found that neither maternity facility complied with the Law of Accompaniment, which gave pregnant women the right to have someone accompany them during childbirth. In addition, the facilities did not have contact with the municipal or state Committees to Combat Maternal Mortality, nor did they conduct investigations of the causes of maternal deaths. The conditions outlined in the Commission's report highlighted continuing problems and failures in the provision of quality maternal care in the Baixada Fluminense region.

The Dhesca Commission made recommendations to the Commission for Human Rights and Minorities (*Commissão de Direitos Humanos e Minorias*) in the Brazilian Senate, which included calling for the immediate closing of *Casa de Saúde Nossa Senhora da Gloria* and the immediate deactivation of the maternity ward of the *Hospital Geral de Nova Iguaçu*. The Dhesca Commission also recommended that the Federal Public Ministry, civil society organizations, and U.N. agencies such as UNFPA and U.N. Women be included in the process of implementing the CEDAW recommendations and pressed for the federal government to pay the pecuniary reparations that were determined by the CEDAW Committee to Alyne's family (Plataforma Dhesca Brasil 2014).

A longer report on the *Alyne* case and CEDAW decision was published by the Dhesca Commission in 2015 that included recommendations for several levels of government, including the president, the Ministry of Health, the Federal Public Ministry, and the Rio de Janeiro State Health Secretariat (Galli et al. 2015). The national-level recommendations called for the implantation of maternal mortality committees in all states and municipalities and reengagement with PNAISM (*Política Nacional de Atenção Integral à Saúde da Mulher,* National Policy for Integral Attention to Women's Health), a policy first developed by feminist health activists in the 1980s. Recommendations at the state level focused on the closure of the health center *Casa de Saúde Nossa Senhora da Gloria* and the guarantee of rapid and efficient transportation of pregnant women to prenatal and maternal health services, among other areas.

On February 28, 2014, the CEDAW Committee backed an agreement between the Brazilian government and the Center for Reproductive Rights, representing Alyne's family, on the monetary compensation Alyne's mother would receive. Individual reparations for Alyne's daughter were still pending after this agreement. The CEDAW Committee also underscored that follow-up dialogue would continue regarding its other recommendations, specifically as they related to the reparations for Alyne's daughter. In addition, a legal decision was still pending in the Brazilian courts (Center for Reproductive Rights 2014). On March 25, 2014, a ceremony was held in Brasília to recognize the payment of reparations to Alyne's mother, who received indemnification in the amount of R\$131,000 on March 17. Three significant symbolic forms of reparation were also scheduled to take place the following month, including renaming of the intensive care unit of the Mariana Bulhões Maternity Facility in Nova Iguaçu after Alyne Pimentel on April 4, 2014. That same day, the federal prosecutor in Rio de Janeiro held the "Alyne Pimentel Case Seminar" on the right to sexual and reproductive health and maternal mortality in Brazil. In addition, the Alyne Pimentel community space was inaugurated in the *Hospital Estadual Mãe de Mesquita* on April 5.

The nearly three-year delay between the CEDAW Committee's decision and the Brazilian government's agreement to provide reparations to Alyne's mother, as well as the continued existence of unsafe and poor-quality maternity services in the Baixada Fluminense region, highlight the gaps that often exist between international human rights norms, symbolic state commitments, and on-the-ground policies and results. The *Alyne* case is an instructive example of the potential limitations of using international human rights norms to enforce change and results at the national level. Though the CEDAW decision was important symbolically, the Brazilian government's failure to implement the decision in a timely manner lessened its intended impact and jeopardized the lives and health of pregnant women in the Baixada Fluminense region, as well as in other areas of the country that had maternal health facilities of similarly poor quality. The implications of the committee's decision were also complicated by the fact that it could set a precedent that the Brazilian government would become obligated to follow in future cases of maternal mortality, with respect to indemnifying the families of women who die from preventable pregnancy-related causes.[18]

Institutional Discrimination, Violence, and the Genocidal Continuum

Alyne da Silva Pimentel's death illuminates the ways in which institutional gender and racial discrimination shape African-descendant women's experiences in the Brazilian public health system. The deplorable quality of care that Alyne received was directly related to her individual social location as a poor, African-descendant woman, as well as the structural location of her community, Belford Roxo, which is a predominantly African-descendant, low-income community. Alyne's experiences in the health system immediately prior to her death underscore the inadequate level of care provided in the local health center and hospitals she visited. As noted in the 2014 Dhesca report, the health center and maternity services Alyne used continued to provide abysmal levels of care to women more than a decade after Alyne's death, further pointing to the lack of interest and commitment on the part of local health authorities and public officials in improving institutional and structural conditions that determine the quality of obstetric and maternal health services in the region (Plataforma Dhesca Brasil 2014).

In addition, the municipality of Belford Roxo is located in the Baixada Fluminense region, which has historically experienced high levels of state violence, most notably in the form of police homicides of residents (Goulart and Gonçalves 2011). One of the most glaring examples of violence occurred on March 31, 2005, when twenty-nine people were killed in the Baixada Fluminense. The killings were attributed to a group believed to consist of military police officers, who drove through the Baixada Fluminense between 8:30 and 11:00 at night, shooting randomly at passersby (Amnesty International 2005). The massacre was denounced by civil society and human rights organizations. In a 2005 report on the massacre, Amnesty International found that it was part of a larger pattern of police and state violence against *favela* (shantytown) communities. The report also highlighted the lack of human rights policing practices and the impunity with which human rights violations by police are treated in Brazil. Importantly, this publication also underscored the failure of the Brazilian state to protect vulnerable and marginalized communities. Amnesty International argued that violent policing practices criminalized the poor and treated all members of *favela* communities as social outcasts whose lives were disposable. The report also found that, in the Sapopemba community in São Paulo, when residents visited the local hospital, "they faced delays in treatment, disrespectful and discriminatory behaviour and were often dismissed as criminals" (Amnesty International 2005, 16). This finding illustrates the ways in which widespread criminalization of poor, largely African-descendant communities influences access to health care and treatment in the health-care system. Taking this larger context of police and state violence into account is vital to understanding how Belford Roxo and the greater Baixada Fluminense region are positioned in relation to the state and state actors with respect to potential, as well as actual, human rights violations.

A noteworthy example of political discourses that link reproduction by poor women and criminality can be seen in statements made by Sérgio Cabral, former governor of the state of Rio de Janeiro, in October 2007 in which he argued that legalizing abortion was important because it could provide a way to decrease the size of the criminal population. According to an online article, Cabral stated, "All you have to do is compare the number of children per mother in Lago, Tijuca, Meier and Copacabana (middle- and upper-class neighborhoods in Rio de Janeiro), where incomes are similar to those in Sweden, with that of Rocinha (the largest poor area of the city), where incomes are at the same levels as Zambia and Gabon. This is a factory for producing marginalized people. . . . To not offer something in the public system for these (poor) girls to terminate their pregnancies is crazy" (Catholic News Agency 2007). While Sérgio Cabral's statements did not explicitly address the issue of maternal mortality, they underscored the devaluation of the lives of women and children who are considered to be incubators and perpetrators of criminal behavior. Cabral's emphasis on terminating the pregnancies of poor women could also be seen as giving little regard for the need to provide adequate or high-quality maternity services to these women or their children. In addition, although Cabral did not make specific references to race, widespread and commonsense notions that link criminality to African-descendant Brazilians could be easily and subliminally invoked by his statements. His apparent support for abortion is also highly problematic given the fact that he was essentially advocating pregnancy termination from an anti-natalist perspective and, thus, as a way to decrease the number of poor and unwanted children, rather than viewing it as an expression of women's reproductive and bodily autonomy.

Structural violence, and everyday forms of violence, have shaped the experiences of poor African-descendant women, such as Alyne, within Brazilian public institutions and the health-care system. João Vargas's (2004, 2005) work has been instrumental in analyzing how racism shapes the ways in which black bodies and communities in Brazil are perceived and the degree to which the lives of black Brazilians are viewed as disposable. Vargas's work offers an important perspective on Brazilian race relations that pushes for the conceptualization of antiblack violence in the country as a form of genocide that threatens the survival of black citizens. Vargas has highlighted the racialization of urban spaces, most notably *favelas,* in Brazil and the ways in which code words are used to "talk about blackness . . . thus substituting race for urban space" (2004, 460). In addition, he argues that danger and criminality are associated with *favelas* in ways that perpetuate state-sanctioned and state-inflicted violence on black bodies (Vargas 2004). Vargas's conceptualization of antiblack violence and homicides in Brazil as a form of genocide underscores how space and race intersect to determine the value accorded to black bodies and black communities. As a result, it is clear that certain communities and certain lives count less than others. In addition, Vargas has argued that both state and everyday forms of violence in Brazil have created a cultural and social context that normalizes the devaluation of black lives (2005).

Christen Smith's (2013) analysis of the 2007 beating of Sirlei Carvalho in Rio de Janeiro highlights the relationship between symbolic and physical violence against black women in Brazil. As Smith notes, Carvalho's beating by several "white-mestizo"[19] middle-class young men was prompted by their perception of her being a prostitute. Smith highlights the ways in which Carvalho's beating was an act of boundary making predicated on dominant understandings of gender, race, class, and sexuality in Brazil; it also served to reinforce and enact the proper place of black women in Brazil by marking Carvalho's body as both black and female. As Smith argues, "black women's bodies are seen as violable in part because black femaleness is always already marked as outside the social contract and thus, by extension, outside the moral social order (the understanding that is the basis of that contract)" (Smith 2013, 108). The beating of Sirlei Carvalho resonates with the death of Alyne da Silva Pimentel as an expression of social violence against black women, although it occurred outside the health-care system and was not fatal. In both cases, the devaluation of black women's lives and bodies led to actions that constituted either criminal offenses or human rights violations.

The provision of adequate health-care facilities in low-income communities and *favelas* is another issue that merits consideration in relation to the *Alyne* case; it is also closely linked to practices of structural violence. In 2005, Belford Roxo had only one emergency obstetric facility for a population of almost 500,000. The neighboring municipality, São João de Meriti, which is more affluent, had five emergency obstetric facilities, though its population was of a similar size (Center for Reproductive Rights 2009). Disparities in the provision of maternity services based on region, typically urban versus rural areas, have been defined as discriminatory practices and violations of the International Covenant on Economic, Social, and Cultural Rights (Yamin and Maine 2005). In addition, the same racial logics that sanction the killing of poor and working-class blacks who reside in Brazil's *favelas* and periphery neighborhoods also minimize the value of black women's reproduction of black children. The lack of high-quality maternity facilities in cities such as Belford Roxo highlights state policies of neglect that devalue reproduction by black women, especially poor black women who live in marginalized communities. As a result, the lives of pregnant women and their offspring are placed in jeopardy by policies that fail to prioritize their health, well-being, and survival.

João Vargas's (2009) conceptualization of a "genocidal continuum" that affects life chances and mortality in African diaspora communities is useful in understanding the links between seemingly disparate practices that threaten these communities. It is also important to make connections between these practices and the population control and sterilization policies discussed in chapters 1 and 2, which have discouraged and limited reproduction by certain Brazilian women, particularly black Brazilian women. As Vargas has noted in an analysis of antiblack genocide in Brazil and the United States, "we should recognize that in a context defined by racial hierarchies—by white supremacy—apparently neutral policies necessarily become molded by the hegemonic social order. The concepts of symbolic violence and genocidal continuum allow us to understand genocide as part of a constellation of phenomena ranging from everyday forms of individualized discrimination, to structural marginalization (residential segregation, unemployment, and barred access to credit), to the historically persistent killing of those deemed less than human" (2009, 93).

Scholars such as Johan Galtung (1969) and Paul Farmer (2004) have often defined structural violence primarily in reference to diminished life chances that result from poverty; however, it is also important to begin to examine racialized and gendered forms of structural violence, as well as forms of structural violence that result from and perpetuate intersecting practices of discrimination. As can be seen in the institutional experiences and premature death of Alyne da Silva Pimentel, intersecting forms of structural violence played a pivotal role in creating conditions that conspired against her life and well-being. Kathleen Ho's (2007) work provides a framework for viewing sexism and racism, as well as class-based structures, as social mechanisms by which structural violence is enacted and perpetrated. One of the great benefits of the concept of structural violence is the way in which it takes the onus off individual actors and, instead, highlights how "violence is built into the structure and shows up as unequal power and consequently as unequal life chances" (Ho 2007, 4). Alyne da Silva Pimentel's experiences in Brazil's public health system, like those of countless Afro-Brazilian women, reflected practices of structural violence that were rooted in her social location and closely linked to her human rights capabilities (Nussbaum 2006). As Ho observes, "When economic and social structures conspire to limit one's agency to the extent that fundamental human rights cannot be met then structural violence becomes a structural violation of human rights" (2007, 15).

Intersectionality and Human Rights

Alyne da Silva Pimentel's experiences in the health-care system and her preventable death underscore the need to develop new perspectives on human rights that attend to the intersectional relationship among gender, race, class, and other forms of social difference and marginalization. Alyne's death and the CEDAW Committee's decision also raise the question: How can human rights norms begin to address intersectional forms of discrimination? Progress was made on this front during the 2001 World Conference against Racism, because the conference addressed racism, racial discrimination, and related forms of intolerance, which provided an opening to bring gender, sexuality, and other forms of difference into policy discussions related to racism. Nonetheless, much work remains to be done in this area, particularly in relationship to the human right to health for women in African diaspora communities.

In a rare discussion of gender, race, and human rights law, Celina Romany's (2000) work highlights some of the shortcomings of human rights documents such as CEDAW and the Convention on the Elimination of All Forms of Racial Discrimination (CERD) in addressing the specific forms of discrimination experienced by black women and women from other nonprivileged racial groups. Romany notes the androcentric bias and tendency to universalize women's experiences found in most human rights law. For Romany, the emphasis placed on the public sphere in human rights law renders women's experiences in the private sphere invisible. Similarly, because notions of womanhood in international law tend to use privileged white women as the norm, the experiences of women of other backgrounds are often overlooked. In addition, the multiple forms of discrimination experienced by racially marginalized women frequently fall between the gaps of existing international human rights treaties, such as CEDAW and CERD, which focus on either gender discrimination or racial discrimination. Romany advocates use of an intersectional approach to human rights law and provides a general, though not detailed outline, of this approach. She also argues that under the equality provisions of the International Covenant on Civil and Political Rights (ICCPR), the International Covenant on Economic, Social, and Cultural Rights (ICESCR), CEDAW, and CERD:

> Black women could be viewed as a separate group entitled to a greater protection than that offered to white women and Black men. . . . It has been argued that for equal protection purposes Black women in the United States can be categorized as a subset of Blacks or of women, or as a separate group characterized as being excluded from the benefits of full citizenship. They can constitute a "discrete and insular minority"—that is, a group possessing immutable characteristics (such as race) that has been the subject of historical prejudice and political powerlessness. This argument is one that could be successfully explored in the international arena because, as in the United States, race discrimination enjoys a higher level of protection than its gender counterpart. [2000, 63]

Romany also advocates use of the "woman/race" question as part of an intersectional methodological strategy. While recognizing that CEDAW and CERD both have primary areas of focus, either gender or race, Romany points out the need to address multiple forms of subordination. She discusses the prohibitions against multiple forms of discrimination in documents such as CERD, the United Nations Charter, and the Universal Declaration of Human Rights, noting,

> Equality, as espoused in such documents, is not an enclosed room full of compartments. Rather, it is an open and encompassing concept—with race and gender among its categories. Furthermore, in alluding to the UN Charter, the Race Convention refers to the "equality inherent in all human beings," a clear recognition that both men and women are entitled to be free of race discrimination. . . . It is important to ask the woman/race question in order to foster an integrated and more coherent use of international instruments. [2000, 64]

Conclusion

The death of Alyne da Silva Pimentel highlights significant failures in Brazil's health system with respect to the provision of timely and effective care to women facing emergency obstetric crises. Her death also highlights the ways in which institutional racism, sexism, and classism affect the well-being and lives of individuals. Alyne's death resulted from a number of problems in the public health system, including those related to diagnosis and having adequate staffing and facilities, as well as problems stemming from inadequate transportation and space in hospital maternity wards. Many of these problems likely could have been remedied by having a better integrated and more effective system in place for meeting the needs of pregnant women during childbirth. The failed implementation of earlier women's health programs, such as PAISM, likely contributed to the health system's lack of adequate services for pregnant women. In addition, despite the creation of numerous programs and policies designed to reduce maternal mortality and ensure the humanization of women's birth experiences, these initiatives did not seem to translate into effective practices in local health centers and hospitals in 2002, when Alyne died, or in 2013, when the Dhesca Commission visited the Baixada Fluminense region.

Institutional discrimination against women, particularly poor Afro-Brazilian women, in the health system was a major factor shaping the quality of services offered in the region in which Alyne lived, as well as the deplorable level of care she received. Moreover, intersectional forms of discrimination tied to gender, race, class, and social location contributed to Alyne's death. Both Alyne da Silva Pimentel's death and the CEDAW Committee's decision underscore the importance of recognizing and addressing the ways in which poor Afro-Brazilian women's marginal social status renders them vulnerable to intersecting forms of structural discrimination and structural violence within Brazil's health-care system.

Close examination of the circumstances leading to Alyne da Silva Pimentel's death illuminates significant inadequacies in the care provided to Brazilian women during pregnancy and childbirth. The *Alyne* case also personalizes and humanizes the crisis of maternal death in Brazil, by putting a human face on a significant public health crisis. Though statistics on maternal death are useful, they fail to capture adequately the human impact of the preventable deaths of thousands of women that occur in Brazil every year. As Rebecca Cook has noted, relying solely on statistics "can too easily become depersonalizing and alienating, disguising the human side of maternal mortality and losing sight of the women themselves. The reliance on statistics might also tend to dissociate the events from human agency, a dislocation of responsibility, with maternal mortality conceptualized as having a simple, objective existence" (2013, 106). Importantly, Cook's statements highlight the fact that institutional and structural forms of discrimination are enacted and performed by human actors, not abstract entities or institutions.

The *Alyne* case is a cautionary tale that underscores the need for both continued state action and civil society mobilization to ensure that intersectional health equity is achieved in Brazil. Civil society mobilization, at both the national and transnational level, was vital to creating a context in which Alyne da Silva Pimentel's death was officially recognized within an international human rights context by the CEDAW Committee, and within a national legal and policy context by the Brazilian government. Civil society organizations and networks, including the Articulation of Black Brazilian Women's Organizations (AMNB) and the Dhesca Platform, were instrumental in creating sustained pressure and demanding that the Brazilian government act on the CEDAW Committee's recommendations. In addition, the Center for Reproductive Rights played a key role in bringing the *Alyne* case before the CEDAW Committee. The existence of human rights norms that recognized women's right to health were important in establishing a basis for recognizing Alyne da Silva Pimentel's death as a human rights violation. Her identity as a poor,

Afro-descendent woman also pushed the limits of existing notions of human rights and health to include multiple forms of discrimination and inequality.

While much can be learned from the tragic death of Alyne da Silva Pimentel and the international and domestic legal battles that ensued following her death, structural and institutional forms of inequality and discrimination in Brazil's health-care system must be addressed at the level of state policy, as well as at the micro-level with respect to the care that individual women receive from health professionals and within the health system, in order for real, concrete, and long-lasting changes to take place. Recognizing the impact of institutional and structural forms of violence and racial discrimination on black Brazilian women's health experiences is essential to achieve such changes.

Making Race and Gender Visible in Brazil's HIV/AIDS Epidemic

Policy, Advocacy, and Research

The 1997 documentary *Odô Yá: Life with AIDS* examines the development of culturally sensitive HIV/AIDS prevention messages for the Afro-Brazilian population (Cypriano 1997). The film is one of few scholarly or popular works to examine the impact of the HIV/AIDS epidemic on Afro-Brazilians. It highlights the experiences of HIV positive individuals and explores the work of *mães* and *paes de santo* (mothers and fathers of saints), leaders in the Afro-Brazilian religion of Candomblé, to bring awareness of HIV to their communities, while at the same time honoring cultural and religious traditions that might be threatened by the imposition of Western beliefs about sexuality. Although it was released in the late 1990s, this film raises important and enduring questions about the efficacy of efforts to address the HIV/AIDS prevention and treatment needs of the African-descendant population in Brazil. The film demonstrates the importance of including issues such as culture and social class as integral components of HIV/AIDS prevention efforts, particularly for marginalized groups whose cultural practices and/or socioeconomic status might make them vulnerable to HIV infection. However, it should also be noted that, while religion and culture are central themes in *Odô Yá*, it does not directly address the issue of race. Instead, the possible existence of racial health disparities with respect to HIV/AIDS diagnosis, prevention, and treatment is raised indirectly in the film.

In contrast to the cultural emphasis in the film *Odô Yá* and the HIV/AIDS prevention program on which it was based, this chapter focuses on efforts to develop race-conscious HIV/AIDS initiatives for the Afro-Brazilian population. Since the mid-1980s, Brazil has been at the forefront of progressive and proactive approaches to slow the spread of the HIV/AIDS epidemic. While HIV/AIDS prevention and treatment efforts undertaken by the Brazilian government and non-governmental organizations have received a good deal of scholarly attention, little research has focused on the impact of the HIV/AIDS epidemic on the country's African-descendant population. This chapter examines efforts to address the HIV/AIDS prevention needs of the Afro-Brazilian population and places such efforts within the broader context of Brazil's universalist HIV/AIDS prevention and treatment programs. The analysis maps the development of Brazil's HIV/AIDS policies and initiatives at the federal level, and explores the extent to which race and the specific needs of the Afro-Brazilian population have been addressed in recent decades. Given the fact that Brazil has been internationally recognized as a model of successful prevention and treatment of HIV/AIDS, it is important to consider the impact of these initiatives on the African-descendant population in order to more fully understand issues of health equity in the country. This chapter also explores HIV prevention initiatives developed by black women's organizations and the ways in which this work has highlighted links between gender, race, and HIV vulnerability. Finally, this chapter examines critiques of racially specific HIV/AIDS prevention initiatives and the tensions between universalism and race consciousness that have characterized the shift toward focusing on the black population in HIV prevention efforts.

Brazil's Response to the HIV/AIDS Epidemic

Since the mid-1980s, the Brazilian government has been at the forefront of developing effective and aggressive HIV/AIDS prevention and treatment initiatives that have been instrumental in curbing the epidemic. Brazil's success in combating HIV/AIDS has owed to a number of factors, including civil society mobilization, proactive responses on the part of the federal government, and, since the late 1980s, the emphasis on universal access to health care as a guiding principle of Brazil's public health system, the SUS (*Sistema Único de Saúde*) (Paim and Silva 2010; Parker 2009). Brazil was also the first developing country to pledge free and universal access to AIDS medications for people living with HIV/AIDS (PLWHA) and has played a major role in shaping global AIDS treatment paradigms (Nunn 2009).

During the 1980s, the emerging gay rights movement and mobilization of hemophiliacs were instrumental in putting HIV/AIDS on the policy agenda of larger cities such as São Paulo and Rio de Janeiro. In 1986, amid significant civil society mobilization following the end of the military dictatorship, the Brazilian Ministry of Health established the National Program for STDs and AIDS (*Programa Nacional de DSTs e AIDS*). Founding of the National Program occurred within a larger context of mobilization by political parties, labor unions, universities, women's rights activists, antiracist activists, and NGOs to reestablish democratic forms of governance and expand political rights as Brazil returned to democratic rule. Owing to the success of the National Program for STDs and AIDS, Brazil has been hailed as a model of government intervention in the spread of HIV/AIDS. By the mid-2000s researchers noted a slowing of the HIV/AIDS epidemic, particularly in cities such as Rio de Janeiro and São Paulo (Galvão 2000). This resulted primarily from the effective use of prevention measures, including dissemination of information about prevention, the increase in condom use among the general population, and the free distribution of antiretroviral therapy (ARVs) to HIV-positive individuals (Galvão 2005). In 1991, the Brazilian Ministry of Health began to distribute combination ARVs free of charge through the national health system, the SUS. President Fernando Henrique Cardoso also signed a law in 1996 mandating the provision of free ARVs to all people living with HIV/AIDS.[1]

Brazil's policy of providing universal and free access to AIDS medications was unprecedented at the time, particularly among developing countries. By the end of 2002, 125,000 people living with HIV had received ARVs without cost through the public health system. At this time, more than a third of ARV-treated patients in the developing world lived in Brazil (Teixeira and Paim 2003). By 2008, the number of people receiving ARVs increased to 185,000 (Nunn 2009). Active participation by civil society, including a high number of non-governmental AIDS organizations, was key to bringing about and ensuring the effectiveness of Brazil's ARV distribution policy (Galvão 2005; Nunn 2009; Parker 2008, 2009). Between 1994 and 2002, over $40 million (U.S.) was invested in more than two thousand projects implemented by civil society organizations, including communities and NGOs of people living with HIV/AIDS (Teixeira and Paim 2003).

In 1992, the World Bank estimated that Brazil would have almost 1.2 million cases of HIV infection by 2000. However, the country succeeded in drastically reducing that number. In fact, in 2000, the number of people living with HIV in Brazil was estimated to be 597,000, which was less than half the amount in earlier World Bank estimates (Teixeira and Paim 2003). By the late 2000s, scholars such as Richard Parker argued the epidemic had not only "reached a plateau but may also have begun to decrease, thanks to an aggressive public health response" (2009, S49). These successes owed largely to the federal government's implementation of a comprehensive and multifaceted National AIDS Plan and the active involvement of civil society in HIV/AIDS prevention, care, and treatment (Safreed-Harmon 2008).

Beginning in the early 1980s, a human rights focus was central to HIV/AIDS prevention and treatment efforts in Brazil. Initiatives developed with human rights as a core value first developed in cities such as São Paulo, where the first governmental AIDS program in the Americas was established in 1983 (Parker 2009; Teixeira and Paim 2003). A human rights focus enabled Brazil to approach the epidemic in ways that challenged stigma and discrimination against people living with HIV and AIDS. It also led to notable successes with regard to universal treatment, which were closely connected to the emphasis on universality as a foundational principle of the SUS. Richard Parker has pointed out the connections between the health reform movement and the development of progressive HIV/AIDS policies in Brazil, noting:

> AIDS activists, together with representatives of the broader sanitary reform movement, would play an important role in the public debates leading up to the drafting of the new constitution in 1988, which articulated the legal basis for universal access to health-care services, the principle of integration between treatment and preventive public health programs, and the principle of "'social control" of health-care policies and programs through citizen representation on health councils at every level of government—all of which would come to have significant implications for the elaboration and implementation of HIV/AIDS-related policies and programs over the next 20 years. [2009, S50]

Human rights were a core principle of early HIV/AIDS prevention and treatment efforts in Brazil. This was largely due to the political context of the 1980s, when various sectors of civil society were organizing for a return to democratic rule, as well as for health reform, and state policies to address the emerging AIDS epidemic. Early AIDS activists included people such as Herbert de Souza, known as *Betinho,* and Herbert Eustáquio de Daniel, known as Herbert Daniel. Both activists later died of AIDS-related complications in 1992 and 1997, respectively. In 1986 Betinho founded the Brazilian Interdisciplinary AIDS Association (ABIA, *Associação Brasileira Interdisciplinar de AIDS*) in the city of Rio de Janeiro, an organization that continues to be at the forefront of HIV/AIDS research and advocacy (Bacon et al., 2004). Herbert Daniel founded the group Pela VIDDA (For the Valorization, Integration and Dignity of People with AIDS, *Pela Valorização, Integração e Dignidade do Doente de AIDS*) in Rio in 1989. Early organizing around AIDS focused on the human rights of individuals living with the disease and also informed the development of government-sponsored AIDS initiatives.

Many observers, including scholars and international agencies, have argued that Brazil has been exemplary in its approach to HIV/AIDS prevention and universal treatment (Berkman et al. 2005; Galvão 2005).[2] The country also stands as a model for the provision of universal AIDS treatment in resource-poor settings, especially in developing countries (Teixeira and Paim 2003). Brazil's AIDS treatment model has been praised by the World Health Organization, as well as the Gates, Clinton, and Ford Foundations (Nunn 2009). Kelly Safreed-Harmon has highlighted factors that have set Brazil apart from other developing countries, noting:

> Brazil's executive and legislative branches have developed a body of law that provides clear direction on how the right to health is to be actualized. The judiciary has provided critical guidance on implementation through rulings that address many different HIV-related issues from a human rights perspective. Finally, a strong community-based movement has conceptualized its objectives in terms of human rights principles. [2008, 4]

The 1988 constitution provided a basis for Brazilian judges to rule favorably when people living with HIV/AIDS sued state or municipal governments for needed medications (Parker 2009). In this way, the constitution provided a foundation for Brazil's successes and advances in HIV prevention and AIDS treatment. As noted above, the active participation of civil society in the citizen control of HIV/AIDS policies was also instrumental in slowing the spread of the epidemic in the country. As one scholar has noted, the history of the mobilization of civil society in response to HIV and AIDS in Brazil "suggests that strengthening a country's response to the epidemic can in fact have important consequences for its entire health system. . . . the energy and commitment of AIDS activism and mobilization of civil society associated with the HIV epidemic has spilled over in important ways to contribute to citizen involvement and greater social control of health care" (Parker 2009, S50).

Race and the HIV/AIDS Epidemic in Brazil

Race and racial disparities have received little attention in most academic research and state policy focusing on HIV/AIDS in Brazil. This has likely resulted from

Brazil's longstanding image as a racially harmonious society and the belief that it has been free of the racial distinctions and inequalities that characterize other multiracial societies, such as the United States. In addition, the universalist principles undergirding the SUS and the National STD/AIDS Program traditionally have emphasized the importance of increasing access and equity for socioeconomically disadvantaged individuals, rather than focusing on racial groups or racial disparities in HIV/AIDS prevention or treatment. Moreover, the tradition of focusing on class, rather than race, as the primary method of discrimination and inequality in Brazil likely influenced how public health researchers and practitioners viewed and responded to the HIV/AIDS epidemic in its early stages.

In a book titled *Boundaries of Contagion: How Ethnic Politics Have Shaped Government Responses to AIDS,* U.S. political scientist Evan Lieberman examines Brazil's AIDS policies and argues that ethnically harmonious social conditions have allowed the country to achieve relative success in its fight against AIDS. Based on a comparative analysis of the impact of ethnic boundaries on AIDS policies in Brazil, South Africa, and India, Lieberman argues that the use of Portuguese as the national language was a unifying factor that enabled Brazil to avoid the establishment of ethnic boundaries. He also highlights the prohibitions against race distinctions and race prejudice in Brazil's 1967 and 1969 constitutions as significant contributors to racial harmony in the country (2009). According to Lieberman, the overall success of Brazil's AIDS policies has owed to the existence of "clearly flexible, if not entirely permeable, ethnic boundaries in the country" (2009, 145).

While noting the increased attention that has been given to racial and ethnic disparities and the implementation of affirmative action in Brazil during the early twenty-first century, Lieberman argues that such developments have been elite led. He further contends that there was "no broad-based social movement leading to such changes" (2009, 148), thus erasing and rendering invisible the efforts of antiracist activists, most notably members of Brazil's black movement, to challenge Brazilian racism since the early decades of the twentieth century (Alberto 2011; Andrews 1991; Butler 1998; Hanchard 1994).

Lieberman's favorable view of Brazil's AIDS policies is premised on the belief that Brazil is a racial democracy. Moreover, while Lieberman's analysis highlights ethnic, racial, and caste divisions in South Africa and India, it gives little regard to the racial divisions that exist in Brazil.[3] In doing so, it fails to recognize ongoing practices of racial discrimination and inequality that place African-descendant Brazilians at a disadvantage with respect to employment, income, education, and health (Beato 2004; Paixão 2013; Telles 2004). Policy and legislative developments during the 2000s and 2010s also challenge Lieberman's view of Brazil as a county in which race holds little or no significance. As noted in chapter 3, during 2009, the Brazilian Ministry of Health promulgated the National Policy for the Integral Health of the Black Population (*Política Nacional de Saúde da População Negra*). This federal policy was designed to address racial health disparities in Brazil and highlights the need for increased governmental and health sector attention to health issues that disproportionately affect the black population. Provisions for addressing racial health disparities were also included in the Statute of Racial Equality (Federal Law 12.288/2010), which President Lula signed into law in July 2010. Though passage of the Statute of Racial Equality took nearly a decade and was the subject of intense controversy, it signaled growing recognition of the need for state action to remedy racial inequality and discrimination in Brazil. It is also important to note that both the National Policy for the Integral Health of the Black Population and the Statute of Racial Equality were the result of sustained pressure by activists in the black women's movement and black movement dating back to the 1980s and 1990s. Acknowledging the impact of antiracist activism on policy development in Brazil challenges Lieberman's assertions that policies developed during the early 2000s were elite led.

Making the Black Population Visible in HIV/AIDS Data and Research

Although some researchers have noted an increase in the spread of HIV/AIDS among low-income and poor Brazilians, minimal research has been done on the links between race and class with regard to the HIV/AIDS epidemic in Brazil (Caldwell and Bowleg 2011). This observation is true of work by acclaimed researchers such as anthropologist João Biehl, whose book, *Will to Live: AIDS Therapies and the Politics of Survival,* examines the development of AIDS treatment policies in Brazil and chronicles the experiences of poor HIV-positive individuals who live in the city of Salvador, Bahia (Biehl 2007). While Biehl's work makes a major contribution to scholarship on access to AIDS treatment in Brazil, it does not situate the experiences of his informants with respect to their racial/ethnic identities or positionalities. This is particularly curious given the fact that the project was carried out in Salvador, a city that has a predominantly black population. In addition, all of the photos included in the book are of individuals of visible African ancestry. Despite the strengths of *Will to Live,* the book serves as a missed opportunity to highlight and address the experiences of African-descendant individuals with respect to AIDS treatment. By eliding discussion of race, this important study fails to address potential racial disparities in access to AIDS treatments, despite the fact that they are theoretically available to all Brazilians without cost as part of universal AIDS treatment policies. Ultimately, Biehl's (2007) study reinforces beliefs that only class and socioeconomic differences should be examined when analyzing gaps and shortcomings in Brazil's AIDS treatment policies.

The documentary *Odô Yá,* mentioned at the beginning of this chapter, focuses on HIV/AIDS in African-descendant communities and, in so doing, stands in sharp contrast to the position of Evan Lieberman, discussed above, as well as João Biehl's analysis of HIV treatment in Salvador. Both authors take a race-neutral or color-blind approach to their study of HIV/AIDS prevention and treatment. In contrast, *Odô Yá* examines the experiences of poor and low-income African-descendant HIV-positive individuals in the city of Salvador, and the lack of services provided for them. It also looks at the Odô Yá HIV prevention campaign in Rio and prevention efforts among Candomblé practitioners in the city of São Paulo (Silva and Guimarães 2000).

A lack of epidemiological data by race has been one of the main impediments blocking efforts to understand the impact of the HIV/AIDS epidemic on the Afro-Brazilian population. As noted in chapter 4, until 1996, Brazil lacked an official policy that would permit the collection of health data by race. Efforts to increase collection of the *quesito cor* (color/race data) that took place in HIV/AIDS services in the state of São Paulo beginning in 2004 highlight the importance of obtaining data on rates of HIV/AIDS in the Afro-descendant community in Brazil to assess the impact of the epidemic on this population (Giovanetti et al. 2007; Souza et al. 2005). São Paulo's pioneering program was implemented to collect the *quesito cor* in HIV/AIDS services throughout the state. These efforts later served as both a catalyst and model for discussions within the Ministry of Health and in the National STD/AIDS Program regarding the collection of HIV/AIDS data by color/race.

Since the early 1990s, black activists and scholars, particularly black women, have been at the forefront of calling attention to the racial dimensions of what researchers have called the increasing "pauperization" (*pauperização*) of the HIV/AIDS epidemic in Brazil (Bastos and Szwarcwald 2000; Parker and Camargo Jr. 2000). The term pauperization refers to the fact that larger numbers of poor people have increasingly been affected by the epidemic. This term also highlights how the epidemic has shifted from primarily affecting middle-class and affluent gay white males to affecting people of lower social status; however, the racial/ethnic background of these individuals has typically been invisible in class-based analyses of the epidemic.

Examining the changing class dimensions of the HIV/AIDS epidemic in Brazil has been an important means of trying to assess its impact on the African-descendant population, particularly in the absence of reliable epidemiological data by race or skin color. Given the traditional lack of health data collection by race, innovative approaches to assessing the links between race and class have been developed by scholar-activists such as Jurema Werneck. A medical doctor who also holds a Ph.D., she is a longtime leader of the black women's NGO Criola in Rio de Janeiro. In her research, Werneck (2001) has used standard measures of socioeconomic standing, such as the educational attainment index, as a proxy for race and has argued that the rise of HIV/AIDS cases among low-income and poor Brazilians during the 1990s also meant that rates of HIV/AIDS were increasing within the Afro-Brazilian population, considering this population is disproportionately impoverished.[4]

When considering how socioeconomic status affects the health of Afro-Brazilians, it is useful to examine racial disparities in Human Development Index (HDI) calculations for Brazil. As a tool used by the United Nations Development Programme (UNDP), the HDI measures life expectancy at birth, education, and standard of living for 174 countries and has been used to assess a country's level of development based on the capabilities of its citizens, rather than solely by Gross Domestic Product (GDP). Wania Sant'Anna and Marcelo Paixão's (1997) analysis evaluated the HDI of African descendants in Brazil and their gender status, and showed that the combination of race/ethnicity and gender caused black women to occupy the lowest social position in comparison to white and black men as well as white women. Racially disaggregated calculations of the human development index for 2000 have shown that the white population had a high level of human development, with a world ranking of thirty-third to thirty-fourth, while the *pardo* (brown) and *preto* (black) populations had a medium level of human development, with world rankings of ninety-ninth and ninety-sixth to ninety-seventh, respectively (Paixão 2013, 66). Furthermore, when the life expectancy and longevity indexes in Brazil were disaggregated by sex and racial group using data from the National Household Sample Survey database for 1997, white Brazilians had a life expectancy of seventy years, while Afro-descendants had a life expectancy of sixty-four (Sant'Anna 2001). The life expectancy for Afro-descendant men and women was sixty-two and sixty-six years, respectively. The life expectancy for white men and women was sixty-nine and seventy-one years, respectively (Sant'Anna 2001). In addition, research by Barbosa (2001) has found that black men and women have disproportionately high mortality rates before the age of fifty.

Data demonstrating the disadvantages experienced by Afro-Brazilians with respect to human development and life expectancy underscore how practices of economic and social marginalization impact the health and well-being of the African-descendant population in Brazil. Race and skin color serve as major determinants of access to wealth, education, housing, public services, health services, and information for members of African-descendant communities (Paixão 2013). These structural conditions may also place low-income Afro-Brazilians at greater risk for HIV infection.

An increasing number of studies have pointed to the importance of focusing on skin color and race for understanding how the HIV/AIDS epidemic affects different segments of the Brazilian population (Lopes et al. 2007; Taquette 2009a; Werneck 2000). Several studies have also highlighted the vulnerability of the Afro-Brazilian population in the face of the HIV/AIDS epidemic (Garcia and Souza 2010; Lopes and Werneck 2009; Miranda-Ribeiro et al. 2010; Taquette 2009a, 2009b). However, research in these areas remain markedly underdeveloped. Research focusing on gender and race also points to the role of poverty and gender violence in shaping women's vulnerability to HIV infection, especially young Afro-Brazilian women (Guimarães 2009; Lopes and Werneck 2009; Meirelles and Ruzany 2009; Taquette 2009b).

Research by Fernanda Lopes and her colleagues (2007) highlights significant differences among black and nonblack Brazilian women with regard to levels of vulnerability to HIV infection and access to adequate AIDS treatment. Lopes et al. (2007) found statistically significant differences between black and nonblack women living with HIV with regard to schooling, monthly income, and number of dependents, as well as in their opportunities to see medical professionals, speak with medical professionals about their sex lives, and have correct knowledge of the significance of T-cell count and viral load.[5] Based on their findings, Lopes et al. (2007) advocate for the inclusion of ethnicity and skin color as variables in HIV/AIDS research. They argue that the inclusion of ethnicity and skin color will enable researchers to gain a better understanding of the relationship among gender, ethnicity/race, and socioeconomic conditions in shaping black women's health risks and in limiting the resources that are invested in treatment services for them. An earlier study by Fernanda Lopes (2003) was one of the first to call attention to the disparities in AIDS treatment experienced by black women. This study provided evidence needed to address the impact of the HIV/AIDS epidemic on black communities in the city and state of São Paulo. It also had an impact on the shift to focus on AIDS and racism within the National STD/AIDS Program in the early 2000s.[6]

Research and Activism Focusing on the Feminization of HIV/AIDS

Despite Brazil's relative success in slowing rates of HIV transmission in the country, since the mid-2000s researchers and public health professionals have focused greater attention on the feminization of the AIDS epidemic, or its growth in the female population. Some Brazilian researchers began calling attention to the increasing feminization of the epidemic in the mid-1990s (Parker and Galvão 1996). Pedro Chequer, former coordinator of the National STD/ AIDS Program, recognized feminization of the epidemic in the late 1990s and highlighted the program's activities in the areas of prevention, mother-to-child transmission, and support for women living with HIV and AIDS (Chequer 1998). The federal government developed its first comprehensive plan to combat the feminization of AIDS in March 2007, when the *Plano Integrado de Enfrentamento da Feminização da Epidemia de AIDS e Outras DST* was launched by the Brazilian Ministry of Health and the Special Secretariat for the Promotion of Women's Policies. Inauguration of the plan strategically coincided with International Women's Day on March 8, 2007, and was given a good deal of attention in the Brazilian media, particularly because then-President Luiz Inácio Lula da Silva participated in a series of events related to the plan's launch. As the first initiative to combat the feminization of HIV/AIDS to be developed by a Latin American country, the plan represented an important move by the Brazilian federal government to recognize and address the impact of HIV/ AIDS on women in Brazil. However, at the same time, it can also be viewed as a decidedly tardy attempt to reverse a trend that had long been neglected.

Brazil has experienced an upsurge in rates of HIV infection among women since the early to mid-1990s. The feminization of HIV/AIDS in Brazil parallels similar developments in other countries. However, some scholars have argued that the rise in cases among women has been more rapid in Brazil than in any other country (Bastos 2001). While HIV/AIDS affected males at much higher rates during the 1980s, in the late 1980s and early 1990s heterosexual transmission had become predominant and the rates of infection among females began to surpass those among males. In 1985, there were twenty-five men for every woman with HIV/AIDS; by 1990, the ratio had reached 6:1, and in 2000 it was 2:1 (Biehl 2007, 60). The spread of the HIV virus among teenage females age thirteen to nineteen has been even more pronounced. The male to female ratio for HIV infection shifted from 0.9:1 in 1998, to 0.8:1 in 2000, and 0.6:1 in 2001. These data demonstrate that almost twice as many females were being infected than males in this age group by 2001 (Werneck 2004). Though a marked increase in rates of HIV infection among Brazilian women has been noted in epidemiological data, it has often been difficult to determine the impact of the HIV/AIDS epidemic on black women because of lack of reliable epidemiological data containing both gender and race/skin color as variables.

A number of black women's organizations have been at the forefront of efforts to bring visibility to the impact of HIV/AIDS on black communities, particularly those located in *favelas* and the urban peripheries, and developing grassroots HIV/AIDS prevention and education initiatives for these communities. Black women's organizations have played a key role in developing intersectional perspectives on HIV/AIDS that highlight the role of gender, race, and class in shaping the HIV/AIDS epidemic in Brazil. It is important to note that these organizations developed HIV/AIDS-related programs and initiatives in black communities long before the federal government and local governments did. They also initiated work in this area despite the absence of official data to verify the impact that the HIV/AIDS epidemic was having on black communities. Rather than relying on epidemiological or statistical evidence to support their work, black women activists responded to what they experienced and observed in local communities (López 2011). Black women's organizations also have engaged in citizen control with the National STD/AIDS Program to ensure that specific initiatives for the black community are developed and maintained.

Several black women's organizations have developed important and innovative HIV/AIDS-related initiatives since the late 1980s and early 1990s. Organizations such as Maria Mulher, Criola, *Associação Cultural de Mulheres Negras* (Black Women's Cultural Association, ACMUN), and the *Rede de Mulheres Negras do Paraná* (Network of Black Women of Paraná) have developed important HIV-prevention programs in cities such as Porto Alegre, Rio de Janeiro, and Curitiba. The health department of Geledés and the organization Fala Preta were also involved with HIV/AIDS-related initiatives in the city of São Paulo during the 1990s. Research has examined black women's activism related to HIV/AIDS in the southern region of Brazil, particularly in the states of Rio Grande do Sul, Paraná, and Santa Catarina (Cruz et al. 2008; López 2011; Santos 2008). Though states in southern Brazil have relatively small black populations when compared to other regions, mobilization around health for black communities has been remarkably strong. Black women's organizations, such as Maria Mulher and ACMUN, both located in the city of Porto Alegre, and the Network of Black Women of Paraná, which is based in the city of Curitiba, have been particularly important advocates of health equity for black communities. Research by Cruz et al. (2008) found that these organizations have been at the forefront of addressing the HIV/AIDS epidemic in black communities in southern Brazil, and have been more active in this area than mixed-gender organizations in the black movement.

Maria Mulher: Innovative and Holistic HIV/AIDS Initiatives

The black women's NGO Maria Mulher has been at the forefront of developing innovative programs for HIV/AIDS prevention, as well as treatment and support for African-descendant women living with HIV/AIDS. Maria Mulher was founded in the city of Porto Alegre, the capital of the state of Rio Grande do Sul, in 1987. The leaders of Maria Mulher made a conscious decision to have a presence in *bairros da periferia*, peripheral, low-income communities that have a largely African-descendant population. As Maria Noelci Teixeira Homero, also known as "Noho," a former technical coordinator for Maria Mulher, noted when I interviewed her in 2008:

> ... we make a point of being in a *vila* (poor neighborhood) because the majority of institutions distance themselves from people who are in a situation of vulnerability. We also do not use this thing of saying that the community is of the *base* (grassroots), people of the *base*, because if we say that there is a *base*, then we are legitimating those who are on top. So [for us] they are the people who are in vulnerability.

In 1999 members of Maria Mulher began to develop HIV/AIDS prevention and support services for women in Vila Cruzeiro do Sul, which is located in the southern region of Porto Alegre. Unlike many of the women served by Maria Mulher, most of the founders and members were professional and college-educated women. The organization's engagement in HIV/AIDS prevention resulted from members' growing recognition of the impact the disease was having in the community. It was also the result of an organic progression that developed from focusing on the issue of child abuse to focusing on the domestic violence experienced by mothers who were abusing their children and then realizing that women who experienced domestic violence were often more vulnerable to HIV infection, owing to unequal power dynamics in their relationships with their male partners.[7] Members of Maria Mulher were initially invited to the Vila Cruzeiro do Sul region in 1997 to develop a research project and do an assessment related to child abuse and family structures in the neighborhood. A year to two years later, they began working in the neighborhood on an ongoing basis.

In 2000 Maria Mulher began to use a two-story community center in Cruzeiro do Sul that belonged to the local Methodist church. The building contained a computer lab, rooms for meetings and film screenings, office space, areas for job training in paper recycling and hairstyling, as well as a kitchen. In 2006, the multipurpose space used for film screenings was designated as a *Ponto de Cultura* (Culture Point) by the Brazilian Ministry of Culture, which was then under the direction of musician Gilberto Gil. Films focusing on women and issues such as domestic violence, including U.S. films like *The Color Purple,* were regularly shown in the Ponto de Cultura at Maria Mulher.

A 2008 study conducted by members of ACMUN and university researchers found that approximately four hundred women living with HIV had been assisted by Maria Mulher by that time (Cruz et al. 2008). The majority of the women were infected by male partners who used intravenous drugs, and only three women had been infected through heterosexual sexual contact. The staff of Maria Mulher realized that most women did not use condoms as a method of HIV prevention, often because they were married or in long-term relationships, and also had difficulty following their treatment regimen after being diagnosed with HIV. In many cases, this owed to women's lack of access to adequate and nutritious food. In addition, many women transmitted the virus to their children because they were unaware of their HIV-positive status (Cruz et al. 2008).

Maria Mulher's decision to focus on HIV/AIDS as a primary area of concern and intervention is supported by epidemiological data for the state of Rio Grande do Sul and the city of Porto Alegre. Between 2009 and 2013 Rio Grande do Sul ranked number one of all units of the Brazilian federation in terms of its AIDS index (Ministério da Saúde 2014). These data ranked all twenty-six Brazilian states and the national capital, Brasília, which is a federal district. The city of Porto Alegre also ranked number one of all Brazilian capitals with respect to its AIDS index for the same time period (Ministério da Saúde 2014). In 2006, the Gloria-Cruzeiro-Cristal region, where Cruzeiro do Sul is located, had an AIDS incidence rate of 107.7 cases per 100,000 residents. This rate was markedly higher than most other areas of the city, which had incidence rates in the range of 56.7 to 79.6 (Secretaria Municipal de Saúde de Porto Alegre 2008).

During the 2000s, Maria Mulher launched several important education and prevention programs, as well as income generation and social and economic support programs for women and adolescents in the Cruzeiro do Sul region. These initiatives were developed based on community needs and input. As Noho observed during our 2008 interview: "We elaborated these services according to the need of the local community. We always work with the local needs. With the local demands . . . of women." She went on to state:

For example every and whatever course of professional formation that we have is the result of the self-esteem encounters, the individual and group encounters that we have with the women. And also from the contact with the community that we have one time per week and that we do for the whole community, not only the women, it is the whole community. It is the result of this.

The holistic nature of Maria Mulher's work related to HIV/AIDS prevention and treatment was unique among organizations that did work in this area during the 2000s and early 2010s. I was impressed by the organization's work when I first visited their site in Cruzeiro do Sul in March 2007. Although I was familiar with several black women's organizations in different cities, prior to visiting Maria Mulher I had never seen an organization with the depth and breadth of its activities and programs. The organization's site also allowed it to have a permanent presence in the community and develop a wide range of programs.

While domestic violence and HIV/AIDS are at the heart of Maria Mulher's mission and the services and programs it provides, the staff is keenly aware of the complex web of factors that make poor, African-descendant women vulnerable to HIV infection. Maria Mulher has developed programs and initiatives that address the continuum of needs experienced by low-income and poor women, adolescents, and families in Vila Cruzeiro do Sul. As noted above, the organization's programs have typically developed out of the perceived needs of women and families in the community. A 2006 study conducted by Maria Mulher identified lack of access to food as a major factor that prevented HIV positive women in Cruzeiro do Sul from taking their medications (Maria Mulher 2006). The study also explored the perspectives of women living with HIV who experienced domestic violence, thus making important empirical and programmatic links between gendered violence and HIV vulnerability. As a result of this research, the staff of Maria Mulher began income generation programs for HIV-positive women in the community.

Research conducted by black women's organizations, such as Maria Mulher and ACMUN, provided evidence of the health needs of local communities and the types of HIV/AIDS initiatives and programs that existed or might work best in the future. They also followed the tradition of documenting the health experiences of black communities, particularly those of black women, that was started by black women's organizations such as Geledés in the early 1990s (Geledés 1991a, 1991b). These studies and publications served as important informational and documentation sources, given the lack of research on the health of the black population and black women during the 1990s and 2000s (Lebon 2007).

During the 2000s, Maria Mulher developed job training and income generation programs with partners such as the National Network of People Living with HIV/AIDS (*Rede Nacional de Pessoas Vivendo com HIV/Aids*), which donated machines so HIV-positive women could make bags with recycled plastic. Women who participated in this program at Maria Mulher sold the bags to earn money that enabled them to buy food and adhere to their HIV treatment regimen. Paper recycling, food and clothing production, computer classes, and hair care were other key areas in which Maria Mulher provided job training for women in the community. The organization also launched a literacy program for women in the community to enable those living with HIV to read their medications and take them properly. These programs strengthened women's professional and life skills and also increased their self-esteem.

Though Maria Mulher provides social services and nutritional programs, such as distributing the *cesta básica* (food basket), with support from the municipal government, members of the organization have attempted to avoid creating a relationship of dependence for women who receive assistance and instead has tried to promote self-sufficiency and economic independence, particularly through job training programs. Maria Mulher's programs and activities have been funded by the Fund for Mini-Projects of the Southern Region of Porto Alegre and federal ministries, including the Ministry of Health, the Ministry of Justice, and the Ministry of Culture. International organizations such as the Global Fund for Women and UNESCO (United Nations Educational, Scientific, and Cultural Organization) have also funded Maria Mulher's programs. In addition, the organization formed partnerships with the municipal, state, and federal STD/AIDS programs. Members of Maria Mulher and ACMUN were also part of the coordinating committee of the Feminist Health Network/RedeSaúde from 2008 to 2010, when the Rede was based in the city of Porto Alegre. Both organizations were able to push for discussions of black women's reproductive health and issues such as HIV/AIDS through their close involvement with the Rede during this time.

Maria Mulher's HIV/AIDS prevention work focused on the links between gender, race, class, and HIV/AIDS vulnerability. As Cruz et al. note:

> The work of Maria Mulher integrates various dimensions: a view of the family as the nucleus of cooperation; the perception of how the racial factor (*recorte*) operates in everyday life; the implementation of income generation projects that improve living conditions and care for one's health in a holistic manner. [2008, 47]

To encourage HIV/AIDS prevention among adolescents in Vila Cruzeiro do Sul, members of Maria Mulher began programs that engaged youth in the community, both young women and men. In 2007 a six-month pilot project called *Jovens Lideranças* (Young Leaders) was launched with adolescents and young adults between sixteen and twenty-two years of age. The project included a cohort of twenty young people, ten young women and ten young men. Sessions were held on Friday afternoons and all day on Saturdays and included discussion topics such as domestic violence and relationships between men and women.

Maria Mulher's staff also provided social services and psychological support to women living with HIV/AIDS. Maria Mulher's project "Caring for Health is a Woman's Thing" (*Cuidar da Saúde é Coisa de Mulher*) offered services in Cruzeiro do Sul through home visits and weekly services provided by the staff for the entire community, including men, women, children, and senior citizens (Cruz et al. 2008). Orientations and referrals were offered for medical and hospital services, as well as juridical assistance. The team was comprised of social workers, psychologists, nurses, educators, and nutritionists. This project also involved showing videos and distributing information about prevention of STDs and HIV/AIDS, as well as about violence. In addition to collective meetings, individual assistance was also provided to community members as part of this project.

Maria Mulher's work in the Vila Cruzeiro do Sul region is deeply anchored in members' awareness of the "social vulnerability" that characterizes the lives of women in the community. As Noho noted:

> It is this social vulnerability. They are subjected to all of the atrocities that come from being people who do not have access to information, to work, to education, to schooling, to health and this really is extremely precarious. The living conditions, the conditions of habitation.

In addition to the social vulnerability described above, women who participate in Maria Mulher's programs also experience a community context of violence, which according to Noho, made them "hostages to the drug traffic, hostages of the drug traffickers, hostages of drugs. . . . This situation grabs these women and kills these women."

On several occasions, Noho also spoke of the "perverse" impact that being diagnosed with HIV had on women. For women who resided in Cruzeiro do Sul, an HIV diagnosis could often lead to a better quality of life than they experienced prior to being diagnosed, because they were provided access to food, health care, and social services not previously available to them. Ironically, their lives improved after being informed of their HIV diagnosis. According to Noho:

> . . . before for people who were not living with AIDS the health care (*atenção*) was very precarious. When a woman begins living with AIDS, she begins to have health care (*atenção*) she did not have. These people even begin to valorize and even say this perversity. [They say] "My life improved after I had AIDS." This is cruel, very cruel. And it really did improve . . .

While Noho's observations highlight Brazil's effectiveness in providing low-income and poor women with benefits and improved care after being diagnosed with HIV, they also point to gaps in existing health-care and social service programs. Her comments suggest that although, in theory, the SUS provides universal and free access to health care for all Brazilian citizens, the reality is bleaker. This leads to average citizens not receiving the best quality care, unless perhaps they are diagnosed with a serious illness, such as HIV, for which social and medical support services are offered.

Anthropologist João Biehl has written extensively about AIDS treatment in Brazil and its relationship to poor individuals living with HIV/AIDS (Biehl 2004, 2007, 2009). In an analysis of the services provided at a house of support for individuals living with HIV/AIDS in Salvador, Biehl noted that, "former noncitizens have an unprecedented opportunity to claim a new identity around their politicized biology, with the support of international and national, public and private funds" (2004, 122). Biehl has also noted that poor and marginalized individuals have access to a "novel social and biomedical inclusion" as AIDS patients (2004, 122), a phenomenon similar to what has happened for many of the women Maria Mulher serves.

State Action to Address the HIV/AIDS Epidemic among the Black Population

During the early 2000s, the National STD/AIDS Program began to acknowledge potential racial differences in how the HIV/AIDS epidemic was affecting black and white Brazilians. The shift toward increased discussion of race, racism, and AIDS occurred within a broader context of the post-Durban race policy environment, as well as the debate over affirmative action policies in Brazil. In addition, the creation of the Special Secretariat for the Promotion of Racial Equality Policies (SEPPIR) by President Lula in March 2003 increased discussion and implementation of race-conscious policies at the federal level.[8]

In 2004 the National STD/AIDS Program published an Epidemiological Bulletin that highlighted the growth of the HIV/AIDS epidemic within the *preto* and *pardo* segments of the population, as well as among individuals with low levels of education (Ministério da Saúde 2004). In response to these data, the National STD/AIDS Program began to develop initiatives focusing on the black population in 2004, and the national campaign for HIV/AIDS prevention targeted black Brazilians the following year. The slogan for the 2005 campaign was "AIDS and Racism—Brazil has to live without Prejudice." The campaign featured a poster with an image of a smiling black woman with long, braided hair, holding a condom in her hands as if she were serving it to the viewer (figure 6.1). Because many black Brazilian women continue to work in service jobs, particularly domestic work, this image can be seen as reinforcing a social representation of black women as servants. The fact that the woman was serving the condom also implies that it would be used by someone else, rather than

FIGURE 6.1. Poster for National 2005 HIV-Prevention Campaign. Health Ministry of Brazil

being used by the woman in her own sexual encounters as a form of protection or HIV risk reduction. It should also be noted that black Brazilian feminists criticized HIV prevention campaigns that featured images of black women that were viewed as being hypersexualized (Fry et al. 2007a). Critical examination of these images and representations highlights the potential for black women to be portrayed in HIV prevention campaigns in stereotypical and problematic ways. This also underscores the need for an intersectional approach that goes beyond race-only or gender-only framework with respect to the imagery and forms of representation used in HIV prevention campaigns.

The caption on the poster from the 2004 national HIV/AIDS campaign states, "You have the right to information, prevention, and treatment for AIDS. Your color does not matter." By calling attention to racism, this caption provided an important challenge to common beliefs within the Brazilian health system, and Brazilian society more generally, that most people were color blind and, thus, racial discrimination was not an important issue. It should also be noted that use of the phrase "Your color does not matter" implied that nonwhite Brazilians faced particular forms of discrimination, while at the same time suggesting that having a "colored" phenotype was socially undesirable. Saraiva Felipe, then minister of health in Brazil, made a statement when the campaign was launched, observing:

> We decided to have a special view for the Afro-descendant Brazilians because we verified an increase in the number of AIDS cases in this population. We decided along with NGOs, with the Special Secretariat for the Promotion of Racial Equality Policies (SEPPIR) and with black celebrities to give a focus, calling attention to the links between racism, poverty, and the increase in cases in this segment of the Brazilian population. These are people who, by being in the most poor stratum of society, have less access to health information and services, within the context of poverty and racial discrimination in the country. [Quoted in Fry et al. 2007a, 498]

Saraiva Felipe's statements were important for several reasons: (1) they expressed official state acknowledgement of the growth of AIDS cases within the Afro-descendant population; (2) they highlighted the relationship between race and class in the spread of HIV/AIDS in the Afro-descendant population; and (3) they recognized how racial and class inequalities might lead to disparities in access to health information and services. Felipe's comments constituted the first public acknowledgment by a Brazilian minister of health of the impact of racial discrimination on black Brazilians' health status. As noted in chapter 3, Felipe's successor, José Agenor Álvares da Silva, publicly recognized the existence of institutional racism in the SUS the following year, in 2006, further highlighting the Ministry of Health's role in calling attention to and taking responsibility for challenging racial inequities in health.

Shifts in official discourse within the Ministry of Health were similar to President Fernando Henrique Cardoso's acknowledgment of the existence of racism in Brazil. This acknowledgment came in a November 1995 speech given during an event related to the march commemorating the three hundredth anniversary of the death of Zumbi of Palmares, also known as the Marcha Zumbi (Zumbi March). In all of these cases, leading government officials played a pivotal role in creating new possibilities for developing policy proposals focused on redressing racial inequalities. Prior to this point, government officials often dismissed political demands made by black movement activists. However, by the mid-2000s, the Brazilian state, particularly at the federal level, had become both a stakeholder and an advocate in efforts to challenge racism, both symbolically and substantively, particularly through the establishment of SEPPIR.

As part of the National STD/AIDS Program's efforts to address the impact of HIV/AIDS on black communities, it launched Afroatitude: Integrated Program of Affirmative Action for Blacks during the December 2004 commemorations for World AIDS Day (Bruck 2006). The Afroatitude Program resulted from a collaboration among the National AIDS Program, the Secretariat for Higher Education in the Ministry of Education, the Special Secretariat for Human Rights, and SEPPIR. Afroatitude was originally conceptualized as a way to promote affirmative action policies within the health sector and support African-descendant college students financially, because many students from low-income backgrounds often had to choose between working to support their families and/or themselves and studying full time. The program provided one-year research fellowships to five hundred undergraduate affirmative action students (*cotistas,* or quota students) at ten federal and state universities where affirmative action programs were in place.[9] The program offered these students opportunities to engage in HIV/AIDS-related research and other research focusing on black communities. Karen Bruck, a staff member in the National Program for STDs and AIDS who was responsible for the Afroatitude Program, wrote in a 2006 publication:

> Although the objectives of the Brasil Afroatitude Program are at the interfaces between racial inequalities and vulnerability to HIV/AIDS, this governmental policy deems the camp of affirmative action as a strategy to minimize these inequalities and, consequently, vulnerability to HIV. With this Program, the PN-DST/AIDS (National Program for STDs/AIDS) assumed

the commitment to promote a strategy of strengthening the policy of affirmative action, through means of granting scholarships, related to the theme "AIDS and Racism" for black quota students. [Bruck 2006, 15]

The Afroatitude Program was a direct result of policy discussions and initiatives related to affirmative action that were taking place in the federal government, as well as at public universities throughout the country during the early 2000s. It should also be noted that this initiative likely would not have come about without broader discursive and policy shifts related to race. In addition, the program sought to meet two critical needs related to health research and support of diversity in higher education by funding black affirmative action students to undertake HIV/AIDS research. As I discuss below, the program was criticized for not being solely focused on HIV/AIDS research, as well as for promoting racialized notions of health. The National AIDS Program funded Afroatitude for two years (2005–2007). Funding for the program was initially only supposed to last for one year, but owing to the successes achieved during the program's first year, it extended the funding.[10] After that time, funding needed to come from individual universities and other sectors of the federal government, such as the Ministry of Education, to continue the program at each university. Though the National AIDS Program provided initial funding for Afroatitude as a pilot project, the program was not sustainable without financial support, particularly given the high number of students who participated.[11]

In March 2006, the Brazilian Ministry of Health launched a Strategic Affirmative Action Program focusing on the black population and AIDS (*Programa Estratégico de Ações Afirmativas: População Negra e Aids*). This program was developed in collaboration with SEPPIR, the Special Secretariat for Human Rights, and the Ministry of Education. A publication outlining the program's goals stated that it "comes from the perspective that racism, like sexism and homophobia, are factors in the production of vulnerability to HIV/AIDS for people and communities of the black population" (Ministério da Saúde 2006b, 10).

The Strategic Affirmative Action Program focused on four areas: 1) Policy Implementation; 2) Promotion of Partnerships; 3) Knowledge Production; and 4) Capacity-building and Communication (Ministério da Saúde 2006a). The overall objective of the program was to promote equity and the human rights of the black population. In the area of policy implementation, the program sought to encourage inclusion of race/color and socioeconomic variables in all of the information systems controlled by the National AIDS Program, and also to include these variables in all epidemiological analyses, research, and projects developed by the National AIDS Program. Challenging racism was a transversal, or crosscutting, theme in all projects developed by the National AIDS Program and was also an important policy action item. Support for the Afroatitude Program was prioritized as an action item in the areas of policy implementation and partnership promotion. As part of the partnership promotion goals related to Afroatitude, the Strategic Affirmative Action Program outlined the need for support meetings, seminars, and other activities focusing on racism and vulnerability to HIV/AIDS in partnership with social movements and universities participating in the Afroatitude Program. The program's goals in the areas of communication and capacity building focused on including race/color in instructional and reference materials, as well as including racism as a transversal theme in publications, posters, and pamphlets produced by the National AIDS Program.

As can be seen from table 6.1, most of the programs and initiatives described above took place within a three-year period, from 2004 to 2006. During this time, there was increased discussion of the need to develop specific federal-level HIV/AIDS research and prevention initiatives for the black population. In addition, the presence of two ministers of health, Saraiva Felipe (2005–2006) and José Agenor Álvares da Silva (2006–2007), who demonstrated sensitivity to racial issues and a willingness to speak openly about them, seemed to create an opening for initiatives focusing on the black population within the National AIDS Program. It should also be noted that these developments paralleled the increasing discussion of other race-conscious policy and legislative proposals that took place during the early 2000s, most notably the Statute of Racial Equality and the Law of Quotas within the Brazilian Congress, in addition to affirmative action policies more generally. Both the Statute of Racial Equality and the Law of Quotas generated a great deal of controversy and public debate, as well as opposition (Santos et al. 2011). Any progress, as well as setbacks, that

Table 6.1. National HIV/AIDS Programs and Initiatives Focusing on the Black Population

2004	Epidemiological Bulletin published by Brazilian Ministry of Health highlights growth of HIV/AIDS epidemic in black population
2004	National STD/AIDS Program begins to develop prevention initiatives for black population
2004/2005	Afroatitude Program is launched in ten federal and state universities for black quota students
2005	"AIDS and Racism" HIV/AIDS Prevention Campaign is launched by National STD/AIDS Program
2006	Brazilian Ministry of Health launches Strategic Affirmative Action Program: Black Population and AIDS

occurred with respect to HIV/AIDS prevention for the black population during this time should certainly be considered within this broader and highly complex discursive and policy environment. After 2006, the momentum that had been generated around HIV/AIDS initiatives focusing on the black population seemed to wane. During this time, there was also a marked increase in open critiques of race-conscious policies, which I discuss in the next section.

Challenges to Racially Specific HIV/AIDS Prevention Initiatives

Efforts to develop specific HIV/AIDS initiatives and prevention campaigns for the black community, particularly those initiated by the National STD/AIDS Program, were critiqued by many of the scholars who challenged affirmative action and other race-conscious public policies during the mid and late 2000s. Most of the criticisms of racially specific HIV/AIDS initiatives made by these scholars emphasized the importance of universalist policies and expressed concern that linking race and health would legitimize outdated and scientifically invalid beliefs about race. In 2007, Peter Fry, an anthropology professor at the Federal University of Rio de Janeiro (UFRJ) and several scholars from FIOCRUZ (*Fundação Oswaldo Cruz*), the leading public health institution in Brazil, began to challenge specific HIV/AIDS prevention campaigns for the African-descendant population. In a March 2007 article published in the academic journal *Cadernos de Saúde Pública,* Fry and his colleagues articulated their position on racially specific HIV/AIDS initiatives, stating:

> We are suggesting that the most recent governmental campaign of HIV/AIDS prevention, focused on the racial theme, may prejudice the national effort against the epidemic. This program, which has been widely recognized internationally, continues to be based on the principles of universality, equity and *integralidade* (comprehensiveness) that orient public policies in the area of health in Brazil. However, the racialization of AIDS is, for certain, a new element (and we would affirm it as being a troubling one) in the complex epidemiological and sociopolitical dynamic of the epidemic. [Fry et al. 2007a, 505]

As can be seen above, Fry and his collaborators juxtaposed universal, equitable, and comprehensive health policies, which were viewed as characterizing the SUS, with racialized policies, which they viewed as "troubling."

In March 2007, Fry also published a single-authored op-ed piece in the leading Brazilian newspaper *Folha de São Paulo* titled "Afinal, aids tem cor ou raça no Brasil?" (In the end, does AIDS have a color or race in Brazil?). This commentary provides a strong critique of race-conscious health policies, stating:

> Our interpretation is that the logic of the programs focused on the "health of the black population" have as their presupposition that Brazilians can and should be classified into impervious categories (white and blacks), each with its own specificities in the field of health. As self-fulfilling prophecies, these policies can transform their presuppositions into realities. The emphasis on the association between race and health can have as a consequence the naturalization and strengthening of supposed racial differences between population groups, minimizing the social and historical genesis of them. [Fry 2007]

The positions held by Fry and his collaborators were also articulated, however, in greater detail, in the earlier *Cadernos* article. Both pieces critiqued the growing emphasis on color/race and AIDS in Brazil as being part of a political strategy of racializing HIV/AIDS as a health problem, with the ultimate goal being to strengthen "identities with racial contours" (Fry et al. 2007a, 504). It is important to note that Fry and his collaborators published their work in Brazil's leading newspaper and public health journal. These scholars' access to leading publishing venues underscores the academic capital they held and how it provided entre to influential vehicles of both scholarly and public opinion. This access was also likely facilitated by the fact that the owners and editors of these publishing venues were often sympathetic to views opposing race-conscious public policies, such as affirmative action and health policies for the black population. This degree of access to major media and scholarly outlets has rarely been available to black activists or scholars.

Fry's op-ed in the *Folha de São Paulo* analyzes the role President Cardoso's and President Lula's administrations played in providing an opening for black movement demands between 2000 and 2005, and notes that the state became increasingly more "permeable" to such demands during this time.[12] Fry's commentary expressed a negative view of the level of state responsiveness to civil society concerns and demands. João Biehl's (2004, 2007, 2009) work underscores the increasingly activist role taken on by the state during the Cardoso presidency, particularly with respect to HIV/AIDS and the provision of AIDS pharmaceuticals. In fact, Biehl found that in a 2003 interview with President Cardoso, he discussed AIDS as a "microcosm of a new state-society partnership" and expressed his support for what he termed a "porous state so that society could have room for action in it" (2009, 487). Biehl's research points to Cardoso's self-awareness regarding state-civil society relations and highlights the fact that his administration's openness to civil society was intentional.

The final paragraphs of Fry's commentary critique the "ironies" and "paradoxes" of focusing on the growth of HIV/AIDS cases in the black population, noting that such a focus tends to link racial identities to discussions of high-risk groups. Fry also argues against discussions of race and health, owing to the danger of encouraging beliefs in biological and racial determinism. These critiques also focused on the potential pitfalls of the "racialization" of health.

The article by Fry et al. (2007a) published in *Cadernos de Saúde Pública* was part of a special debate in the journal. The debate contained eight responses to the Fry et al. article, most of which supported the arguments and critiques made by Fry and his collaborators. In a response to the article, public health researcher Claudia Travassos argued that epidemiological data on HIV/AIDS based on race/color is unreliable because the percentages of cases in which color was not recorded (or was ignored) varied between 41.5 and 88 percent (Travassos 2007). In addition, she notes that the quality of existing data had been questioned because the data in SINAN (*Sistema de Informação de Agravos de Notificação*) was based on data coming from two other databases, SIS-CEL (*Sistema de Controle de Exames Laboratoriais*) and SICLOM (*Sistema de Controle Logístico de Medicamentos*). Travassos also argues that universalized access to AIDS treatment in Brazil sought to challenge the discrimination and stigmatization that often characterized the disease and "represent a posture against whatever type of segregation" (2007, 519).[13]

The lone dissenting response to the Fry et al. article was written by Marcelo Paixão and Fernanda Lopes, the only black researchers who participated in the debate. As mentioned earlier, Lopes did pioneering work on HIV/AIDS prevention and treatment for black women in São Paulo and has also been instrumental in the development of health policies for the black population. She worked for the British Department for International Development (DFID) in Brazil during the implementation of the Program to Combat Institutional Racism (PCRI) and later worked with the United Nations Population Fund (UNFPA) on projects related to the health of Brazil's black population. Marcelo Paixão is a sociologist who has done pioneering research on racial differences in the Human Development Index in Brazil.[14] In their response, Paixão and Lopes (2007) recognize some of the same problems regarding the inadequacy of existing HIV/AIDS data highlighted by Fry et al. However, they also argue for the importance of finding ways to assess the impact of the HIV/AIDS epidemic on the black population. Paixão and Lopes openly challenge scholars who oppose a research focus on the black population, noting:

> For Fry et al., in the sole hope of not racializing the debate about public policies in Brazil, these [health] differentials should be maintained as prohibited

terms, taboos; they should be discussed only and exclusively within academic circles and/or research groups. In spite of the gravity of the situations studied, research that analyzes data disaggregated by race/color are seen by the authors as ills in themselves, as if the debate about racial inequalities and their impact on health outcomes necessarily implies the defense of racially supremacist perspectives. [2007, 512]

The positions stated by Fry et al. and Paixão and Lopes highlight the divergent perspectives on the importance of focusing on racial health disparities that existed in Brazilian academic circles during the late 2000s. While Paixão and Lopes advocated the use of race as a variable in public health research, Fry et al. argued that this would reinforce biologically based and scientifically invalid beliefs about racial difference. As noted previously, critiques of specific HIV prevention initiatives for the black population were in line with Fry et al.'s resistance to a variety of race-conscious public policies, including affirmative action. Given this broader political and policy context, the legitimacy of developing a focus on the black population within HIV/AIDS research and policies was hotly contested by the late 2000s.

In addition to opposing affirmative action and specific health policies for the black population, as noted in chapter 3, some of the scholars who were part of the group mentioned above were also critical of programs such as Afroatitude. One member of this group, Simone Monteiro, published an essay that describes an unpleasant encounter with students in the Afroatitude Program during the VI Brazilian Congress for STD and AIDS Prevention in November 2006 (Monteiro 2007). During a congress session in which she was a speaker, an Afroatitude student openly accused Monteiro of being racist for opposing specific health policies for the black population and also for the critiques made by Monteiro and some of her colleagues in a recently published newspaper op-ed. In this piece titled, "O SUS é Racista?" ["The SUS is Racist?'] Marcos Chor Maio, Simone Monteiro, and Paulo Henrique Almeida Rodrigues question Minister of Health José Agenor Álvares da Silva's proclamation that racism was present in SUS services on the October 2006 National Day of Mobilization for the Health of the Black Population (Maio et al. 2007). The authors argue that, while there might be "manifestations of prejudice and discrimination" on the part of some health professionals, there was not sufficient evidence to prove that institutional racism existed within the SUS (Maio et al., 2007, 237). In doing so, the authors challenge the idea that racism was systemic and institutional; instead arguing that "prejudice" and "discrimination" took individual forms. These perspectives also reinforced longstanding cultural beliefs that focused on prejudice rather than racism, as well as individual versus structural and systemic forms of discrimination. They also ran counter to the type of work the Program to Combat Institutional Racism (PCRI) initiated in cities such as Salvador and Recife in the mid-2000s.

In Monteiro's essay on the Afroatitude Program, "Programa Afroatitude: a fabricação de uma identidade racial?" (Afroatitude Program: The Fabrication of a Racial Identity?), she openly critiques the Afroatitude Program for promoting racialized approaches to health and HIV/AIDS prevention and treatment (Monteiro 2007). Monteiro argues that the research projects carried out by students who participated in Afroatitude linked race, racial discrimination, and AIDS and many of the projects did not focus on HIV/AIDS, although this was one of the program's stated goals. On this basis, Monteiro argues that Afroatitude could not be considered a valid research program. According to Monteiro, "this initiative is an affirmation of the Brazilian racial collision, the strengthening of networks of black students and the celebration of racialized affirmative action" (2007, 248). Monteiro also states that in highlighting the importance of universalist policies, she and her colleagues are not promoting a destructive perspective, and encourage students in Afroatitude to reconsider their characterization of such critiques as "racist." Monteiro closes her essay by pointing to the risks of legitimating the biological concept of race "and, in this way, reinforcing racial prejudice and preventing actions of [HIV/AIDS] prevention and assistance" (2007, 249).

The writings discussed above offer important insights into critiques that have been made of race-conscious HIV/AIDS prevention and research initiatives. The critiques articulated by Peter Fry, Simone Monteiro, and their colleagues portrayed universalist HIV/AIDS policies and programs as being preferable to ones that were racially specific or targeted the black population. These scholars also suggested that invocations of race would lead to problematic conceptualizations of health in Brazil that would legitimize erroneous, biologically based notions of racial difference. Given the fact that many of the scholars in this group are anthropologists, it is useful to consider these critiques in light of the racialist and racist history of the field. As a number of scholars have noted, the fields of ethnology and physical anthropology played a central role in the development of scientific racism, as well as in providing scholarly justifications for European imperialism in Africa and other regions of the world during the nineteenth and twentieth centuries (Baker 1998; Gould 1996[1981]; Harrison 1995).

While many of the criticisms of race-specific HIV/AIDS initiatives discussed above may be viewed as part of a larger scholarly attack on affirmative action and policies for the black population, they also highlight the complexities of implementing these initiatives in the Brazilian context. Moreover, they raise a series of important questions regarding the use of race in HIV/AIDS initiatives in Brazil, such as: Is it ever necessary to invoke and utilize race in HIV/AIDS prevention efforts as a way to reach the black population and also call attention to potential disparities in access to testing, diagnosis, and treatment? Perhaps put a slightly different way, when is race a useful category of analysis and policy making with respect to HIV/AIDS prevention and treatment in Brazil? In addition, can the HIV/AIDS prevention and treatment needs of the black population adequately be addressed through universalist policies that do not acknowledge or address race or racial inequalities?

White Racial Privilege and/in the Brazilian Academy

In addition to the issues discussed above, it is also important to consider how race- and class-based differentials in social capital, access, and opportunity shape the research process in Brazil with respect to HIV/AIDS research, as well as health research more generally. Researchers such as Kátia Guimarães (2009) have argued that white racial privilege and power have perpetuated the lack of HIV/AIDS research focusing on race and the experiences of Afro-Brazilians. The majority of the critics of race-conscious health policies discussed in this chapter, as well as in chapter 3, are either white Brazilians or white foreigners who reside in Brazil; however, the question of white academic privilege was never explicitly marked or mentioned in their critiques of health policies for the black population. Moreover, critics of race-conscious health policies have rarely acknowledged the underrepresentation of black health researchers within Brazilian universities and prestigious research institutions, such as FIOCRUZ. As one example, Monteiro's aforementioned criticisms of the Afroatitude Program elide and downplay very real racial inequalities and inequities that exist at all levels of higher education in Brazil, from undergraduate students to high-level faculty and administrators.

Anthropologist José Jorge de Carvalho, one of the architects of the affirmative action program at the University of Brasília, has written about the "racial confinement" of universities and academic spaces in Brazil (Carvalho 2005). Carvalho's work calls attention to the fact that 1 percent or less of faculty at major Brazilian universities, such as the University of São Paulo, the Federal University of Rio de Janeiro, the University of Campinas, and the Federal University of Minas Gerais, were black. Importantly, Carvalho's analysis highlights the near absence of black faculty at major universities in Brazil and discusses the implications of racial "segregation" and "apartheid" in the academy for the production of knowledge about race from a nondominant perspective (Carvalho 2005). It should also be noted that Carvalho's observations regarding white racial privilege at the University of Brasília were a major motivation leading to his advocacy of affirmative action policies at the university in the early 2000s. In a 2010 study of the number of black women with doctorates in Brazil, Brazilian sociologist Joselina da Silva found that between 1991 and 2005, out of a total of 63,234 individuals, both male and female, holding doctorates only 251 black women did (Silva 2011). This amounted to black women holding 0.39 percent of doctorates and had important consequences for the types of research and teaching that could be carried out on questions of race and gender in Brazil, including in health-related areas.

Organizations such as the Association of Black Brazilian Researchers (*Associação Brasileira de Pesquisadores/as Negros/as*, ABPN) and congresses of black researchers, such as COPENE (*Congresso de Pesquisadores/as Negros/as*), were launched in the early 2000s as a way to increase the visibility of black researchers in Brazil, as well as to provide networking opportunities for them. Along with the ABPN, these congresses regularly included thematic discussions on the health of the black population and were instrumental in building a new cadre of researchers and publications in this area.

Though affirmative action policies in undergraduate admissions have highlighted the fact that affluent, white Brazilians have long comprised the majority of public university students, issues yet to be resolved include promoting the advancement of black students into graduate programs, the professoriate, and respected research positions. Recognition of these issues can be seen in developments such as the approval of affirmative action in all graduate programs at the *Universidade Federal de Goiás* (Federal University of Goiás, UFG) in May 2015. This policy called for 20 percent of all graduate school admission slots to be filled by students who are *negro, pardo,* or indigenous (Túlio 2015).

Conclusion

This chapter opened by referring to the film *Odô Yá* as a representation of efforts to bring visibility to the cultural dimensions of HIV/AIDS prevention and treatment within Afro-Brazilian communities. While the *Odô Yá* project and film provide a point of departure for thinking about the potential role of Afro-Brazilian culture and religion in promoting HIV/AIDS prevention efforts, they also raise the important question of cultural specificity with respect to HIV/AIDS prevention and treatment. Though culture and race are distinct concepts, they are closely interrelated, and often inseparable, for groups that are marginalized on the basis of both. In addition, consideration of culture can open the door to consider potential racial disparities in the effectiveness of HIV/AIDS policies. However this may not always happen.

It is important to note that most HIV/AIDS-related initiatives for the black population have focused on prevention, rather than treatment. This likely owes to the assumption or presumption that Brazil's universal AIDS treatment policies adequately meet the needs of all individuals living with HIV. However, studies such as Biehl's (2007) highlight gaps in universal AIDS treatment. As mentioned earlier, Biehl's analysis calls attention to the class-based dimensions of these gaps, for poor and low-income individuals, yet fails to address how race may also serve as a factor in terms of access to treatment for African-descendant individuals. The work of organizations such as Maria Mulher also points to the intersection of gender, race, and class in shaping black women's vulnerability to HIV, as well as their inability to effectively utilize available AIDS treatments because of food insecurity. Further research is also needed to determine the effectiveness of Brazil's AIDS treatment policies in reaching the black population.

As this chapter highlights, efforts to highlight and make visible the specific and differential impact of the HIV/AIDS epidemic on Afro-Brazilians have often been critiqued and viewed as threats to Brazil's recent tradition of universalist approaches to health and HIV/AIDS prevention and treatment. Since the early 2000s, the development of HIV/AIDS prevention initiatives for the black population has also been subject to larger political debates about the efficacy, appropriateness, and legality of race-conscious policy initiatives, most notably affirmative action.

Conclusion

The Limits of Universality and the Urgency of Intersectionality

This book has examined some of the key issues shaping efforts to achieve gender and racial health equity in Brazil. While Brazil continues to face a number of challenges in fully achieving health equity, it is important to recognize areas in which substantial progress has been achieved. During the 1990s, Brazil's public health policies and the establishment of the Unified Health System (SUS) placed the country far ahead of many of its Latin American neighbors, as well as more economically developed countries, such as the United States. In addition, Brazil's pioneering HIV/AIDS prevention and treatment initiatives and notable successes in curbing the HIV/AIDS epidemic have served as important models globally.

Significant improvements in the collection of health data by color/race also took place during the 2000s and early 2010s, which placed Brazil at the forefront of collecting data by color/race for health issues such as maternal mortality within the Latin American region (Paixão 2013). Brazil's National Policy for the Integral Health of the Black Population (PNSIPN) and the existence of federal government institutions focusing on policies to address racial inequalities, such as SEPPIR (Secretariat for the Promotion of Racial Equality Policies), also made Brazil a pioneer with respect to acknowledging and addressing racial disparities in health when compared to most other Latin American countries. These developments were due, at least in part, to decades-long activism by black health activists, particularly black women, as well as changes in state discourse and policy following the 2001 World Conference against Racism.

On the Limits of Universality

As noted throughout this study, the principle of universality has been central to the development and functioning of the SUS in Brazil. Though grounded in socialist principles and a commitment to provide universal access to health care for all Brazilians, many of the health equity issues examined in this study highlight the shortcomings of a universalist approach to health. During her tenure as the first federal minister in charge of SEPPIR, Matilde Ribeiro wrote about the limitations of universalist government policies in the areas of education, work, and health. As she observed: "Universalist policies, which should not have their merit diminished, since they allow for the citizenship inclusion of a great number of the population, are not an end in themselves" (UNDP 2005, 127).

The increased expansion of and legitimacy accorded to affirmative action policies in Brazilian higher education since the early 2000s highlights growing recognition of the limits of universal education policies. The development of specific health policies for the black population, such as the National Policy for the Integral Health of the Black Population (PNSIPN), also underscores increasing state acknowledgment of the role that differentiated policies can play in mitigating and challenging health disparities. While the concept of universality is laudable in theory, in practice it can serve to elide various forms of inequality, because emphasis is placed on the notion of equal access to health care. However, the issue of equality with respect to health outcomes for different groups is often overlooked. Universality also shares a number of similarities with the Brazilian ideology of racial democracy and the concept of *mestiçagem* (race mixing), both of which focus on blending and mixture, and downplay ethnic/racial differences and inequalities. Important links can also be made between the concept of universality and some health professionals' resistance to collect the *quesito cor* (color/race data), based on the belief that all Brazilians are equal and color differences do not need to be acknowledged or addressed in or by the public health system. Given this situation and longstanding Brazilian practices of downplaying the importance of color/race identification, universality may be one of the greatest challenges that will be faced as the PNSIPN is implemented in the years to come.

Recognizing the limits of universality is also critical to advancing gender health equity in Brazil, particularly considering that women's health needs and health outcomes are often quite different from those of men. Through policies such as PAISM, feminist health activists in Brazil have sought to achieve gender health equity by focusing on the provision of holistic or integral health services to women, meaning that all phases of women's lives and health needs are addressed, rather than solely focusing on women's experiences as reproducers. In doing so, activists have attempted to emphasize the specificities of women's health needs and experiences without locking them into a reproductive role that would limit their sexual and reproductive autonomy. However, as noted in chapter 1, growing conservative and religious influence in Brazilian politics has posed a threat to the strong feminist health tradition that has been built for more than three decades in Brazil.

On the Urgency of Intersectionality

In many ways, black women's health needs and experiences exist at the intersection of many of the aforementioned issues, while also reflecting how gender, racial, and class inequalities shape access to health care, as well as patterns of illness and wellness. Most of the policies and initiatives examined in this study focus on either women or black Brazilians, thus overlooking the ways in which black women are simultaneously members of both groups, yet often minimally acknowledged in or by either. Activists in the black women's movement have for several decades been at the forefront of calling attention to the need for intersectional political practices and public policies. Through their insistence in calling attention to *both* race and gender, black women activists have challenged the single-identity focus of the women's movement and black movement and also have pushed for state acknowledgment of black women's intersectional identities and experiences.

Though this study has examined health policies and issues of health equity using an intersectional framework, much work remains to be done with respect to developing and implementing intersectional public policies. In fact, the development of such policies is a complex undertaking that requires engagement with multiple forms of identity, experience, and inequality. It also requires that black women not just be added to groups such as "women" or "blacks." Instead, active recognition of and engagement with intersecting identities, experiences, and inequalities is essential.

In order to achieve health equity for groups who are simultaneously affected by multiple vectors of social experience, such as black women, it is critical that researchers and public health practitioners move toward the development and implementation of intersectional frameworks. These frameworks require careful consideration of the ways that various forms of difference and inequality shape health access, health experiences, and health outcomes, thus leading to richer and more nuanced understandings of health and wellness. While the use of intersectional frameworks is critical to the development of health policies that respond to the needs of multiply marginalized individuals and communities, they are also an important means of improving the relevance and efficacy of health policies for all populations. By recognizing and highlighting how multiple social identities and social locations shape health experiences and health outcomes for both marginalized and nonmarginalized groups, researchers and health practitioners will be better positioned to improve the health of all Brazilians.

Current and Future Challenges

As noted in earlier sections of this book, the guiding principles of the SUS—equity, universality, and integrality, or comprehensiveness—undergirded public health efforts in Brazil following the implementation of health reform in the early 1990s and emphasized the importance of making health care accessible to the entire population. However, although the SUS was designed to provide free health care to all Brazilians, regardless of income level, the fact that middle-class and more affluent Brazilians have typically been able to afford private health insurance has meant that poor and low-income Brazilians rely most heavily on the SUS for their health-care needs. Moreover, because Afro-descendant Brazilians are disproportionately represented among the country's poor, they have tended to utilize the SUS in greater numbers than their white counterparts. Nationwide data from 1998 showed that while 66.05 percent of white Brazilians were served by the SUS, 76.23 percent of Afro-descendants were. Similarly, 54.65 percent of hospitalizations among whites and 78.99 percent of hospitalizations among Afro-descendants were covered by the SUS nationwide in 1998. In addition, while 32.39 percent of whites had private health plans, 14.62 percent of blacks did nationwide in 1998 (Rede Feminista de Saúde 2003).

Race-conscious health policies that were developed during the 2000s, such as the *Política Nacional de Atenção Integral às Pessoas com Doença Falciforme* (National Policy for Integral Attention to People with Sickle Cell Anemia) and the PNSIPN were major advances in efforts to address racial health disparities in Brazil. As noted in chapter 3, the PNSIPN was developed alongside other important race-conscious public policies and legislation, such as affirmative action, the Statute of Racial Equality, and the Law of Quotas in Higher Education, all of which resulted from longstanding demands by black movement activists and reflected an unprecedented shift in public and state acknowledgment of racism and racial inequalities in the country. As a relatively new policy, it is somewhat difficult to gauge the efficacy of the PNSIPN in addressing racial health disparities or meeting the health needs of the Afro-descendant population. To date, few, if any, studies have examined the extent of implementation that has taken place or how effective implementation of the PNSIPN has been. Moreover, as a federal policy, the PNSIPN must be implemented at state and municipal levels throughout Brazil. This process will likely be uneven, given the vast regional, economic, and political differences that characterize municipalities and states across Brazil.

It is also important to consider the role that having government agencies involved in addressing racism and racial inequality at the local and state level might potentially have on the implementation of the PNSIPN at these levels in the future. Though limited in number, cities and states that had government agencies and technical committees focused on the health of the black population prior to or soon after the promulgation of the PNSIPN in 2009 were likely in a more favorable position to implement the policy. As noted in chapter 4, the city and state of São Paulo and the city of Salvador have been leaders with respect to health policies for the black population, as well as in addressing institutional racism; however, more research is needed to assess how the PNSIPN has been implemented in these places, as well as in other areas of Brazil. In addition, as discussed in chapter 3, the removal of provisions to create an implementation plan for the PNSIPN from the 2010 Statute of Racial Equality will likely compromise the effective and timely implementation of this policy. Due to the lack of an implementation plan, few accountability measures were put in place within the first few years of the PNSIPN's implementation. This highlights the fact that policies for the health of the black population can exist without being implemented or adequately funded. In fact, at the end of 2013, black health activists openly critiqued then–Minister of Health Alexandre Padilha for the slow pace at which the PNSIPN was being implemented.

Although there was increased development of race-conscious public policies, including those focused on health, in Brazil during the 2000s and early 2010s, gains made with respect to gender-conscious public policies began to be rolled back in the early 2010s. As noted in chapter 1, increasing conservative pressure on Dilma Rousseff's administration led to the enactment of policies that constrained women's reproductive autonomy and led to an increasing emphasis on a maternalist framework for women's health during her first term in office. Rousseff's reelection in October 2014 took place within a context that promised similar measures during her second term. While Brazil had one of the strongest feminist and women's health movements in the world in the mid-2010s, efforts to decriminalize abortion and promote gender equity in health were severely circumscribed by this time. As noted in chapter 5, Brazil's public proclamations regarding women's health in areas such as the Millennium Development Goals and maternal mortality stand in sharp contrast to on-the-ground realities that severely constrain women's reproductive autonomy and, in many cases, place women's well-being and very lives at risk.

During the early 2010s, a conservative political shift also undermined Brazil's longstanding tradition of progressive approaches to HIV prevention. In response to an HIV prevention campaign that featured prostitutes, called "I'm happy being a prostitute," on June 4, 2013, then–Minister of Health Alexandre Padilha removed the posters from the Department of HIV/AIDS, STDs and Viral Hepatitis' Web site (Malta and Beyrer 2013). The director of the department, Dirceu Greco, was also removed from his position by the end of the day and his two deputy directors resigned. Later that month, in response to Greco's firing, all civil society organizations resigned from the National AIDS Commission (Malta and Beyrer 2013).

The federal government's decision to halt an HIV prevention campaign featuring prostitutes was seen as a sign that the commitment to human rights in the federal government's HIV/AIDS programs was eroding, owing to conservative pressure and an emphasis on improving and sanitizing the country's international image. These became increasingly important concerns as Brazil's international stature was elevated as an emerging economy and member of the BRIC nations (Brazil, Russia, India, China) during the early 2010s. As one sexuality rights activist told me in 2013, "Brazil can't be seen as a crazy place anymore." The federal government's response to the 2013 AIDS campaign signaled a significant move away from Brazil's tradition of centering human rights and combating stigma and discrimination in its response to the AIDS epidemic.

Significant public health and political developments during 2015 and 2016 highlighted the lack of effective reproductive rights policies in Brazil. During 2015 and 2016, people around the world observed Brazil's struggle to curb the spread of the Zika virus and address its impact on unborn fetuses and newborn infants. The growing number of microcephaly cases, in which infants were born with small heads and brains, caused panic in Brazil and raised concerns as the country prepared for the 2016 Summer Olympics in Rio de Janeiro. While much of the media coverage of the Zika virus focused on infants who were born with microcephaly, there was less discussion of how the Zika crisis was both shaped by and a reflection of the lack of reproductive rights for women in Brazil and many other Latin American nations. Perhaps most striking was that comments made by government representatives from the region demonstrated a lack of commitment to, as well as concern about, women's reproductive rights. Rather than using the Zika virus as an opportunity to address longstanding policy failures with respect to reproductive health or providing expanded contraceptive and pregnancy termination options, most governments encouraged women to postpone pregnancies as a way to avoid potential complications from the virus (Roa 2016).

As media coverage of the Zika and microcephaly crisis in Brazil peaked in early 2016, the country's political crisis and calls for the impeachment of Dilma Rousseff were also reaching a fever pitch. On May 12, 2016, the Brazilian Senate voted to begin impeachment hearings against Rousseff. Senate hearings took place in August 2016, following the Olympics in Rio de Janeiro, to determine Rousseff's fate. The Brazilian Senate decided to impeach Rousseff on August 31, 2016, with a vote of sixty-one to twenty.

Progressive members of Brazilian civil society and many members of the international community viewed Rousseff's ouster as a coup orchestrated by rich and powerful elites. By 2016, the right wing of Brazilian politics had been out of power for thirteen years, owing to the presidencies of Rousseff and her predecessor, Lula. Though Rousseff was accused of maneuvering funds and tampering with budgets, at the time of her impeachment, there was no proof that a crime of responsibility had been committed (Council on Hemispheric Affairs 2016). In addition, many of the politicians who fought for Rousseff's impeachment were accused of personal embezzlement themselves, and nearly a third of the 594 members of Congress were under scrutiny by the courts over claims of violating laws.

Vice President Michel Temer, of the *Partido do Movimento Democrático Brasileiro* (Brazilian Democratic Movement Party, PMDB), assumed the role of acting president in May 2016. However, there was widespread discontent with him assuming office given corruption allegations against him, as well as his central role in orchestrating Rousseff's impeachment. Temer was accused of illegal financing during the 2014 elections, and there were allegations he was involved with the *Lava Jato* (car wash) scandal that precipitated Rousseff's impeachment.

Like Temer, many members of Congress were implicated in the *Lava Jato* scandal, a multibillion-dollar kickback and bribery scheme involving the state-owned oil company Petrobras. The Lava Jato scandal was viewed by many as the cause of Rousseff's impeachment, since politicians accused of involvement in the scandal would not be charged if Rousseff was removed from office. Comparisons to the 1964 *golpe* (coup) by the military regime, which forced

President João Goulart out of office and ushered in Brazil's twenty-one-year dictatorship, were commonly made and there were deep concerns that democratic and social justice gains attained over the previous decades were being quickly eroded. The movement to impeach Rousseff was also highly gendered and drew on sexist beliefs and imagery to prematurely end her presidency and diminish her accomplishments as Brazil's first female president.

When Michel Temer assumed office as acting president in May 2016, he immediately came under criticism for the lack of gender and racial diversity in his cabinet. Of the twenty ministers he initially named, none were women; all were white men whose self-presentation indicated that they were heterosexual (CLADEM 2016). Temer's decision to have an all-male cabinet would have made his administration the first since President Ernesto Geisel (1974–1979) to not include a woman. It is also important to note that Geisel was in office during the military dictatorship. The lack of gender diversity in Temer's cabinet stood in sharp contrast to those of Presidents Luiz Inácio Lula da Silva and Dilma Rousseff, who appointed eleven and fifteen women to serve in their respective cabinets (Arbex and Bilenky 2016). As leading Brazilian feminist Eva Blay noted in a May 2016 newspaper interview, "We will have to struggle again. It will be a waste of energy. We were at a level where we could have advanced a lot more. It is a setback" (Arbex and Bilenky 2016).

After taking office, Temer appointed Flávia Piovesan, a well-respected attorney and specialist in human rights and international law, to lead the newly created *Secretaria dos Direitos Humanos* (Secretariat for Human Rights). Piovesan's appointment received strong criticism by many feminists in Brazil, including members of the *Comitê Latino Americano e do Caribe para a Defesa dos Direitos da Mulher* (Latin American and Caribbean Committee for the Defense of Women's Rights, CLADEM), an organization of which she was a member. In an open letter to Piovesan, members of CLADEM urged her to reconsider her appointment in Temer's administration based on a series of decisions he made after assuming office, as well as the generally antidemocratic tenor of the new government (CLADEM 2016). The letter detailed Temer's dismantling of important government ministries related to women's rights and racial equality, and those that represented civil society interests soon after taking office, including the *Ministério de Mulheres, Direitos Humanos e Igualdade Racial* (Ministry for Women, Human Rights and Racial Equality), the *Ministério da Cultura* (Ministry of Culture), the *Ministério das Comunicações* (Ministry of Communications), the *Ministério de Desenvolvimento Agrário* (Ministry of Agrarian Development), and the *Controladora Geral da União* (the General Comptroller of the Union). By dismantling the Ministry for Women, Human

Rights, and Racial Equality, Temer dealt a final blow to the institutionalization of racial equality and gender equality policies within the federal government. Dilma Rousseff created this ministry in October 2015, which collapsed several ministries, including SEPPIR (Secretariat for the Promotion of Racial Equality Policies) and the SPM (Secretariat for the Promotion of Women's Policies), into one entity, a move that substantially weakened work in these areas at the federal level and indicated a lack of support for racial and gender equality policies in Rousseff's government.

As this book goes to press, the political and public policy situation in Brazil is extremely bleak and uncertain. Given the increasingly conservative political context and policy challenges outlined above, the future development and implementation of policies to promote and ensure racial and gender equity in health will likely face an uphill battle in Brazil. However, given the country's strong history of civil society mobilization related to health and health equity, this battle is far from over.

Notes

Introduction

1. The International Covenant on Civil and Political Rights forms part of the Universal Bill of Human Rights, along with the Universal Declaration of Human Rights and the International Covenant on Economic, Social, and Cultural Rights. The International Covenant on Civil and Political Rights went into force in 1976. Brazil became a state party of the covenant in 1992.

2. Paim et al. 2011 provides an excellent overview of the Brazilian health-care system.

3. According to Negri Filho (2013), during Collor de Mello's administration a constitutional rule that called for guaranteed minimum funding for the public health sector was eliminated.

4. Most scholarly analyses of the post-Durban period have focused on policy developments with regard to affirmative action for the African-descendant population in employment and university admissions. This may largely owe to the controversial nature of affirmative action policies in Brazil, as well as in countries such as the United States.

5. The references cited here represent a small sample of written critiques of official racial/color classification methods in Brazil. It should also be noted that black activists have critiqued these methods at meetings and conference for several decades.

6. Research on racial/ethnic health disparities in Brazil is still in its early stages. Doctoral thesis research by Maria Ines Barbosa (1998) and Fernanda Lopes (2003), two Afro-Brazilian researchers, offered some of the earliest examinations of racial/ethnic health disparities in the field of public health in Brazil. The 2005 publication of an edited volume on the health of the black population by the National Health Foundation (*Fundação*

Nacional de Saúde, or FUNASA) reflected increasing discussion of racial/ethnic health disparities within the Brazilian federal government during the mid-2000s.

7. Abortion is illegal in Brazil. Feminist health researchers and activists have long argued that the country's high rates of maternal mortality are linked to the frequency of unsafe, clandestine abortions.

8. See Weber and Parra-Medina (2003) and essays in Shulz and Mullings (2006) for discussions of intersectional approaches to health in the United States. Other key texts on intersectionality and health include Hankivsky and Christoffersen (2008), Hankivsky and Cormier (2009), Hankivsky et al. (2010), and Hankivsky (2012).

9. A nationwide march in Brasília, the capital of Brazil, was organized by black activists on November 20, 1995, to commemorate the three-hundredth anniversary of the death of Zumbi, the leader of the renowned fugitive slave community of Palmares. Several important discursive and policy shifts regarding racism took place after this march and during the presidency of Fernando Henrique Cardoso, who served for two terms.

Chapter 1. Feminist Dreams and Nightmares

1. According to Alvarez (1990), in the state of São Paulo, a feminist approach to women's health was developed as part of the state's *Programa da Saúde da Mulher* (Women's Health Program). Feminists were also active in the development of this program since they feared that, without their influence, the program would be coercive and anti-natalist in nature.

2. By the early 1990s, councils on women existed in at least twelve cities and six states in addition to the National Council on Women's Rights (Dixon-Mueller 1993).

3. The Commission on Reproductive Rights included a working group that reviewed how contraceptive methods, such as IUDs, injectables, and implants, were tested and used, as well as potential abuses. See Barroso (1990, 17, 23–24).

4. Bohn (2010) discusses the backlash against the Council's efforts to promote progressive policies for women. During 1989 individuals without ties to the women's movement were appointed to the executive body of the CNDM and the Council was reduced to being a consultative unit. The Council's power and influence was further diminished under the Collor administration beginning in 1990.

5. Dixon-Mueller (1993) mentions that 135 private planning agencies in addition to BEMFAM were operating in Brazil at this time.

6. Chapter 2 discusses the contributions of black women's non-governmental organizations, such as Fala Preta, in greater detail.

7. The original name of the Rede Saúde was the Rede Nacional Feminista de Saúde e Direitos Reproductives.

8. The CNDM, which is comprised of civil society representatives, became part of the SPM and has played an important role in providing advocacy for the women's movement and serving as a means to critique the state, which would be difficult for the SPM because it was a state entity (Bohn 2010).

9. Chapter 5 provides a detailed discussion of maternal mortality in Brazil.

10. I discuss the formation of the AMNB in chapter 2. It has played an important role in organizing black women at the national level in Brazil and was formed during the preparatory process for the 2001 World Conference against Racism.

11. This national policy was passed in 2009 and is examined in greater detail in chapter 3.

12. In 2013, President Rousseff sanctioned Federal Law 12.845, which ensured women's access to abortion in the public health system for cases allowed by the Penal Code. In 2014 the Minister of Health suspended the technical protocol and revoked funding for this law.

Chapter 2. Black Women's Health Activism and the Development of Intersectional Health Policy

1. This quote is from an interview I conducted with Edna Roland in December 1994 when she was the director of the Health Program at Geledés in São Paulo.

2. Table 2.1 does not provide an exhaustive discussion of all of these organizations' programs. Readers may consult the organizations' Web sites for additional information on their programs and areas of focus. Maria Mulher (http://mariamulher.org.br); Geledés (http://www.geledes.org.br); Associação de Mulheres Negras (http://www.acmun.org.br); Criola (http://criola.org.br).

3. The names of these organizations highlight their efforts to challenge racism and sexism in Brazil. Here I provide English translations of the organizations' names, as well as descriptions found on their Web sites where relevant. The phrase "Maria Mulher" means "Maria woman" in English. Since Maria is a common name in Brazil, use of it in the organization's name is a way to refer to women as a collectivity. The term "Criola" refers to black women born in the Americas and dates back to the colonial slave era. It has often been used as a racial slur. "Associação Cultural de Mulheres Negras" is translated as "Black Women's Cultural Association" in English. The phrase "Fala Preta!" means "Speak Black Woman!" According to English-language material available on the Geledés Web site, "Geledés is originally a kind of female secret society of a religious nature existing in traditional yorubás [*sic*] societies, it expresses the female power over the land fertility, procreation and the community's well-being. The Geledés cult aims at easing and revering the ancestral mothers to assure the world's balance." http://geledes.org.br (accessed March 24, 2008).

4. Sonia Santos's (2008) research highlights the existence of black women's organizations in Brazil since the 1950s. It should also be noted that black women's organizations and networks in northeastern Brazil, such as *Odara-Instituto da Mulher Negra* and the *Rede de Mulheres Negras do Norte e Nordeste* (the North and Northeast Network of Black Women), began to take a leading role in national-level organizing in the 2010s. These groups were the primary organizers of the March of Black Women that took place in Brasília in November 2015 (Alvarez 2016).

5. U.S. feminist scholars such as Vivian May and Beverly Guy-Sheftall have argued that the concept of intersectionality predates the work of black feminists such as Kimberlé Crenshaw. May (2012) and Guy-Sheftall have called attention to the ways in which the

concept of intersectionality is present in the writings of nineteenth-century black feminists in the United States, such as Anna Julia Cooper.

6. The writings of U.S. black feminists such as Barbara Smith, the Combahee River Collective, Angela Davis, and bell hooks provide insightful critiques of capitalism and class exploitation.

7. November 20, 1695, is the date on which the death of Zumbi, the famous leader of the *quilombo* of Palmares is remembered. November 20 is now recognized as an official holiday in many Brazilian cities and states.

8. See da Silva's biography for a discussion of her experience of having a hysterectomy and the impact of the practice on her physical and mental health (Benjamin et al. 1997).

9. During the 1990s, activists in the black women's movement became involved in significant forms of transnational organizing. A number of black women participated in the First and Second Encounters of Afro–Latin American and Afro-Caribbean Women in 1992 and 1995. These encounters were sponsored by the Network of Afro–Latin American and Afro-Caribbean Women and sought to foster dialogue among black women in the region. Black Brazilian women also played a visible role in the preparatory process for the Fourth World Conference on Women held in Beijing during 1995.

10. Alvarez (2000) discusses the significance of transnational advocacy networks and the United Nations conference process for Latin American feminists in terms of both gender-conscious policy development and broader social change.

11. Oliveira (2002).

12. Carneiro (2002).

13. See Caldwell (2007) for a discussion of perspectives on national-level organizing within the black women's movement.

14. Versions of this document were published in Portuguese, English, and Spanish, and copies were presented to governmental and non-governmental representatives for all of the countries participating in the Durban conference.

15. Personal interview, Nilza Iraci, March 12, 2007, São Paulo, Brazil.

16. Alvarez (2000) discusses Latin American feminists' views of the U.N. process and transnational advocacy networks in terms of both gender-conscious policy development and broader cultural change.

17. Almeida (2001).

18. Personal interview, Nilza Iraci, March 12, 2007, São Paulo, Brazil.

19. Ibid.

20. See Carneiro (2003) for an extended discussion of black women's involvement in the preparatory process for the WCAR.

21. Personal interview, Nilza Iraci, March 12, 2007, São Paulo, Brazil.

22. Carneiro (2002).

23. Fátima Oliveira has published extensively on issues related to black women's health, women's health, and racial/ethnic health disparities. See, for example, Oliveira (2002).

24. The Pan-American Health Organization also released a publication focused on racial/ethnic equity in health. See Torres and del Rio 2001.

25. U.S. legal scholar Kimberlé Crenshaw presented a document to the WCAR preparatory meeting in Croatia during November 2000. This paper, "Background Paper for the Expert Meeting on Gender-Related Aspects of Race Discrimination" was published as part of a special dossier on the III World Conference against Racism that appeared in the Brazilian feminist journal *Estudos Feministas* during 2002. It has since become a highly influential and often-cited conceptualization of intersectionality in Brazil. Essays by Bentes (2002), Carneiro (2002), and Oliveira and Sant'anna (2002) also appeared in the dossier. This dossier is an important example of knowledge production by activists in the black women's movement. See Lebon (2007) for a detailed discussion of knowledge production by black women activists in Brazil.

26. Ribeiro resigned as minister of SEPPIR in February 2008 amid charges that she had used government funds for personal purposes. Edson Santos served as minister following Ribeiro's departure.

27. Bentes (2002) offers personal observations on the conference process for Durban from the perspective of an activist who is from a less established organization and one that had not previously participated in U.N. conference processes.

Chapter 3. Mapping the Development of Health Policies for the Black Population

1. An individual must receive the hemoglobin S gene from both parents in order to have sickle cell anemia.

2. Werneck (2005) provides a sobering critique of the Cardoso and Lula administrations' actions with regard to racism after the Durban conference.

3. Htun (2004) describes members of the race-based issue network in Brazil as being part of various sectors of society, including journalists, state officials, researchers, public intellectuals, human rights NGOs, politicians in Congress, and black activists.

4. As Edward Telles has noted: "Affirmative action implies setting aside formal equality and seeking real and material equality. It means breaking the logic by which we are all equal, when in fact, we are not" (2004, 71).

5. Health initiatives and policies for indigenous communities pre-date those developed for the black population. The Subsystem for Attention to the Health of Indigenous Peoples (*Subsistema de Atenção à Saúde dos Povos Indígenas*) was established in 1999. The National Policy of Attention to the Health of Indigenous Peoples (*Política Nacional de Atenção à Saúde dos Povos Indígenas*) was promulgated by the Ministry of Health in 2002.

6. For criticisms of Lula's administration by black women activists, see Oliveira (2005b) and Reis (2007).

7. *Portarias* are decrees issued by municipal secretariats and federal ministries, such as the Ministry of Health or a municipal Secretariat of Health.

8. I discuss the Program to Combat Institutional Racism (PCRI) and activities sponsored by the British Agency for International Development in greater detail in chapter 4.

9. Chapter 4 provides a more detailed analysis of institutional racism in the health sector in Brazil and efforts to combat it.

10. In 2010 the National Council of Municipal Health Secretaries publicly affirmed their commitment to health equity and distributed the National Policy for the Integral Health of the Black Population during their XXVI National Congress. This decision signaled growing acknowledgement of the importance of specific health policies for the black population across the country.

11. "Lai Lai Apejo" is a Yoruba phrase that means *encounter forever.*

12. During the 2006 election for the National Health Council, the Articulation of Black Brazilian Women's Organizations (AMNB) gained a seat on the council. Two black organizations were elected as substitutes, the *Coordenação Nacional de Entidades Negras* (CONEN) and the *Congresso Nacional Afro-Brasileira* (CNAB).

13. Many of the essays contained in the book were previously published either as newspaper articles and commentaries or as scholarly journal articles. The book also includes excerpts from articles published in Brazilian newspapers by non-Brazilian scholars, such as Paul Gilroy and Kwame Appiah, whose work can be viewed as being in line with a neoracial democracy perspective on race in Brazil. Much like the twentieth-century ideology of Brazilian racial democracy, this perspective downplays the significance of race and racism in Brazil and emphasizes racial egalitarianism and harmony.

14. The Law of Social Quotas (Federal Law no. 12.711) was signed by President Dilma Rousseff in August 2012. It mandates that 50 percent of public university students come from public schools. Within this group, the number of black (*preto*), brown (*pardo*), and indigenous students is required to be proportional to the percentage of each group in the state population for a given university.

15. An example of this can be seen in the publication of Ali Kamel's (2006) book *Não Somos Racistas* (We Are Not Racists), which critiqued affirmative action policies and argued that they would introduce racial antagonisms into Brazilian society. Kamel is a high-profile journalist and executive with TV Globo, Brazil's largest television network, and the Brazilian newspaper *O Globo.*

16. The 2013 documentary *Raça* by Joel Zito Araujo documents the approval process for the Statute of Racial Equality.

17. The documentary *Raça* by Joel Zito Araujo captures the use of this language when Demosthenes Torres comments on the dangers of the Statute of Racial Equality leading to the racialization of Brazilian society. This highlights the likely impact academic writings opposed to race-conscious policies likely had on politicians who also opposed such policies.

18. Torres left the DEMS Party (*Partido Democratas*) in April 2012 and was expelled from the Senate on corruption charges in July 2012.

Chapter 4. Strategies to Challenge Institutional Racism and Color Blindness in the Health Sector

1. See Hernandez (2013) for an important analysis of race and the law in Latin America.

2. Interview with Silvia Augusto, June 27, 2012, Salvador, Bahia.

3. Findings in Telles (2014) indicate that both respondents and interviewers in a survey of Brazilian racial attitudes recorded similar color identifications for respondents.

4. See Nobles (2000, 2011) and Telles (2004) for excellent analyses of the role of the national census in struggles over racial categories and the racialized counting of bodies in Brazil.

5. The indigenous category was added to the 1991 census.

6. Interview with Luis Eduardo Batista, June 22, 2011, São Paulo, Brazil.

7. Ibid.

8. For scholarly analyses of race and skin color in Brazil, see Guimarães (2005[1999]), Nogueira (1985), Sheriff (2001), Telles (2004), and Twine (1998).

Chapter 5. The *Alyne* Case

1. This private health-care center was providing public health services under a special agreement with the municipality of Belford Roxo.

2. http://www.who.int/healthinfo/statistics/indmaternalmortality/en/ (accessed September 27, 2013).

3. Data SUS, "Painel do Monitoramento da Mortalidade Materna," http://svs.aids.gov.br/ dashboard/mortalidade/materna.show.mtw (accessed September 28, 2013).

4. Ibid.

5. World Health Organization, "Brazil: Health Profile." http://www.who.int/gho/countries/ bra.pdf (accessed September 26, 2013).

6. Convention on the Elimination of All Forms of Discrimination against Women, http://www.un.org/womenwatch/daw/cedaw/text/econvention.htm#intro (accessed July 16, 2014).

7. The CEDAW decision notes that the British Department for International Development also called attention to maternal mortality as the Millennium Development Goal Brazil was least likely to achieve.

8. The shadow letter presented to the CEDAW by the Center for Reproductive Rights in 2007 notes that maternal mortality was not prioritized in federal planning efforts such as the Multi-Year Plan for 2004–07 (Center for Reproductive Rights 2007).

9. "Programa de Humanização no Pré-natal e Nascimento," http://www.datasus.gov.br/ SISPRENATAL/SPN_PHPN.php (accessed September 27, 2013).

10. Other reproductive health measures issued during Lula's presidency include a 2005 law guaranteeing women the right to have someone accompany them during childbirth.

11. Shadow letters are submitted to the United Nations by non-governmental organizations. They typically highlight issues not raised in official government reports or point out misleading information that may be presented by governments. The Center for Reproductive Rights' shadow letter on the *Alyne* case is available at: http://reproductiverights .org/sites/crr.civicactions.net/files/documents/sl_brazil_eng_2007.pdf (accessed July 16, 2014).

12. The Center for Reproductive Rights also submitted a shadow letter on maternal mortality in Brazil in April 2006 to the Committee on Economic, Social and Cultural Rights, which monitors the International Covenant on Economic, Social and Cultural Rights. The letter highlights racial disparities in maternal death in Brazil. The letter is

available at: http://reproductiverights.org/sites/crr.civicactions.net/files/documents/Brazil%20CESCR%202009.pdf (accessed July 16, 2014).

13. Brazil signed the Facultative Protocol for CEDAW on March 13, 2001. The Protocol was approved by the Brazilian Congress on June 5, 2002 (Legislative Decree no. 107), ratified on June 28, 2002, and promulgated by Presidential Decree no. 4.316 on July 30, 2002.

14. Discrimination on the basis of race or gender is also considered to be a violation of the International Covenant on Social, Economic, and Cultural Rights (Yamin and Maine 2005).

15. The Dhesca special rapporteur's role is similar to that of the special rapporteurs for the U.N. Human Rights Council, which monitors the implementation of the International Covenant on Civil and Political Rights. These special rapporteurs investigate and issue reports on specific human rights concerns.

16. Skype video interview with Beatriz Galli, July 4, 2013.

17. Ibid.

18. Ibid.

19. Smith uses this term to refer to the assailants. The term "white-mestizo" calls into question the racial identity of the assailants as being purely white.

Chapter 6. Making Race and Gender Visible in Brazil's HIV/AIDS Epidemic

1. In November 1996, President Fernando Henrique Cardoso signed Law 9.313, requiring the federal government to provide free AIDS medications through the public health system to all who needed them.

2. Brazil's approach to HIV prevention and treatment anticipated recent initiatives among HIV researchers and professionals regarding treatment as a form of prevention.

3. One example can be seen in Lieberman's assertion that there is "no significant 'ethnic' press in the form of a large circulation newspaper that is read by groups identifiable in terms of race or skin color. The idea of a major 'Moreno' [brown] newspaper would be nonsensical in Brazil" (2009, 148). Scholars such as Paulina Alberto (2011), Kim Butler (1998), Michael Hanchard (1994), and George Reid Andrews (1991) have documented black activism in Brazil and the existence of a black press in cities such as São Paulo since the early decades of the twentieth century. Their research challenges Lieberman's erroneous assertions regarding the nonexistence of ethnic or black newspapers in Brazil.

4. Werneck mapped data for educational attainment by race and sex and the illiteracy index from 1992 and 1999 onto data about the educational attainment of persons twenty to sixty-nine years by year of HIV/AIDS diagnosis because data by race did not exist for those years. Data used in her analysis was obtained from the Brazilian Institute of Geography and Statistics (IBGE) and the National Household Survey (PNAD).

5. Measuring T-cell count and viral load are techniques that are routinely used to determine immune response and the progression of HIV/AIDS for people living with the disease.

6. Interview with Karen Bruck, National STD/AIDS Program, Brasília, July 22, 2010.

7. Nilo (2008) examines the relationship between interpersonal violence and women's vulnerability to HIV/AIDS. The feminist NGO Gestos also does work focused on these issues in the city of Recife, Pernambuco.

8. The National STD/AIDS Program participated in the federal government's affirmative action program that was established by Presidential Decree 4.228 in 2002. President Cardoso initiated the federal affirmative action program.

9. The following universities participated in the Afroatitude Program: Universidade de Brasília, Universidade Federal da Bahia, Universidade Federal do Paraná, Universidade Federal de Alagoas, Universidade Estadual de Montes Claros, Universidade do Estado da Bahia, Universidade Estadual de Londrina, Universidade Estadual do Mato Grosso do Sul, Universidade Estadual do Rio de Janeiro, and Universidade Estadual de Minas Gerais.

10. Interview with Karen Bruck, National STD/AIDS Program, Brasília, July 22, 2010.

11. It has been difficult to gauge which universities continued the program after 2007, because it was no longer centralized within the National AIDS Program.

12. See Htun (2004) for an insightful discussion of the black movement's relationship with the Brazilian state during this time period.

13. A version of Travassos's essay was republished in the 2007 book edited by Peter Fry et al., *Divisões Perigosas*.

14. For examples of Lopes and Paixão's research, see Lopes (2005), Lopes and Werneck (2009), Sant'Anna and Paixão (1997), and Paixão (2003, 2013).

Bibliography

Adesse, Leila, and Mario Monteiro. 2007. "Magnitude do Aborto no Brasil: Aspectos Epidemiológicos e Sócio-Culturais." Sao Paulo.

Ahmed, Sara. 2012. *On Being Included: Racism and Diversity in Institutional Life*. Durham, N.C.: Duke University Press.

Alberto, Paulina. 2011. *Terms of Inclusion: Black Intellectuals in Twentieth-Century Brazil*. Chapel Hill: University of North Carolina Press.

Almeida, Eliana Fonseca. 2001. "Mulheres Documentam o Racismo no Brasil." *O Tempo*, July 4.

Alvarez, Sonia. 1990. *Engendering Democracy in Brazil: Women's Movements in Transition Politics*. Princeton, N.J.: Princeton University Press.

———. 2000. "Translating the Global: Effects of Transnational Organizing on Local Feminist Discourses and Practices in Latin America." *Meridians* 1 (1): 29–67.

———. 2012. "Feminismos e Antirracismos: Entraves e Intersecções. Entrevista com Luiza Bairros, Ministra da Secretaria de Políticas de Promoção da Promoção da Igualdade Racial (Seppir)." *Revista Estudos Feministas* 20 (3): 833–50.

———. 2016. "'Vem Marchar com a Gente,' Come March with Us." *Meridians: Feminism, Race, Transnationalism* 14 (1): 70–75.

Anderson, Cora Fernandez. 2016. "Reproductive Inequalities: As Latin America's Pink Tide Recedes, the Struggle for Reproductive Health Reform Continues." *NACLA Report on the Americas* 48 (1): 15–17.

Andrews, George Reid. 1991. *Blacks & Whites in São Paulo, Brazil, 1888–1988*. Madison: University of Wisconsin Press.

Arbex, Thais, and Thais Bilenky. 2016. "Ministério de Temer Deve Ser o Primeiro Sem Mulheres Desde Geisel." *Folha de São Paulo,* May 12, 2016. Accessed June 14, 2016. http://www1.folha.uol.com.br/poder/2016/05/1770420-ministeriado-de-temer-deve-ser-o-primeiro-sem-mulheres-desde-geisel.shtml.

Articulação de Mulheres Brasileiras. 2001. "Mulheres Negras: Um Retrato da Discriminação Racial no Brasil." Brasília: Articulação de Mulheres Brasileiras.

Articulação de Organizações de Mulheres Negras Brasileiras. 2012. *Saúde da Mulher Negra Guia para a Defesa dos Direitos.* Porto Alegre: Articulação de Organizações de Mulheres Negras Brasileiras.

Arvitzer, Leonardo. 2009. *Participatory Institutions in Democratic Brazil.* Washington, D.C.: Woodrow Wilson Center Press and Baltimore: The Johns Hopkins University Press.

Bacon, Oliver, Maria Lúcia Pecoraro, Jane Galvão, and Kimberly Page-Shafer. 2004. *HIV/AIDS in Brazil.* University of California, San Francisco: AIDS Policy Research Center.

Baker, Lee D. 1998. *From Savage to Negro: Anthropology and the Construction of Race, 1896–1954.* Berkeley: University of California Press.

Bairros, Luiza and Sonia E. Alvarez. 2016. "Feminism and Anti-Racism: Intersections and Challenges." *Meridians: Feminism, Race, Transnationalism* 14 (1): 50–69.

Barbosa, Maria Inês. 1998. "Racismo e Saúde." Ph.D. diss., University of Sao Paulo.

Barbosa, Maria Inês da Silva. 2001. "It's a Woman, but She's a Black Woman: Mortality Profile in the 'Dumping Closet.'" *Jornal da RedeSaúde* 23(August): 34–36

Barros, Fernando C., Alicia Matijasevich, Jennifer Harris Requejo, Elsa Giugliani, Ana Goretti Maranhão, Carlos a Monteiro, Aluísio J. D. Barros, Flavia Bustreo, Mario Merialdi, and Cesar G. Victora. 2010. "Recent Trends in Maternal, Newborn, and Child Health in Brazil: Progress toward Millennium Development Goals 4 and 5." *American Journal of Public Health* 100 (10): 1877–89.

Barroso, Carmen. 1989. "Fecundidade e Políticas Públicas." *São Paulo em Perspectiva,* 3 (3): 15–19.

Bastos, Eloísa Solange Magalhães, and Liliane de Jesus Bittencourt. 2010. "O Programa de Combate ao Racismo Institucional (PCRI) e a Criação da Rede de Saúde Da População Negra de Salvador: Alguns Elementos Metodológicos." *BIS—Boletim do Instituto de Saúde* 12: 179–84.

Bastos, Francisco. 2001. *A Feminização da Epidemia de AIDS no Brasil: Determinantes Estruturais e Alternativas de Enfrentamento.* Rio de Janeiro: Associaçao Interdisciplinar de Aids.

Bastos, Francisco Inácio, and Célia Landmann Szwarcwald. 2000. "AIDS e Pauperização: Principais Conceitos e Evidências Empíricas." *Cadernos de Saúde Pública* 16 (Suppl. 1): 65–76.

Batista, Luís Eduardo, and Rosana Batista Monteiro. 2010. "Política de Saúde da População Negra no Estado de São Paulo: Focalizando para Promover a Universalização do Direito à Saúde." *BIS—Boletim do Instituto de Saúde* 12 (2): 172–78.

Batista, Luis Eduardo, Rosana Batista Monteiro, and Araujo Rogério Medeiros. 2013. "Iniquidades Raciais e Saúde: O Ciclo da Política de Saúde da População Negra." *Saúde em Debate* 37 (99): 681–90.

Beato, Lucila Bandeira. 2012. "Inequality and Human Rights of African Descendants in Brazil." *Journal of Black Studies* 34 (6): 766–86.

Beatriz, Sônia. 2009. "As ONGs de Mulheres Negras no Brasil." *Sociedade e Cultura Goiânia,* 12 (2): 275–288.

Benjamin, Medea, Maisa Mendonça, and Benedita da Silva. 1997. *Benedita da Silva: An Afro-Brazilian Woman's Story of Politics and Love.* Oakland, CA: Institute for Food and Development Policy.

Bentes, Nilma. 2002. "Brasil-Durban-Brasil: Um Marco da Luta Contra o Racismo." *Estudos Feministas* 10 (1): 229–236.

Berkman, Alan, Jonathan Garcia, Miguel Muñoz-Laboy, Vera Paiva, and Richard Parker. 2005. "A Critical Analysis of the Brazilian Response to HIV/AIDS: Lessons Learned for Controlling and Mitigating the Epidemic in Developing Countries." *American Journal of Public Health* 95 (7) (July): 1162–72.

Biehl, João. 2004. "The Activist State: Global Pharmaceuticals, AIDS, and Citizenship in Brazil." *Social Text* 22 (3): 105–32.

———. 2007. *Will to Live: AIDS Therapies and the Politics of Survival.* Princeton, N.J.: Princeton University Press.

———. 2008. "Drugs for All: The Future of Global AIDS Treatment." *Medical Anthropology* 27 (2): 99–105.

———. 2009. "The Brazilian Response to AIDS and the Pharmaceuticalization of Global Health." In *Anthropology and Public Health: Bridging Differences in Culture and Society,* 480–511. New York: Oxford University Press.

Blackwell, Maylei, and Nadine Naber. 2002. "Intersectionality in the Era of Globalization: The Implications of the UN World Conference against Racism for Transnational Feminist Practices." *Meridians* 2 (2): 237–48.

Bohn, Simone R. 2010. "Feminismo Estatal sob a Presidência Lula: O Caso da Secretaria de Políticas para as Mulheres." *Revista Debates* 4 (2): 81–106.

Bond, Johanna. 2003. "International Intersectionality: A Theoretical and Pragmatic Exploration of Women's International Human Rights Violations." *Emory Law Journal* 52 (1): 171–86.

Bonin, Robson. 2010. "Dilma Divulga Carta Para 'Pôr Um Fim Definitivo À Campanha de Calúnias.'" *G1,* October 15, 2010. Accessed June 15, 2015. http://g1.globo.com/especiais/eleicoes-2010/noticia/2010/10/dilma-divulga-carta-para-por-um-fim-definitivo-campanha-de-calunias.html.

Braveman, Paula. 2010. "Social Conditions, Health Equity, and Human Rights." *Health and Human Rights* 12 (2): 31–48.

Bruck, Karen. 2006. "A Iniciativa de Implantação do Programa Brasil Afroatitude: Contexto de Surgimento." In *Brasil Afroatitude: Primeiro Ano do Programa.* Brasilia: Ministério da Saúde/Secretaria de Vigilância em Saúde/Programa Nacional de DST e Aids.

Butler, Kim D. 1998. *Freedoms Given, Freedoms Won: Afro-Brazilians in Post-Abolition São Paulo and Salvador.* New Brunswick, N.J.: Rutgers University Press.

Caldwell, Kia Lilly. 2007. *Negras in Brazil: Re-Envisioning Black Women, Citizenship, and the Politics of Identity.* New Brunswick, N.J.: Rutgers University Press.

————. 2009. "Intersectional Health Policy in Brazil: Race and Gender as Determinants of Health and Wellness." In *The Intersectional Approach: Transforming Women's and Gender Studies through Race, Class, and Gender,* ed. Michele Tracy Berger and Kathleen Guidroz, 118–35. Chapel Hill: University of North Carolina Press.

————. 2016. "Charting a Path toward Racial Health Equity in Brazil: Health Activism, the State, and Policy Development." *National Political Science Review* 18: 89–109.

Caldwell, Kia Lilly, and Lisa Bowleg. 2011. "Mirror Opposites: Examining Race and Socioeconomic Status in HIV/AIDS Research and Policies in Brazil and the United States from an Intersectional Perspective." In *Saúde da População Negra,* edited by Luis Eduardo Batista, Jurema Werneck, and Fernanda Lopes, 287–302. Petrópolis, Rio de Janeiro: DP et Alii.

Cançado, Rodolfo D., and Joice A. Jesus. 2007. "A Doença Falciforme no Brasil." *Revista Brasileira de Hematologia e Hemoterapia* 29 (3): 204–6.

Carneiro, Sueli. 2000a. "Matriarcado da Miseria." *Correio Braziliense.* September 15.

————. 2000b. "Raça e Etnia no Contexto da Conferência de Beijing." In *O Livro da Saúde das Mulheres Negras,* edited by Jurema Werneck, Maisa Mendonça, and Evelyn C. White. 247–56. Rio de Janeiro: Pallas/Criola.

————. 2002. "A Batalha de Durban." *Estudos Feministas* 10 (1): 209–14.

"Carta Pública: Todos Têm Direitos Iguais na República Demócratica." 2007. In *Divisões Perigosas: Políticas Raciais No Brasil Contemporâneo,* edited by Peter Fry, Yvonne Maggie, Marcos Chor Maio, Simone Monteiro, and Ricardo Ventura Santos, 345–47. Rio de Janeiro: Editora Civilização Brasileira.

Carvalho, José Jorge de. 2005. "O Confinamento Racial do Mundo Acadêmico Brasileiro." *Revista USP* (68): 88–103.

Catholic News Agency. 2007. "Rio de Janeiro governor promotes legalization of abortion to reduce number of criminals." October 29, 2007. Accessed March 3, 2017. http://www .catholicnewsagency.com/news/rio_de_janeiro_governor_promotes_legalization_of _abortion_to_reduce_number_of_criminals/

Center for Reproductive Rights. 2007. Letter to the Committee on the Elimination of All Forms of Discrimination against Women (CEDAW). July 24, 2007.

————. 2009. "Re: Supplementary Information on Brazil, Submitted to the Committee on Economic, Social and Cultural Rights for the Periodic Review of Brazil in Its 42nd Session." http://www.reproductiverights.org/sites/crr.civicactions.net/files/documents/ Brazil CESCR 2009.pdf.

————. 2010. "Reproductive Rights Violations as Torture and Cruel, Inhuman, or Degrading Treatment or Punishment: A Critical Human Rights Analysis." New York: Center for Reproductive Rights. http://www.reproductiverights.org/sites/crr.civicactions.net/ files/documents/TCIDT.pdf.

————. 2014. "Brazil Takes Step to Implement Historic United Nations Ruling in Maternal Death Case." March 11, 2014. Accessed March 25, 2014. https://www.reproductiverights .org/press-room/Brazil-Takes-Step-to-Implement-Historic-United-Nations-Ruling-in -Maternal-Death-Case%20

Chapman, Audrey R. 2010. "The Social Determinants of Health, Health Equity, and Human Rights." *Health and Human Rights* 12 (2) (January): 17–30.

Chequer, Pedro. 1998. "AIDS e Mulheres." *Fêmea* (June): 6–7.

Cicalo, André. 2012. *Urban Encounters: Affirmative Action and Black Identities in Brazil.* New York: Palgrave Macmillan.

CLADEM. 2016. *Carta Aberta do CLADEM À Jurista Flávia Piovesan.* Accessed June 13, 2016. http://www.cladem.org/brasil/Carta_Flávia-Piovesan.pdf.

Collins, Patricia Hill. 1998. *Fighting Words: Black Women and the Search for Justice.* Minneapolis: University of Minnesota Press.

Convention on the Elimination of All Forms of Discrimination against Women (CEDAW). 2011. "Views of the Committee for the Elimination of Discrimination against Women under Article 7, Paragraph 3, of the Optional Protocol to the Convention Concerning Communication No. 17/2008. Forty-Ninth Session, 11 to 29 July 2011."

Cook, Rebecca. 2013. "Human Rights and Maternal Health: Exploring the Effectiveness of the Alyne Decision." *Global Health and the Law* 41 (1): 103–23.

Cook, Rebecca J., and Bernard M. Dickens. 2012. "Upholding Pregnant Women's Right to Life." *International Journal of Gynaecology and Obstetrics: The Official Organ of the International Federation of Gynaecology and Obstetrics* 117 (1) (April): 90–94.

Cook, Rebecca J., Bernard M. Dickens, O. Andrew Wilson, and Susan Scarrow. 2001. *Advancing Safe Motherhood Through Human Rights.* Geneva: World Health Organization.

Cornwall, Andrea, and Alex Shankland. 2008. "Engaging Citizens: Lessons from Building Brazil's National Health System." *Social Science & Medicine* 66 (10): 2173–84.

Corrêa, Sonia. 1993. "PAISM: Uma Historia Sem Fim." *Revista Brasileira de Estudos de População* 10 (1): 2–12.

———. 2010a. "Abortion and Human Rights: Will Brazil Be the Next Nicaragua?" *RH Reality Check.* June 15. http://rhrealitycheck.org/article/2010/06/15/abortion-human-rights-current-controversy-brazil/.

———. 2010b. "Abortion and Human Rights in Brazil—Part 2." *Sexuality Policy Watch.* http://sxpolitics.org/abortion-and-human-rights-in-brazil-part-2/5184.

———. 2014a. "Sexuality and Human Rights in Brazil: The Long and Winding Road." In *The Making of Social Contracts: Feminists in a Fierce New World,* edited by Gita Sen and Marina Durano, 233–35. London: Dawn/Zed Books.

———. 2014b. "Abortion and the General Elections: A Chronicle of Announced Tragedies." *Sexuality Policy Watch.* September 27. http://sxpolitics.org/around-the-world-393/9778.

Corrêa, Sonia, Peter McIntyre, Carla Rodrigues, Anabela Paiva, and Cecilia Marks. 2005. "The Population and Reproductive Health Programme in Brazil 1990–2002: Lessons Learned." *Reproductive Health Matters* 13 (25): 72–80.

Corrêa, Sonia, Sérgio Piola, and Margareth Arilha. 1998. "Reproductive Health in Policy and Practice." http://www.prb.org/pdf/RHPPBrazil.pdf.

Costa, Ana Maria, and Estela Leão Aquino. 2000. "Saúde da Mulher na Reforma Sanitária Brasileira." In *Saúde, Eqüidade e Gênero: Um Desafio Para as Políticas Públicas,* edited by Ana Maria Costa, Edgar Merchán-Hamann, and Débora Tajer, 181–202. Brasília: Universidade de Brasília.

Cottingham, Jane, Eszter Kismodi, Adriane Martin Hilber, Ornella Lincetto, Marcus Stahlhofer, and Sofia Gruskin. 2010. "Using Human Rights for Sexual and Reproductive Health: Improving Legal and Regulatory Frameworks." *Bulletin of the World Health Organization* 88 (7): 551–55.

Council on Hemispheric Affairs. 2016. "Soft Coup in Brazil: A Blow to Brazilian Democracy." May 12, 2016. Accessed June 15, 2016. http://www.coha.org/soft-coup-in-brazil-a -blow-to-brazilian-democracy/.

Covin, David. 2006. *The Unified Black Movement in Brazil, 1978–2002.* Jefferson, N.C., and London: McFarland.

Crenshaw, Kimberlé. 1989. "Demarginalizing the Intersection of Race and Sex: A Black Feminist Critique of Antidiscrimination Doctrine, Feminist Theory and Antiracist Politics." *University of Chicago Legal Forum* 1: 139–67.

———. 1995. "Demarginalizing the Intersection of Race and Sex: A Black Feminist Critique of Antidiscrimination Doctrine, Feminist Theory and Antiracist Politics." In *Critical Race Theory: The Key Writings that Formed the Movement,* edited by Kimberlé Crenshaw, Neil Gotanda, Gary Peller, and Kendall Thomas, 357–83. New York: New Press.

———. 2002. "Documento para o Encontro de Especialistas em Aspectos da Discriminação Racial Relativos ao Gênero." *Estudos Feministas* 10(1): 171–88.

Cruz, Simone, Laura López, Daniel Etcheverry, and Miriam Steffen Vieira. 2008. *Saúde da População Negra Como Ação Afirmativa: Estratégias de Enfrentamento ao HIV/Aids na Perspectiva de Entidades do Movimento Negro na Região Sul do Brasil.* Porto Alegre: Metropole.

Cypriano, Tania. 1997. *Odo-Ya! Life with AIDS.* New York: Filmmakers Library.

Da Costa, Alexandre Emboaba. 2014. *Reimagining Black Difference and Politics in Brazil.* New York: Palgrave Macmillan.

Damasco, Mariana Santos, Marcos Chor Maio, and Simone Monteiro. 2012. "Feminismo Negro: Raça, Identidade E Saúde Reprodutiva No Brasil (1975–1993)." *Estudos Feministas* 20 (1): 133–51.

Davis, Darién J., Tianna S. Paschel, and Judith A. Morrison. 2012. "Pan-Afro-Latin Americanism Revisited: Legacies and Lessons for Transnational Alliances in the New Millennium." In *Afro-Descendants, Identity, and the Struggle for Development in the Americas,* edited by Bernd Reiter Simmons and Kimberly Eisen, 19–48. East Lansing: Michigan State University Press.

Dhamoon, Rita Kaur. 2001. "Considerations on Mainstreaming Intersectionality." *Political Research Quarterly* 64(1): 230–43.

Dhesca Brasil. 2012. "Letter to Dilma Roussef Regarding CEDAW Decision." http://www .dhescbrasil.org.br/attachments/614_alyne_case_english_version/pdf.

Dias, Jussara, Mária R. Giovanetti, and Naila J. Seabra Santos. 2009. *Perguntar Não Ofende. Qual é Sua Cor ou Raça/Etnia? Responder Ajuda a Prevenir.* Sao Paulo: Centro de Referência e Treinamento DST/Aids.

Diniz, Simone. 2012. "Materno-Infantilism, Feminism and Maternal Health Policy in Brazil." *Reproductive Health Matters* 20 (39): 125–32.

Dixon-Mueller, Ruth. 1993. *Population Policy & Women's Rights: Transforming Reproductive Choice*. Westport, CT: Praeger.

Dulitzky, Ariel E. 2005. "A Region in Denial: Racial Discrimination and Racism in Latin America." In *In Neither Enemies Nor Friends: Latinos, Blacks, Afro-Latinos*, edited by Anani Dzidzienyo and Suzanne Oboler, 39–59. New York: Palgrave Macmillan.

Dzidzienyo, Anani. 2005. "The Changing World of Brazilian Race Relations?" In *Neither Enemies Nor Friends: Latinos, Blacks, Afro-Latinos*, edited by Anani Dzidzienyo and Suzanne Oboler, 137–55. New York: Palgrave Macmillan.

Ewig, Christina. 2010. *Second-Wave Neoliberalism: Gender, Race and Health Sector Reform in Peru*. University Park: Pennsylvania State University Press.

Farmer, Paul. 2004. "Sidney W. Mintz Lecture for 2001, An Anthropology of Structural Violence." *Current Anthropology* 45 (3): 305–25.

Ferraz, Octavio Luiz Motta. 2009. "The Right to Health in the Courts of Brazil: Worsening Health Inequities?" *Health and Human Rights* 11 (2): 33–45.

Fonseca Sobrinho, Délcio da. 1993. *Estado e População: Uma História do Planejamento Familiar no Brasil*. Rio de Janeiro: Editora Rosa dos Tempos.

Freyre, Gilberto. 1959. *New World in the Tropics: The Culture of Modern Brazil*. New York: Knopf.

Friedman, Elisabeth. 1999. "The Effects of 'Transnationalism Reversed' in Venezuela: Assessing the Impact Of UN Global Conferences on the Women's Movement." *International Feminist Journal of Politics* 1 (3): 357–81.

Fry, Peter. 2005. "O Significado da Anemia Falciforme no Contexto da 'Política Racial' do Governo Brasileira." *História, Ciências, Saúde-Manguinhos* 12 (2): 347–70.

———. 2007. "Afinal, aids tem cor ou raça no Brasil?" *Folha de São Paulo*, March 11, J5.

Fry, Peter, Simone Monteiro, Marcos Chor Maio, Francisco I. Bastos, and Ricardo Ventura Santos. 2007a. "AIDS Tem Cor ou Raça?: Interpretação de Dados e Formulacão de Políticas de Saúde no Brasil." *Cadernos de Saúde Publica* 23: 497–507.

Fry, Peter, Yvonne Maggie, Marcos Chor Maio, Simone Monteiro, and Ricardo Ventura Santos. 2007b. *Divisões Perigosas: Políticas Raciais No Brasil Contemporâneo*. Rio de Janeiro: Editora Civilização Brasileira.

———. 2007c. "Apresentação." In *Divisóes Perigosas: Políticas Raciais No Brasil Contemporâneo*, edited by Peter Fry, Yvonne Maggie, Marcos Chor Maio, Simone Monteiro, and Ricardo Ventura Santos, 17–22. Rio de Janeiro: Editora Civilização Brasileira.

Fundação Nacional de Saúde. 2005. *Saúde da População Negra no Brasil: Contribuições Para a Promoção da Eqüidade*. Brasilia: Fundação Nacional de Saude.

Galli, Maria Beatriz. 2005. *Mortalidade Materna e Direitos Humanos*. Rio de Janeiro: Advocacia Cidadã pelos Direitos Humanos.

———. 2011. "Negative Impacts of Abortion Criminalization in Brazil: Systematic Denial of Women's Reproductive Autonomy and Human Rights." *University of Miami Law Review* 65 (3): 969–80.

Galli, Beatriz, Helena Rocha, and Jandira Queiroz. 2015. *Relatório Sobre Mortalidade Materna no Contexto do Processo de Implementação da Decisão do Comitê CEDAW Contra o Estado brasileiro no Caso Alyne da Silva Pimentel* Brasília: UNFPA.

Galtung, Johan. 1969. "Violence, Peace and Peace Research." *Journal of Peace Research 6* (3): 167–91.

Galvão, Jane. 2005. "Brazil and Access to HIV/AIDS Drugs: A Question of Human Rights and Public Health." *American Journal of Public Health* 95: 1110–16.

Garcia, Sandra, and F. M. Souza. 2010. "Vulnerabilities to HIV/AIDS in the Brazilian Context: Gender, Race and Generation Inequities." *Saúde e Sociedade* 19 (2): 9–20.

Geledés. 1991a. *Cadernos Geledés 1: Mulher Negra e Saúde*. São Paulo: Geledés - Instituto da Mulher Negra, Programa de Saúde.

———. 1991b. *Cadernos Geledés 2: Esterilização: Impunidade ou Regulamentação*. São Paulo: Geledés - Instituto da Mulher Negra, Programa de Saúde.

———. 2013a. *Guia de Enfrentamento Do Racismo Institucional*. São Paulo: Geledés - Instituto da Mulher Negra, Programa de Saúde.

———. 2013b. *Racismo Institucional: Uma Abordagem Conceitual*. São Paulo: Geledés - Instituto da Mulher Negra, Programa de Saúde.

Germain, Adrienne, Gita Sen, Claudia Garcia-Moreno, and Mridula Shankar. 2015. "Advancing Sexual and Reproductive Health and Rights in Low- and Middle-Income Countries: Implications for the Post-2015 Global Development Agenda." *Global Public Health* 10 (February): 137–48.

Giovanetti, Márcia Regina, Naila J. Seabra Santos, Caio Westin, Dulcimara Darre, and Maria Clara Gianna. 2007. "The Implementation of the Question Regarding Color/Race in STD/AIDS Services in the State of São Paulo." *Saude e Sociedade* 16 (2): 163–70.

Goulart, Henrique Rodrigues de Andrade, and Leandro Pereira Gonçalves. 2011. "O Regime do Extermínio: A Concretização da Violência Ilegal Enquanto Ferramenta Política no Brasil Pós-Golpe em 1964." *CES Revista* 25: 159–72.

Gould, Stephen Jay. 1996[1981]. *The Mismeasure of Man*. New York, NY: Norton.

Gruskin, Sofia, Jane Cottingham, Adriane Martin Hilber, Eszter Kismodi, Onella Lincetto, and Mindy Jane Roseman. 2008. "Using Human Rights to Improve Maternal and Neonatal Health: History, Connections and a Proposed Practical Approach." *Bulletin of the World Health Organization* 86: 589–93.

Guimarães, Antonio Sérgio Alfredo. 1995. "Racism and Anti-racism in Brazil: A Postmodern Perspective." In *Racism and Anti-racism in World Perspective*, ed. Benjamin P. Bowser, 208–26. Thousand Oaks, Calif.: Sage Publications.

———. 2005 [1999]. *Racismo e Anti-Racismo no Brasil*. São Paulo: Editora 34.

Guimarães, Kátia. 2009. "Estigma, Discriminação e Contextos de Vulnerabilidade: Gênero, Racismo, Pobreza e a Infecção pelo HIV/AIDS." In *Aids e Juventude: Gênero, Classe e Raça*, edited by Stella R. Taquette, 235–46. Rio de Janeiro: EdUERJ.

Hanchard, Michael George. 1994. *Orpheus and Power: The Movimento Negro of Rio de Janeiro and São Paulo, 1945–1988*. Princeton, N.J.: Princeton University Press.

Hankivsky, Olena. 2012. "Women's Health, Men's Health, and Gender and Health: Implications of Intersectionality." *Social Science & Medicine* 74: 1712–20.

Hankivsky, Olena, and Ashlee Christoffersen. 2008. "Intersectionality and the Determinants of Health: A Canadian Perspective." *Critical Public Health* 18 (3): 271–83.

Hankivsky, Olena, and Renee Cormier. 2009. *Intersectionality: Moving Women's Health Research and Policy Forward*. Vancouver: Women's Health Research Network.

———. 2011. "Intersectionality and Public Policy: Some Lessons from Existing Models." *Political Research Quarterly* 64 (1): 217–29.

Hankivsky, Olena, Colleen Reid, Renee Cormier, Colleen Varcoe, Natalie Clark, Cecilia Benoit, and Shari Brotman. 2010. "Exploring the Promises of Intersectionality for Advancing Women's Health Research." *International Journal for Equity in Health* 9(6): 1–16.

Harrison, Faye V. 1995. "The Persistent Power of 'Race' in the Cultural and Political Economy of Racism." *Annual Review of Anthropology* 24: 47–74.

Hernandez, Tanya. 2013. *Racial Subordination in Latin America: The Role of the State, Customary Law, and the New Civil Rights Response*. New York: Cambridge University Press.

Ho, Kathleen. 2007. "Structural Violence as a Human Rights Violation." *Essex Human Rights Review* 4 (2): 1–17.

Htun, Mala. 2004. "From 'Racial Democracy' to Affirmative Action: Changing State Policy on Race in Brazil." *Latin American Research Review* 39 (1): 60–89.

Instituto AMMA Psique e Negritude. n.d. *Identificação e Abordagem do Racismo Institucional*.

Instituto Brasileiro de Geografia e Estatística. 2011. "Censo Demográfico 2010: Caraterísticas da População e dos Domicílios. Resultados do Universo." Rio de Janeiro: Instituto Brasileiro de Geografia e Estatística.

Jaccoud, Luciana. 2009. *A Construção de Uma Política de Promoção da Igualdade Racial: Uma Análise dos Ultimos 20 Anos*. Brasilia: IPEA.

Jeronimo, Josie. 2010. "Senadores aprovam Estatuto da Igualdade Racial, mas retiram cotas." *Correio Braziliense*. June 17. http://www.correiobraziliense.com.br/app/noticia/brasil/2010/06/17/interna_brasil,198091/index.shtml.

Jesus, Joice Aragão. 2010. "Doença Falciforme no Brasil." In *Nascer Com Equidade,* edited by Suzana Kalckmann, Luís Eduardo Batista, Claúdia Medeiros de Castro, Tânia Di Giacomo do Lago, and Sandra Regina de Souza, 285–88. São Paulo: Instituto de Saúde.

Johnson, Ollie A. III. 1998. "Racial Representation and Brazilian Politics: Black Members of the National Congress, 1983–1999." *Journal of Interamerican Studies and World Affairs* 40 (4): 97–118.

———. 2015. "Blacks in National Politics." In *Race, Politics, and Education in Brazil: Affirmative Action in Higher Education,* edited by Ollie A. Johnson III and Rosana Heringer, 17–58. New York: Palgrave Macmillan.

Kalckmann, Suzana, Luís Eduardo Batista, Cláudia Medeiros de Castro, Tânia Giacomo do Lago, and Sandra Regina de Souza, ed. 2010. *Nascer com Equidade*. São Paulo: Instituto de Saúde.

Kalckmann, Suzana, Claudete Gomas dos Santos, Luís Eduardo Batista, and Vanessa Martins da Cruz. 2007. "Racismo Institucional: Um Desafio Para a Eqüidade No SUS / Institutional Racism: A Challenge to Equity in the National." *Saúde e Sociedade São Paulo* 16 (2): 146–55.

Kamel, Ali. 2006. *Não Somos Racistas*. Nova Fronteira.

Kane, Gillian, Beatriz Galli, and Patty Skuster. 2014. *When Abortion Is a Crime: The Threat to Vulnerable Women in Latin America*. Chapel Hill, NC: IPAS.

Kluchin, Rebecca M. 2009. *Fit to be Tied: Sterilization and Reproductive Rights in America, 1950–1980*. New Brunswick, NJ: Rutgers University Press.

Koshimizu, Ricardo Koiti. 2011. "Ilegalidade do Aborto Prejudica Mulheres Pobres e Negras, Avaliam Participantes de Audiência." *Senado Federal*. August 18. http://www12 .senado.gov.br/noticias/materias/2011/08/18/ilegalidade-do-aborto-prejudica-mulheres -pobres-e-negras-avaliam-participantes-de-audiencia.

Laguardia, Josué. 2007. "Raça e Epidemiologia: As Estratégias para Construção de Diferenças Biológicas." *Ciência & Saúde Coletiva* 12 (1): 253–61.

Laurenti, Ruy, Sabina Léa, and Davidson Gotlieb. 2004. "A Mortalidade Materna nas Capitais Brasileiras : Algumas Características e Estimativa de Um Fator de Ajuste." *Revista Brasileira de Epidemiologia* 7 (4): 449–60.

Leal, Maria do Carmo, Silvana Granado Nogueira da Gama, and Cynthia Braga da Cunha. 2005. "Racial, Sociodemographic, and Prenatal and Childbirth Care Inequalities in Brazil, 1999–2001." *Revista de Saúde Pública* 39 (1): 100–7.

Lebon, Natalie. 2007. "Beyond Confronting the Myth of Racial Democracy: The Role of Afro-Brazilian Women Scholars and Activists." *Latin American Perspectives* 34 (6): 52–76.

Leme, Conceição. 2009. "Alaerte Martins: A Morte Materna Invisível Das Mulheres Negras." *Viomundo* Blog. February 23. http://www.viomundo.com.br/denuncias/alaerte -martins-a-morte-materna-invisivel-das-mulheres-negras.html.

Lewis, Hope. 2015. "Embracing Complexity: Human Rights in Critical Race Feminist Perspective." *Columbia Journal of Gender and Law* 12 (3): 510–20.

Lieberman, Evan S. 2009. *Boundaries of Contagion: How Ethnic Politics Have Shaped Government Responses to AIDS*. Princeton, N.J.: Princeton University Press.

Lopes, Fernanda. 2003. "Mulheres Negras e Não Negras Vivendo com HIV/AIDS no Estado de São Paulo: Um Estudo Sobre Suas Vulnerabilidades." Ph.D. diss., University of São Paulo.

———. 2005. "Experiências Desiguais ao Nascer, Viver, Adoecer e Morrer: Tópicos Em Saúde da População Negra No Brasil." In *Saúde da População Negra no Brasil: Estudos e Pesquisas*, 9–48. Brasilia: Fundação Nacional de Saúde.

Lopes, Fernanda, Cassia Maria Buchalla, José Ricardo de Carvalho, and Mesquita Ayres. 2007. "Black and non-Black women and vulnerability to HIV/AIDS in São Paulo, Brazil." *Revista de Saúde Pública* 41, Suppl. 2: 1–7.

Lopes, Fernanda, and Raquel Quintiliano. 2007. "Racismo Institucional e o Direito Humano a Saúde." *Democracia Viva* 34:8–16.

Lopes, Fernanda, and Jurema Werneck. n.d. "Saúde da População Negra: da Conceituação às Políticas Públicas de Direito." In *Mulheres Negras: Um Olhar Sobre as Lutas Sociais e as Políticas Públicas no Brasil*, 5–22. Rio de Janeiro: Criola.

———. 2009. "Mulheres Jovens Negras e Vulnerabilidade ao HIV/AIDS: O Lugar do Racismo." In *Aids e Juventude: Gênero, Classe e Raça*, edited by Stella R. Taquette, 247–66. Rio de Janeiro: EdUERJ.

López, Laura Cecilia. 2011. "Analysis of the HIV/AIDS Policies from a Gender and Race Intersectional Perspective." *Saude e Socieade* 20 (3): 590–603.

———. 2012. "The concept of institutional racism: applications within the healthcare field." *Interface—Comunicão, Saúde, Educação* 16(40): 121–34.

Maggie, Yvonne. 2005a. "Políticas de Cotas e o Vestibular da UnB ou a Marca Que Cria Sociedades Divididas." *Horizontes Antropológicos* 11 (23): 286–91.

———. 2005b. "Uma Nova Pedagogia Racial." *Revista da USP* 68: 112–29.

Maio, Marcos Chor, and Simone Monteiro. 2005. "Tempos de Racializacao: O Caso da 'Saude da Populacao Negra' No Brasil." *História, Ciências, Saúde - Manguinhos* 12 (2): 419–46.

Maio, Marcos Chor, Simone Monteiro, and Paulo Henrique Almeida Rodrigues. 2007. "O SUS é Racista?" In *Divisões Perigosas: Políticas Raciais no Brasil Contemporâneo*, edited by Peter Fry, Yvonne Maggie, Marcos Chor Maio, Simone Monteiro, and Ricardo Ventura Santos, 235–239. Rio de Janeiro: Civilização Brasileira.

Malta, Monica, and Chris Beyrer. 2013. "The HIV Epidemic and Human Rights in Brazil." *Journal of the International AIDS Society* 16: 1–3.

Maria Mulher. 2006. *Subjetividade de Mulheres em Situação de Violência Doméstica Infectadas Pelo Vírus HIV Frente Adesão ao Tratamento para AIDS*. Porto Alegre: Maria Mulher.

Mariz, Renata, Julia Chaib, and Ana Pompeu. 2014. "Cerca de 865 mil mulheres fizeram abortos no Brasil em 2013." *Estado de Minas*, September 28, 2014. Accessed January 28, 2015. http://www.em.com.br/app/noticia/nacional/2014/09/28/interna_nacional ,573606/cerca-de-865-mil-mulheres-fizeram-abortos-ilegais-no-brasil-em-2013.shtml

Martins, Alaerte Leandro. 2006. "Maternal Mortality among Black Women in Brazil." *Cadernos de Saúde Pública* 22 (11): 2473–79.

———. 2011. "Antigos Temas, Novos Desafios dos Direitos Reprodutivos e Direitos Sexuais—Mortalidade Materna." *Jornal da Rede Feminista de Saúde* December: 15–17.

Martins, Sérgio da Silva, Carlos Alberto Medeiros, and Elisa Larkin Nascimento. 2004. "Paving Paradise: The Road from 'Racial Democracy' to Affirmative Action in Brazil." *Journal of Black Studies* 34: 787–816.

Meirelles, Zilah, and Maria Helena Ruzany. 2009. "O Impacto da Pobreza na Vida das Mulheres Jovens Afrodescendentes e o Risco de DST/AIDS." In *Aids e Juventude: Gênero, Classe e Raça*, edited by Stella R. Taquette, 123–34. Rio de Janeiro: EdUERJ.

Merry, Sally Engle. 2006. *Human Rights and Gender Violence: Translating International Law into Local Justice*. Chicago: University of Chicago Press.

Ministério da Saúde. 2004. *Boletim Epidemiológico—Aids e DST*. Brasília: Ministério da Saúde/Secretaria de Vigilância em Saúde/Programa Nacional de DST e AIDS.

———. 2005. *Perspectiva da Eqüidade no Pacto Nacional pela Redução da Mortalidade Materna e Neonatal: Atenção à Saúde das Mulheres Negras*. Brasília: Ministerio da Saúde.

———. 2006a. *Programa Estratégico de Ações Afirmativas: População Negra e AIDS*. Brasília: Ministerio da Saúde.

———. 2006b. *Brasil Afroatitude: Primeiro Ano do Programa*. Brasília: Ministério da Saúde.

———. 2007a. *Plano Integrado de Enfrentamento da Feminização da Epidemia de AIDS e Outras DST*. Brasília: Ministério da Saúde.

————. 2007b. *Relatório de Gestão 2003 à 2006: Política Nacional de Atenção Integral à Saúde da Mulher.* Brasília: Ministerio da Saúde.

————. 2007c. *Manual dos Comitês de Mortalidade Materna.* Brasília: Ministerio da Saúde.

————. 2009. "Portaria No. 993." *Diário Oficial Da União.*

————. 2010. *Politica Nacional de Saúde Integral da População Negra: Uma Política do SUS.* Brasília: Ministério da Saúde.

————. 2014. *Boletim Epidemiológico—Aids e DST.* Brasília: Ministério da Saúde/Secretaria de Vigilância em Saúde/Departamento de DST, Aids e Hepatites Virais.

Miranda-Ribeiro, Paula, Andréa Branco Simão, André Junqueira Caetano, Marisa Alves Lacerda, and Maria Eponina de Abreu e Torres. 2010. "Perfis de Vulnerabilidade Feminina ao HIV/AIDS em Belo Horizonte e Recife: Comparando Brancas e Negras." *Saúde e Sociedade* 19 (S2): 21–35.

Monteiro, Mário, Leila Adesse, and Jacques Levin. 2008. *"Mulheres Negras e a Mortalidade Materna no Brasil."* São Paulo: Comissão de Direitos Humanos/Center for Reproductive Rights.

Monteiro, Simone. 2004. "Desigualdades em Saúde, Raça e Etnicidade: Questões e Desafios." In *Etnicidade da América Latina: Um Debate Sobre Raça, Saúde e Direitos Reprodutivos,* edited by Simone Monteiro and Livio Sansone, 45–56. Rio de Janeiro: Fiocruz.

————. 2007. "Programa Afroatitude: A Fabricação de Uma Identidade Racial?" In *Divisões Perigosas: Políticas Raciais No Brasil Contemporâneo,* edited by Peter Fry, Yvonne Maggie, Marcos Chor Maio, Simone Monteiro, and Ricardo Ventura Santos, 241–49. Rio de Janeiro: Editora Civilização Brasileira.

"Mortalidade Materna Persiste Por Conta da Omissão dos Governos." 2006. *Boletim PCRI-Saúde* 2 (3): 5–6. http://www.saude.sp.gov.br/resources/ses/perfil/profissional-da-saude/ grupo-tecnico-de-acoes-estrategicas-gtae/saude-da-populacao-negra/artigos-e-teses/ boletim_pcri_saude_-_maio2006.pdf.

Mullings, Leith. 2004. "Race and Globalization: Racialization from Below." *Souls* 6 (2): 1–9.

Negri Filho, Armando de. 2013. "Brazil: A Long Journey Towards A Universal Healthcare System." In *Advancing the Human Right to Health,* edited by José M. Zuniga, Stephen P. Marks, and Lawrence O. Gostin, 173–80. Oxford and New York: Oxford University Press.

Nelson, Jennifer. 2003. *Women of Color and the Reproductive Rights Movement.* New York: New York University Press.

Network of Black Brazilian Women Preparing for the 3rd World Conference against Racial Discrimination, Xenophobia and Related Intolerance. 2001. *We, Brazilian Black Women: Analysis and Proposals.*

Nilo, Alessandra. 2008. *Mulher, Violência & AIDS: Explorando Interfaces.* Edited by Alessandra Nilo. Recife: Gestos.

Nobles, Melissa. 2000. *Shades of Citizenship: Race and the Census in Modern Politics.* Stanford, Calif.: Stanford University Press.

————. 2011. "The Challenge of Census Categorization in the Post-Civil Rights Era." In *Identity Politics in the Public Realm: Bringing Institutions Back In,* edited by Avigail

Eisenberg and Will Kymlicka, 31–51. Vancouver and Toronto: University of British Colombia Press.

Nogueira, Oracy. 1985. *Tanto Preto Quanto Branco: Estudos de Relações Raciais*. São Paulo: T.A. Queiroz.

Nunn, Amy. 2009. *The Politics and History of AIDS Treatment in Brazil*. New York: Springer.

Nussbaum, Martha. 2006. "Capabilities, Human Rights, and the Universal Declaration." In *Human Rights in the World Community: Issues and Action,* edited by Richard Pierre Claude and Burns H. Weston, 27–39. Philadelphia: University of Pennsylvania Press.

Oliveira, Fátima. 1998. *Oficinas Mulher Negra e Saúde*. Belo Horizonte: Mazza Edições, Ltda.

———. 2002. *Saúde da População Negra, Brasil 2001*. Brasília: Pan American Health Organization.

———. 2005a. "Saúde Integral Para as Mulheres: Ontem, Hoje e Perspectivas." *Jornal de Rede Feminista de Saúde* 7: 6–9.

———. 2005b. "Governo Lula e Combate ao Racismo: Há Intenções, Mas Faltam Gestos!" *Cadernos ABONG* 32: 11–14.

Pagano, Anna. 2014. "Everyday Narratives on Race and Health in Brazil." *Medical Anthropology Quarterly* 28 (2): 221–41.

Paim, Jairnilson Silva. 2006. "Eqüidade e Reforma em Sistemas de Serviços de Saúde: O Caso do SU." *Saúde e Sociedade* 15(2): 34–46.

———. 2005. "Decision-Making Process and Administrative Practice : Managing the State Health Secretariat in Bahia, Brazil." *Cadernos de Saúde Pública* 21 (5): 1373–82.

———. 2007. "Reforma Sanitária Brasileira: Contribuição Para a Compreensão e Crítica." Ph.D. diss., Universidade Federal da Bahia.

———. 2008. "O Sistema Único de Saúde : Dialogando com Hipóteses Concorrentes." *Physis* 18(4): 625–44.

———. 2012. "O Futuro do SUS, The Future of the Brazilian Unified National Health System." *Cadernos de Saúde Pública* 28 (4): 612–13.

Paim, Jairnilson Silva, and Lígia Maria Vieira da Silva. 2010. "Universalidade, Integralidade, Equidade e SUS." *Boletim do Instituto de Saúde* 12: 109–14.

Paim, Jairnilson, Claudia Travassos, Celia Almeida, Ligia Bahia, and James Macinko. 2011. "The Brazilian Health System: History, Advances, and Challenges." *Lancet* 377 (9779) (May 21): 1778–97.

Paixão, Marcelo. 2003. *Desenvolvimento Humano e Relações Raciais*. Rio de Janeiro: DP&A.

———. 2013. *500 Anos de Solidão: Estudos Sobre Desigualdades Raciais No Brasil*. Curitiba: Editora Appris Ltda.

Paixão, Marcelo, and Fernanda Lopes. 2007. "Incidência da AIDS nos Contingentes Populacionais: Existem Clivagens." *Cadernos de Saúde Pública* 23 (3): 511–13.

Parker, Richard. 2008. "AIDS Solidarity as Policy: Constructing the Brazilian Model." *NACLA Report on the Americas* (July/August): 20–24.

———. 2009. "Civil Society, Political Mobilization, and the Impact of HIV Scale-up on Health Systems in Brazil." *Journal of Acquired Immune Deficiency Syndromes* 52 (S1) (November): S49–51.

Parker, Richard, and Jane Galvão, ed. 1996. *Quebrando O Silêncio: Mulheres e AIDS no Brasil*. Rio de Janeiro: Relume Damará.

Parker, Richard, and Kenneth Rochel de Camargo Jr. 2000. "Pobreza e HIV/AIDS: Aspectos Antropológicos e Sociológicos." *Cadernos de Saúde Pública* 16 (Suppl. 1): 89–102.

Paschel, Tianna. 2009. "Re-Africanization and the Cultural Politics of Bahianidade." *Souls* 11 (4): 423–40.

———. 2016. *Becoming Black Political Subjects: Movements and Ethno-Racial Rights in Colombia and Brazil*. Princeton, N.J.: Princeton University Press.

Peard, Julyan G. 1999. *Race, Place, and Medicine: The Idea of the Tropics in Nineteenth-Century Brazilian Medicine*. Durham, N.C.: Duke University Press.

Pereira, Leonardo. 2010. "'Carta Aberta ao Povo de Deus' Confira na Integra as Palavras de Dilma Rousseff." *Noticias Cristas Atualizadas*. August 28. http://noticias.gospel prime.com.br/carta-aberta-ao-povo-de-deus-confira-na-integra-as-palavras-de-dilma -rousseff/.

Perry, Keisha-Khan. 2013. *Black Women Against the Land Grab: The Fight for Racial Justice in Brazil*. Minneapolis: University of Minnesota Press.

Petchesky, Rosalind Pollack. 2003. *Global Prescriptions: Gendering Health and Human Rights*. London & New York: Zed Books.

Pinho, Patricia de Santana. 2008. "African-American Roots Tourism in Brazil." *Latin American Perspectives* 35 (3): 70–86.

———. 2010. *Mama Africa: Reinventing Blackness in Bahia*. Durham, N.C.: Duke University Press.

Pinto, Elizabete Aparecida, and Raquel Souzas. 2002. "Etnicidade e Saúde da População Negra no Brasil." *Cadernos de Saúde Pública* 18 (5): 1144–45.

Pitanguy, Jacqueline. 1999. "'O Movimento Nacional E Internacional de Saúde e Direitos Reprodutivos.'" In *Questões da Saúde Reprodutiva*, edited by Karen Giffin and Sarah Hawker Costa, 19–38. Rio de Janeiro: Editora FIOCRUZ.

Plataforma Dhesca Brasil. 2014. "Resumo Executivo Missão à Baixada Fluminense Relatoria Do Direito Humano à Saúde Sexual e Reprodutiva."

Prefeitura Municipal de Salvador. 2006. *Diagnóstico de Saúde da População Negro do Salvador*. Salvador: Prefeitura Municipal de Salvador/Secretaria Municipal de Saúde/ Grupo de Trabalho de Saúde da População Negra.

Presidência da República. 1940. *Decreto-Lei No. 2.848, de 7 de dezembro de 1940*. http:// www.planalto.gov.br/ccivil_03/decreto-lei/Del2848.htm, accessed June 11, 2016.

———. 1988. *Constituição da República Federativa do Brasil de 1988*. Brasília: Brasil.

———. 2010. *Objetivos de Desenvolvimento do Milênio: Relatório Nacional de Acompanhamento*. Brasília: IPEA.

Programa das Nações Unidas para o Desenvolvimento [UNDP]. 2005. "Relatório de Desenvolvimento Humano—Brasil 2005." Brasília.

Programa Nacional de DST e AIDS. 2004. "Boletim Epidemiológico—Aids E DST." http://www.aids.gov.br/final/dados/BOLETIM2.pdf.

Racusen, Seth. 2010. "Affirmative Action and Identity." In *Brazil's New Racial Politics*, edited by Gladys L. Reiter, Bernd, and Mitchell. Boulder, Colo.: Lynne Rienner.

———. 2012. "The Grammar of Color Identity in Brazil." In *Afro-Descendants, Identity, and the Struggle for Development in the Americas,* edited by Bernd Reiter and Kimberly Eison Simmons, 141–75. East Lansing: Michigan State University Press.

Rede Feminista de Saúde. 2003. *Assimetrias Raciais no Brasil: Alerta para a Elaboração de Políticas.* Belo Horizonte: Rede Feminista de Saúde.

———. 2005. *Dossiê Aborto: Morte Preveníveis e Evitáveis. Rede Feminista de Saúde.* Belo Horizonte: Rede Feminista de Saúde.

Reduction of Maternal Mortality: A Joint WHO/UNICEF/UNFPA/World Bank Statement. 1999. Geneva: WHO. Accessed March 3, 2017. http://apps.who.int/iris/bitstream/10665/42191/1/9241561955_eng.pdf.

Reichmann, Rebecca. 1999. "Introduction." In *Race in Contemporary Brazil: From Indifference to Inequality,* edited by Rebecca Reichmann. University Park: Pennsylvania State University Press.

Reis, Lenice Gnocchi da Costa, Vera Lucia Edais Pepe, and Rosângela Caetano. 2011. "Maternidade Segura no Brasil: O Longo Percurso para a Efetivação de um Direito." *Physis: Revista de Saúde Coletiva* 21 (3): 1139–59.

Reis, Vilma. 2007. "Black Brazilian Women and the Lula Administration." *NACLA Report on the Americas* March/April: 38–41.

"Relatório do Seminário Mortalidade Materna e Direitos Humanos." 2009. São Paulo: CEBRAP.

Rios, Luís Felipe, Cinthia Oliveira, Jonathan Garcia, Miguel Muñoz-Laboy, Laura Murray, and Richard Parker. 2011. "Blood, Sweat and Semen: The Economy of Axé and the Response of Afro-Brazilian Religions to HIV and AIDS in Recife." *Global Public Health* 6 (S2): S257-S270.

Roa, Mónica. 2016. "Zika Virus Outbreak: Reproductive Health and Rights in Latin America." *The Lancet* 387 (10021): 843.

Roberts, Dorothy. 1997. *Killing the Black Body: Race, Reproduction, and the Meaning of Liberty.* New York: Vintage Books.

———. 2011. *Fatal Invention: How Science, Politics, and Big Business Re-create Race in the Twenty-First Centtury.* New York and London: The New Press.

Rocha, Maria Isabel Baltar da. 2006. "A Discussão Política Sobre Aborto no Brasil : Uma Síntese." *Revista Brasileira de Estudos de Populacão* 23 (2): 369–74.

Roland, Edna. 1999. "The Soda Cracker Dilemma: Reproductive Rights and Racism in Brazil." In *Race in Contemporary Brazil,* edited by Rebecca Reichmann, 237–56. University Park: Pennsylvania State University Press.

———. 2000. "Eu Fiz Aborto: Aborto e Clandestinidade." In *O Livro da Saúde das Mulheres Negras,* edited by Maisa and Evelyn C. White Werneck, Jurema, Mendonça, 130–36. Rio de Janeiro: Pallas/Criola.

Romany, Celina. 2000. "Themes for a Conversation on Race and Gender in International Human Rights Law." In *Global Critical Race Feminism: An International Reader,* edited by Adrien Katherine Wing, 53–66. New York: New York University Press.

Roseman, Mindy Jane. 2009. "Bearing Human Rights: Maternal Health and the Promise of ICPD." In *Reproductive Health and Human Rights and Human Rights: The Way Forward,* edited by Laura Reichenbach and Mindy Jane Roseman, 91–109. Philadelphia: University of Pennsylvania Press.

Rouse, Carolyn. 2009. *Uncertain Suffering: Racial Health Disparities and Sickle Cell Disease.* Berkeley: University of California Press.

Safa, Helen. 2005. "Challenging Mestizaje: A Gender Perspective on Indigenous and Afrodescendant Movements in Latin America." *Critique of Anthropology* 25: 307–30.

Safreed-Harmon, Kelly. 2008. "Human Rights and HIV/AIDS in Brazil." *GMHC Treatment Issues* April: 1–4.

"Salvador é Capital Mais Negra do País, Aponta IBGE." 2011. *G1 Bahia*, November 14. http://g1.globo.com/bahia/noticia/2011/11/salvador-e-capital-mais-negra-do-pais -aponta-ibge.html.

Sant'Anna, Wania. 2001. "Racial and Gender Inequalities in Brazil: Possible Revelations of the HDI and the GDI." *Jornal da Redesaúde* 23 (August): 16–19.

Sant'Anna, Wania, and Marcelo Paixão. 1997. "Desenvolvimento Humano e População Afrodescendente no Brasil: Uma Questão de Raça." *Proposta* 26 (73): 20–37.

Santos, Adson Roberto Franca, and Maria Jose de Oliveira Araujo. 2006. "Balanço de Dois Anos do Pacto Nacional pela Redução da Mortalidade Materna e Neonatal." *Jornal de Rede Feminista de Saude* 28: 27–29.

Santos, Ivanir Augusto Alves dos. 2007. *O Movimento Negro e O Estado, 1983–1987.* São Paulo: CONE, Coordenadoria dos Assuntos da População Negra. Secretaria Especial para Participação e Parceria, Prefeitura da Cidade de São Paulo.

Santos, Ivanir dos, and José Geraldo da Rocha, eds. 2007. *Diversidade e Ações Afirmativas.* Rio de Janeiro: Centro de Articulação de Populações Marginalizadas—CEAP.

Santos, José Alcides Figueiredo. 2011. "Desigualdade Racial de Saúde e Contexto de Classe no Brasil." *Dados-Revista de Ciências Sociais* 54 (1): 5–40.

Santos, Sales Augusto dos. 2006. "Who Is Black in Brazil? A Timely or a False Question in Brazilian Race Relations in the Era of Affirmative Action?" *Latin American Perspectives* 33 (4): 30–48.

———. 2009. "Ações Afirmativas: racialização e privilégios ou justiça e igualdade?" *Sísifo: Revista de Ciências da Educação* 10: 111–20.

———. 2014. *Educação: Um Pensamento Negro Contemporâneo.* Jundiaí: Paco Editorial.

Santos, Sales Augusto dos, Eliane Cavalleiro, Maria Inês da Silva Barbosa, and Matilde Ribeiro. 2008. "Ações Afirmativas: Polêmicas e Possibilidades sobre Igualdade Racial e o Papel do Estado." *Revista Estudos Feministas* 16 (3) (December): 913–29.

Santos, Sales Augusto dos, João Vitor Moreno, and Dora Lúcia Bertulio. 2011. *O Processo de Aprovação do Estatuto da Igualdade Racial.* Brasília: INESC.

———. 2015. "The Defeat of Quotas within the Racial Equality Statute." In *Race, Politics, and Education in Brazil: Affirmative Action in Higher Education,* edited by Ollie A. Johnson III and Rosana Heringer, 199–221. New York: Palgrave Macmillan.

Santos, Sonia Beatriz. 2008. "Brazilian Black Women's NGOs and Their Struggles in the Area of Sexual and Reproductive Health: Experiences, Resistance, and Politics." Ph.D. diss., University of Texas at Austin.

———. 2012. "Controlling Black Women's Reproductive Health Rights: An Impetus to Black Women's Collective Organizing." *Cultural Dynamics* 24 (1): 13–30.

Schoen, Johanna. 2005. *Choice and Coercion: Birth Control, Sterilization, and Abortion in Public Health and Welfare*. Chapel Hill, NC: University of North Carolina Press.

Schulman, Barbara. 2004. "Effective Organizing in Terrible Times: The Strategic Value of Human Rights for Transnational Anti-Racist Feminisms." *Meridians: Feminism, Race, Transnationalism* 4 (2): 102–8.

Schwarz, Lilia. 1999. *The Spectacle of the Races: Scientists, Institutions, and the Racial Question in Brazil, 1870–1930*. New York: Hill and Wang.

Secretaria Especial de Políticas de Promoção da Igualdade Racial. 2005 *Relatório de Atividades 2005*. Brasília: Secretaria Especial de Políticas de Promoção da Igualdade Racial.

Secretaria Municipal de Reparação. 2012a. *Observatório da Discriminação Racial, Violência Contra a Mulher e LGBT: 2005–2011*. Salvador: Prefeitura Municipal de Salvador.

———. 2012b. *Plano Municipal de Políticas de Promoção de Igualdade Racial*. Salvador: Prefeitura Municipal de Salvador.

Secretaria Municipal de Saúde de Porto Alegre. 2008. *Boletim Epidemiológico, Fevereiro*. Porto Alegre: Secretaria Municipal de Saúde de Porto Alegre.

Shalev, Carmel. 2000. "Rights to Sexual and Reproductive Health: The ICPD and the Convention on the Elimination of All Forms of Discrimination against Women." *Health and Human Rights* 4 (2): 39–66.

Shepard, Bonnie. 2000. "The 'Double Discurse' on Sexual and Reproductive Rights in Latin America: The Chasm between Public Policy and Private Actions." *Health and Human Rights* 4 (2): 110–43.

Sheppard, Dalila de Sousa. 2001. "A Literatura Médica Brasileira Sobre a Peste Branca: 1870–1940." *História, Ciências, Saúde—Manguinhos* 7 (1): 173–92.

Sheriff, Robin E. 2001. *Dreaming Equality: Color, Race, and Racism in Urban Brazil*. New Brunswick, NJ: Rutgers University Press.

Shulz, Amy J., and Leith Mullings, ed. 2006. *Gender, Race, Class, and Health: Intersectional Approaches*. San Francisco: Jossey-Bass.

Silva, Carlos Benedito Rodrigues da. 2012. "State and Social Movements in Brazil: An Analysis of the Participation of Black Intellectuals in State Agencies." In *Black Social Movements in Latin America: From Monocultural Mestizaje to Multiculturalism*, edited by Jean Muteba Rahier, 185–99. New York: Palgrave Macmillan.

Silva, Federico Barbosa da, Luciana Jaccoud, and Nathalie Beghin. 2009. "Políticas Sociais no Brasil: Participação Social, Conselhos e Parcerias." In *Questão Social e Políticas Sociais no Brasil*, edited by Luciana Jaccoud, 373–407. Brasilia: IPEA.

Silva, Joselina da. 2011. "Doutoras Professoras Negras: O Que Nos Dizem os Indicadores Oficiais." *Perspectiva* 28 (1): 19–36.

———. 2012. "From the Black Councils to the Federal Special Secretariat for the Adoption of Policies that Promote Racial Equality (SEPPR): New Identities of the Black Brazilian Movement." In *Black Social Movements in Latin America: From Monocultural Mestizaje to Multiculturalism*, edited by Jean Muteba Rahier, 201–11. New York: Palgrave Macmillan.

Silva, José Marmo, and Marcos Antonio Chagas Guimaráes. 2000. "Odo-Ya Project: HIV/ AIDS Prevention in the Context of Afro-Brazilian Religion." *Journal of Health Communication* (Supplement) 5:119–22.

Silva, José Marmo da. 2007. "Religiões e Saúde: A Experiência da Rede Nacional de Religiões Afro-Brasileiras e Saúde." *Saúde e Sociedade São Paulo* 16 (2): 171–77.

Silva, Marta de Oliveira da. 2005. "Crítica sobre Politicas, Ações e Programas de Saúde Implementados no Brasil." In *Saúde da População Negra no Brasil: Contribuições para a Promoção da Eqüidade,* 387–435. Brasília: Funasa.

Smedley, Brian, Adrienne Y. Stith, and Alan R. Nelson, ed. 2003. *Unequal Treatment: Confronting Racial and Ethnic Disparities in Health Care.* Washington, D.C.: National Academies.

Smiderle, Carlos Gustavo, Sarmet Moreira, and Wania Amelia Belchior Mesquita. 2016. "Political Conflict and Spiritual Battle: Intersections between Religion and Politics among Brazilian Pentecostals." *Latin American Perspectives* 43 (3): 85–103.

Smith, Christen. 2013. "Putting Prostitutes in Their Place: Black Women, Social Violence, and the Brazilian Case of Sirlei Carvalho." *Latin American Perspectives* 41 (1): 107–23.

———. 2016. *Afro-Paradise: Blackness, Violence and Performance in Brazil.* Urbana: University of Illinois Press.

Souza, Edna Muniz de, Shirley Santos, Mario Rogerio Bento, and Chindalena Barbosa. 2005. "Histórico da Implementação do Quesito Cor: Um Relato de Experiências." In *Saúde Da População Negra no Brasil: Contribuições para a Promoção da Eqüidade,* 437–46. Brasília: Fundação Nacional de Saúde.

Souza, Jesse. 1997. *Multiculturalismo E Racismo: Uma Comparação Brasil—Estados Unidos.* Brasilia: Paralelo 15 editores.

Souza, Renilson Rehem de, José Dínio Vaz Mendes, Silvany Lemes Cruvinel Portas, Sonia Barros, and Suely Vallim. 2008. *Plano Estadual da Saúde 2008–2011.* São Paulo: Secretaria da Saúde.

Stepan, Nancy Leys. 1991. *The Hour of Eugenics: Race, Gender, and Nation in Latin America.* Ithaca, N.Y.: Cornell University Press.

Sweig, Julia. 2012. "Brazil's Strong Stance on Women's Rights." http://www.thedailybeast .com/articles/2012/04/24/brazil-s-strong-stance-on-women-s-rights.html.

Tanaka, Ana Cristina d'Andretta. 2006. "Uma Aula e Muitas Lições Sobre a Mortalidade Materna." *Jornal da Rede Feminista de Saúde* 28: 7–9.

Tapper, Melbourne. 1999. *In the Blood: Sickle Cell Anemia and the Politics of Race.* Philadelphia: University of Pennsylvania Press.

Taquette, Stella R., ed. 2009a. *Aids e Juventude: Gênero, Classe e Raça.* Rio de Janeiro: EdUERJ.

———. 2009b. "Estudo das Representações Sociais de Saúde e Doença de Adolescentes Femininas Afrodescendentes." In *Aids e Juventude: Gênero, Classe e Raça,* edited by Stella R. Taquette, 19–40. Rio de Janeiro: EdUERJ.

Teixeira, Carmen Fontes, and Jairnilson Silva Paim. 2003. "A Política de Saúde no Governo Lula e a Dialética do Menos Pior." In *Saúde em Debate,* edited by Benjamin Coriat

Jean-Paul Moatti, Yves Souteyrand Barnett, Tony Jérôme Dumoulin, and Yves-Antoine Flori, 69–88. Paris: Agence Nationale de Recherches Sur le Sida.

Telles, Edward. 2004. *Race in Another America: The Significance of Skin Color in Brazil.* Princeton, N.J.: Princeton University Press.

———. 2014. *Pigmentocracies: Ethnicity, Race, and Color in Latin America.* Chapel Hill: University of North Carolina Press.

Thayer, Millie. 2010. *Making Transnational Feminism: Rural Women, NGO Activists, and Northern Donors in Brazil.* New York: Routledge.

"They Come in Shooting: Policing Socially Excluded Communities." 2005. http://www.amnesty.org/en/library/asset/AMR19/025/2005/en/b922b931-d49c-11dd-8a23-d58a49c0d652/amr190252005en.pdf.

Torres, Cristina, and Mercedes del Rio. 2001. *Equity in Health from an Ethnic Perspective.* Washington, D.C.: Pan American Health Organization.

Travassos, Claudia. 2007. "Fry Debate." *Cadernos de Saúde Pública* 23 (3): 516–18.

Túlio, Silvio. 2015. "UFG Aprova Cotas Raciais para Todos os Cursos de Pós-Graduação em GO." May 13. G1. http://g1.globo.com/goias/noticia/2015/05/ufg-aprova-cotas-raciais-para-todos-os-cursos-de-pos-graduacao-em-go.html.

Turner, J. Michael. 2002. "The Road to Durban—and Back." *NACLA Report on the Americas* 35: 31–35.

Twine, France Winddance. 1998. *Racism in a Racial Democracy: The Maintenance of White Supremacy in Brazil.* New Brunswick, N.J.: Rutgers University Press.

"Uma Oportunidade Ímpar na Luta Contra o Racismo, Uma Entrevista Com Sueli Carneiro." 2001. *Jornal da RedeSaúde* (23): 21–26.

Vargas, J.H.C. 2005. "Genocide in the African Diaspora: United States, Brazil, and the Need for a Holistic Research and Political Method." *Cultural Dynamics* 17 (3): 267–90.

———. 2009. "The Liberation Imperative of Black Genocide: Blueprints from the African Diaspora in the Americas." In *New Social Movements in the African Diaspora: Challenging Global Apartheid,* edited by Leith Mullings, 79–104. New York, NY: Palgrave Macmillan.

Victora, Cesar G, Estela M. L. Aquino, Maria do Carmo Leal, Carlos Augusto Monteiro, Fernando C. Barros, and Celia L. Szwarcwald. 2011. "Maternal and Child Health in Brazil: Progress and Challenges." *Lancet* 377: 2042–53.

Vieira, Elisabeth Meloni, and Nicholas John Ford. 1996. "Regret after Female Sterilization among Low-Income Women in São Paulo, Brazil." *International Family Planning Perspectives* 22: 32–40.

Volochko, Anna. 2010. "Mortalidade Materna: Determinantes Sociopolíticos." In *Nascer com Equidade,* edited by Suzana Kalckmann, Luís Eduardo Batista, Cláudia Medeiros de Castro, Tânia Di Giacomo do Lago, and Sandra Regina de Souza, 111–28. São Paulo: Instituto de Saúde.

Wagley, Charles. 1952. *Race and Class in Rural Brazil,* edited by Charles Wagley. Paris: UNESCO.

Wailoo, Keith. 2001. *Dying in the City of Blues: Sickle Cell Anemia and the Politics of Race and Health.* Chapel Hill: University of North Carolina Press.

Weber, Lynn. 2006. "Reconstructing the Landscape of Health Disparities Research: Promoting Dialogue between Feminist Intersectional and Biomedical Paradigms." In *Gender, Race, Class, and Health: Intersectional Approaches,* edited by Amy J. Shulz and Leith Mullings, 21–59. San Francisco: Jossey-Bass.

Weber, Lynn, and Deborah Parra-Medina. 2003. "Intersectionality and Women's Health: Charting a Path to Eliminating Health Disparities." In *Advances in Gender Research: Gender Perspectives on Health and Medicine,* edited by Marcia Texler Segal and Vasilikie Demos, 181–203. Amsterdam: Elsevier.

Werneck, Jurema. 2000. "O Desafio das Ialodês: Mulheres Negras e a Epidemia de HIV/ AIDS." In *O Livro da Saúde das Mulheres Negras,* edited by Jurema Werneck, Maisa Mendonça, and Evelyn C. White, 95–102. Pallas/Criola.

———. 2003. "O Dia Seguinte: A Conferência Mundial Contra o Racismo e Suas Conseqüencias." *Revista da Articulação de ONGs de Mulheres Negras Brasileiras* 1: 10–13.

———. 2005. "Inclusão Racial e de Gênero: Desafio ou Presupposto da Política Pública?" *Cadernos ABONG* 32: 17–22.

———. 2007. "Of Ialodês and Feminists: Reflections on Black Women's Political Action in Latin America and the Caribbean." *Cultural Dynamics* 19 (1): 99–113.

———. 2010. *Saúde da População Negra.* (Passo a Passo: Defesa, Monitoramento e Availação de Políticas Públicas.) Rio de Janeiro: Criola.

World Health Organization (WHO). 1996. "Revised 1990 Estimates of Maternal Mortality: A New Approach."

———. 2015a. "Brazil: Health Profile." http://www.who.int/gho/countries/bra.pdf.

———. 2015b. *Trends in Maternal Mortality: 1990 to 2015. Estimates by WHO, UNICEF, UNFPA, World Bank Group and the United Nations Population Division.* http://apps .who.int/iris/bitstream/10665/194254/1/9789241565141_eng.pdf?ua=1.

Yamin, Alicia Ely. 1993. "Empowering Visions: Toward a Dialectical Pedagogy of Human Rights." *Human Rights Quarterly* 15 (4): 640–85.

———. 2010. "Toward Transformative Accountability: Applying a Rights-Based Approach to Fulfill Maternal Health Obligations." *International Journal on Human Rights* 7(12): 95–122.

———. 2016. *Power, Suffering, and the Struggle for Dignity: Human Rights Frameworks for Health and Why They Matter.* Philadelphia: University of Pennsylvania Press.

Yamin, Alicia Ely, and Deborah P. Maine. 1999. "Maternal Mortality as a Human Rights Issue: Measuring Compliance with International Treaty Obligations." *Human Rights Quarterly* 21: 563–607.

Index

KIA LILLY CALDWELL is an associate professor of African, African American, and Diaspora studies at the University of North Carolina, Chapel Hill. She is the author of *Negras in Brazil: Re-envisioning Black Women, Citizenship, and the Politics of Identity*.

The University of Illinois Press
is a founding member of the
Association of American University Presses.

University of Illinois Press
1325 South Oak Street
Champaign, IL 61820-6903
www.press.uillinois.edu